Star Wars really happened!

Long ago great battles raged in the universe. A great war caused vast destruction throughout the cosmos and upon the earth. Super beings battled for control of the universe, space, and time. The furious struggle continued down through time. Awesome cataclysms shook the planet earth repeatedly. The earth survived. Other planets may not have been so lucky.

The evidence for these ancient celestial conflicts is profound. It exists in the heavens above us; in the rocks of the earth, beneath our feet; and hidden in the hoary records and musty legends of ancient peoples.

It is time that incredible story was told.

LIVING BOOKS
Tyndale House Publishers, Inc.
Wheaton, Illinois

BEYOND STAR WARS

William F. Dankenbring

New Facts on Atlantis—Easter Island—The Exodus—Joshua's Long Day—Noah's Flood—Hezekiah and the Sun Dial—Tower of Babel—The Great Pyramid—Neanderthal Man—Berezovka Mammoth Mystery—and other Cosmic Encounters.

Tyndale House
Publishers, Inc.
Wheaton, Illinois

Library of Congress
Catalog Card Number 78-78244
ISBN 0-8423-0145-3

First Printing, August 1979
Printed in
the United States of America

Star Wars really happened! Long ago great battles raged in the universe. A great war caused vast destruction throughout the cosmos and upon the earth. Super beings battled for control of the universe, space, and time.

The furious struggle continued down through time. Awesome cataclysms shook the planet earth repeatedly. The earth survived. Other planets may not have been so lucky.

The evidence for these ancient celestial conflicts is profound. It exists in the heavens above us; in the rocks of the earth, beneath our feet; and hidden in the hoary records and musty legends of ancient peoples.

It is time that incredible story were told.

CONTENTS

Dedicated to Nathan,
Natalie and Nancy, whose
avid interest in *Star Wars*
helped inspire this book.

Chapter One

Star Wars Before Our Time?

The greatest motion picture of all time, seen by more people than any other movie, grossing well over $200 million within its first year of release, was the action-filled *STAR WARS.* But this book is about something which is not fiction. Something which goes back in time long before the period of "Star Wars," the movie—something which is as ancient as the Universe itself, and which is still an unfolding drama, in which we are writing our own parts in our own humble lives upon this speck of a planet called Earth.

Men have always wondered where they came from. Is life on earth a mere accident? Did ancient space voyagers who reached the earth, leave precious "seed" behind which itself evolved over millions of years into the vast panoply of life forms we see around us today?

What about the mystery of Atlantis? Did Atlantis once exist? Super beings—did they perhaps even engage in galactic warfare and tremendous cosmic battles in olden times mentioned in the annals of the Biblical epic?

In the greatest box office smash hit of all time, *Star Wars,* playwright George Lucas tells us the fascinating adventures of Luke Skywalker, a handsome young lad who lived on the sun-scorched planet of Tatooine, a desert-like planet where water was only marginally accessible. Luke becomes a prime figure, caught up in a Rebellion against the Empire. The Empire had supplanted the Old Republic, once under the wise rule of the Senate and the protection of the renown Jedi Knights. But when the Republic reached its height, as so often happens when wealth and power pass beyond the admirable and attain the awesome, evil ones appeared on the scene. The Republic rotted from within. Power hungry individuals, lusting for control, seized the reins of government, exterminating all opposition through treachery and deception. The Jedi Knights, guardians of justice in the galaxy, were overthrown, and a reign of terror was inaugurated through the use of Imperial force. As a symbol of the power of the Empire, a huge Death Star—a gargantuan battle station—was built, with the power to annihilate entire populated planets.

In *Star Wars*, Luke Skywalker, with his companions Hans Solo, pilot and skipper of the freighter *Millennium Falcon*, and the beautiful Princess Leia, unite and use their wits to escape the Death Star and eventually lead the forces of the Rebellion against the cruel and oppressive Galactic Empire.

The arch villain in *Star Wars*, Darth Vader—an awesome and malevolent figure dressed in black flowing robes who keeps his face forever masked in a dark, grotesque breath screen—utilizes extra-sensory powers to keep the wicked Emperor in absolute power. In *Star Wars*, Luke Skywalker is catapulted into the midst of the most savage space war ever. He was armed only with his courage and a light saber which had once belonged to his father, one of the Jedi Knights.

Star Wars was the picture of the year in 1977—if not the picture of the entire decade. The special effects—a whole new special effects shop was built to take advantage of computer technology—pictured in great detail the creatures of Tatooine, the Jawas and the Tusken Raiders, and showed the incredible Death Star's surface in tremendous miniaturization. Sensational battles against the Imperial Tie fighters were depicted.

But why did this space adventure catch the fancy of the public? Why did so many millions flock to see *Star Wars* one, two, three times and more?

I believe the answer to that question lies deep within our collective subconscious. There is a deep yearning within human beings, which we often cannot explain. It defies words. It is part of the mystery of our existence, why we are here, and where we are going.

Did wars take place in the celestial sphere in historical and prehistorical times?

Was planet earth involved? If so, what forces were at war with each other? Who were the combatants? Who were the soldiers, the infantry? What kind of battles raged? What were the consequences?

What facts—historical, geological, astronomical, or otherwise—substantiate the acts of this cosmic drama? Is there evidence of great physical catastrophe in both historic and prehistoric times?

The word "catastrophe" seems singularly appropriate here; it literally means, "the stars are against us." How much can we know about interstellar dramas before our time?

The place to begin, I feel, is the evidence of historical texts of scores of peoples around the globe, classical literature, Norse epics, ancient sacred books in the East and West, traditions, folklore, ancient astronomical inscriptions, and archaeological discoveries; then we can proceed to the geological and paleontological finds. Out of all this evidence, perhaps we can find a unifying thread, a common denominator, or two, or three, which will make it all meaningful.

We will learn that there were incalculable catastrophes within the memory of mankind—earth-shaking orogenies which made man feel tiny and insignificant at the time–paroxysms of nature which baffled and bewildered our forefathers.

We will find, in our study, that the most accurate, reliable, and trustworthy testimony will come from the pages of that perennial best-seller, the Bible. Strange as that may seem to some unacquainted with the Bible, it stands as a supreme witness across the ages—a Book unassailable in its history over the centuries of mankind's existence. It stands as a crucial text to be consulted again and again in the pages of this book. It contains, within its pages, records, genealogies, commentaries, brief historical anecdotes and news summaries of bygone ages, events, and cultures, which will assist us greatly in putting the pieces of the puzzle together.

We will find that the Bible is a most unusual book. It contains inspiration far above and beyond the abilities of mere men. It contains historical and prehistorical data which must go far beyond the first-hand knowledge of mere men. It speaks of ages long before any men trod the earth . . . long before Adam existed, or Eve his wife . . . ages long before the Garden of Eden, guarded by the Cherubim with his sword of flaming light.

We will find much to admire in this Mysterious ancient Book.

* * * * *

Chapter Two

The Exodus Catastrophe

In this respect, then, it is of great interest to note that in the Western Hemisphere, the ancient Mayas of Mexico and Central America counted their ages by the names of their consecutive suns. A new age was heralded by the name of a new sun—the Water Sun, Earthquake Sun, Hurricane Sun, Fire Sun. The word "sun" is substituted for the word "age" in the cosmogonies of many peoples of the world. Says Brasseur in *Sources de l'histoire primitive du Mexique,* "These suns mark the epochs to which are attributed the various catastrophes the world has suffered."

Alexander in *Latin American Mythology* points out that the Water Sun was the first age, terminated by a great deluge which destroyed almost all life on earth. The next age, the Earthquake Age, perished when an enormous earthquake rent the earth and mountains fell down. A cosmic hurricane or wind storm ended the Hurricane Age or Hurricane Sun. The next age collapsed in a rain of fire from the sky, the "Fire Age" or "Fire Sun."

The ancient nations of Mexico believed in the sixteenth century that four world ages have already perished—each one terminated by floods, tempests, earthquakes, or fire. Symbols of these suns are painted on pre-Columbian literary documents of Mexico.

The Incas, Aztecs, and Mayas all had traditions of world ages that concluded in cosmic catastrophes. Stone inscriptions found in Yucatan refer to great catastrophes which at intervals convulsed the entire American continent. In Brasseur's history he records the chronicles of the Mexican kingdom: "The ancients knew that before the present sky and earth were formed, man was already created and life had manifested itself four times."

Similarly, in the Hawaiian islands and in Polynesia a tradition persists that early mankind was rent by successive creations and catastrophes. In these traditions, there were nine ages, and in each one a different sky (different arrangement and positioning of the constellations) existed above the earth.[1] *The Poetic Edda: Voluspa* of the Icelanders also speaks of nine worlds or nine successive world ages of mankind.

Rabbinical literature also abounds with similar sentiments. Seven worlds existed before ours, the Hebrews of the post-Exilic period believed, but God destroyed them all. The earth went through six consecutive reshapings, with new conditions following each set of catastrophes. The fourth earth was the generation of the Tower of Babel.

Louis Ginzberg in *Legends of the Jews* states that each of these earth ages was separated from the others by "abyss, chaos, and water." Seven heavens and seven earths were created: the earliest was Eretz, then Adamah, then Arka, Harabah, and Yabbashah. Then Tevel, and then our own earth, called Heled. Periodically the firmament collapsed, as in the days of Noah's Deluge. These ages lasted 1,656 years, according to the rabbinical tradition.

The sacred Hindu book *Bhagavata Purana* speaks of four ages and cataclysms in which mankind was nearly destroyed. Each age met its catastrophe in the form of fire, flood, and hurricane, similar to the Mayan traditions in Yucatan. The *Zend-Avesta* of the ancient Persians also relates that seven world ages or millennia occur, and Zoroaster, their prophet, tells of the portents and signs which accompany the close of each millennial age.

The Buddhists also have a tradition of world ages, or World Cycles. They also mention the three types of destruction—destruction by fire, water and by wind. The Sibylline

1. R.W. Williamson, *Religious and Cosmic Beliefs of Central Polynesia.*

books record nine ages, or nine suns, with two ages or suns yet to come.

The fact that "sun" and "age" seem interchangeable by peoples of both eastern and western hemispheres may well be significant. Could it mean that the sun itself changed its path across the sky during these periods? If so, this would indicate that the earth's axial rotation itself probably was altered, or shifted. The most likely explanation for such a shift would be extraterrestial forces rather than terrestrial causes. The evidence that this is so we will save for later.

Cosmic upheavals in the time of man seem well established, if we accept ancient historical sources as reliable. And when these sources from around the globe seem to confirm each other, and relate the same or similar episodes, then our suspicion that they are correct stands substantiated.

Documents of the ancient world describe cosmic catastrophes befalling the earth. The *Manuscript Troano* of the Mayas tells of a time when the ocean fell on the continent and a hurricane swept over the earth, carrying away all the forests and inhabited towns and villages. The end of the world age was caused by Hurakan, from which we derive the name hurricane.

The Maoris tell that during a mighty cataclysm stupendous winds, fierce squalls, clouds and dense darkness, wildly burst upon creation, with Tawhirima-tea, the father of winds and storms, in their midst, sweeping away huge forests.

In the *Epic of Gilgamesh,* which describes the universal deluge of Noah's fame, we read that for six days and a night the hurricane, deluge, and tempest continued ravaging the land, and mankind perished for the most part.

In the month of March the Polynesians celebrate a god, Taafanua. In Arabic, Tyfoon is a whirlwind and Tufan is the Deluge, says historian G. Rawlinson. He also mentions that the Chinese use a similar word, Ty-fong.

According to the book of Exodus in the Bible during the time of the Israelite passage of the Red Sea, a mighty hurricane swept the entire world—a "mighty strong west wind" (Exodus 10:19). But before the climax, "the Lord caused the sea to go back by a strong east wind all that night, and made the sea dry land, and the waters were divided" (Exo. 14:21). The Sea of the Passage—Jam Suf—is derived not from "reed" sea, as some scholars suggest, but from "hurricane" in Hebrew, *suf,* or *sufa.* In Egyptian the Red Sea is called shari, which signifies the sea of percussion, or the sea of the disaster.

The Exodus of ancient Israel out of Egypt was simultaneous with the demise or fall of the Middle Kingdom of ancient Egypt, which ended, in the words of the Egyptian historian Manetho, with a "blast of heavenly displeasure," At that time Egypt was smitten with several excruciating plagues, or natural disasters, which are recorded in the book of Exodus of the Old Testament. Astonishingly enough, these plagues were recorded also by an Egyptian eye witness. The Egyptian's name was Ipuwer and his record is known as the Ipuwer Papyrus.

Ipuwer exclaimed, in lamentation, "The river is blood."[2] This parallels the account of Moses, the Hebrew lawgiver and leader of the Exodus, who wrote: "All the waters that were in the river were turned to blood" (Exodus 7:20).

Ipuwer also declared, "Plague is throughout the land. Blood is everywhere." Again, Moses wrote: "There was blood throughout all the land of Egypt" (Exo. 7:21).

The author of Exodus also pointed out that "the river stank" (verse 21). "And all the Egyptians digged round about the river for water to drink; for they could not drink of the water of the river" (verse 24). Ipuwer put it this way: "Men shrink from tasting; human beings thirst after water." He exclaimed, "That is our water! That is our happiness! What shall we do in respect thereof? All is ruin."

Was this merely a local Egyptian disaster? Hardly. The manuscript *Quiche* of the Mayas tells that in the days of one of the great world convulsing catastrophes, when the earth quaked and the sun's motion was interrupted, the waters in the rivers turned to blood. The apostle John in the New Testament book of Revelation sees this cosmic drama as being repeated in the

2. See A. H. Gardiner, *Admonitions of an Egyptian Sage from a hieratic papyrus in Leiden,* 1909.

future, at the close of another world age or cycle (but more about this, later).

The Thracians have a myth wherein the top of their highest mountain was named Haemus ("Red") because of the "stream of blood which gushed out on the mountain" (Apollodorus, *The Library*). This according to the myth was during a heavenly battle between two celestial gods, Zeus and Typhon. A city of Egypt received the same name for the identical reason.

In one Egyptian myth the bloody hue of the world is laid to the blood of Osiris, a mortally wounded god. Another myth says the blood of Seth or Apopi is responsible. But according to Babylonian mythology, the blood of the slain heavenly monster Tiamat colored the world red.

The Finnish *Kalevala* tells how the world was sprinkled with "red milk" in the days of a cosmic disturbance. A legend of the Altai Tatars from central Asia tells of a titanic cataclysm in which "blood turns the whole world red."

Was this indeed a worldwide disturbance of some kind?

Back in Exodus we read next that "small dust" like the "ashes of the furnace" fell in all Egypt (Exo. 9:8). Then fell "a very grievous hail, such as has not been in Egypt since its foundations" (Exodus 9:18). *Barad,* here translated hail, is in most places where found in the Scriptures the term for *meteorites.* According to Midrashic and Talmudic sources, the stones or "hail" which fell on Egypt were hot.[3] In the book of Joshua, about fifty years later, another great meteor shower struck the earth—Joshua refers to them as "great stones." Again, in the book of Revelation the apostle John describes gigantic "hailstones" weighing hundreds of pounds as showering the earth in the future.

These meteorites in ancient Egypt fell "mingled with fire" (Exodus 9:24). That would be ridiculous if the stones were merely hailstones. Meteorites were meant. And their plummet to earth was accompanied with "loud noises," or crashes, and

3. See the Babylonian Talmud, Tractate Berakhot 54b, and Ginzberg, *Legends,* VI, 178.

explosion-like noises, and they were so fierce that people in Egypt were terrified out of their wits (Exo. 9:28).

The Egyptian Ipuwer wrote: "Trees are destroyed." He added: "No fruits, no herbs are found;" "Grain has perished on every side;" "That has perished which yesterday was seen. The land is left to its weariness like the cutting of flax."[4]

Moses corroborated Ipuwer's words: "And the hail (stones of barad) smote every herb of the field, and brake every tree of the field" (Exo. 9:25).

A similar catastrophic destruction is found in the text of the Buddhist *Visuddhi-Magga:* "When a world cycle is destroyed by wind," it relates, "there arises a wind to destroy the world cycle, and first it raises a fine dust, and then coarse dust, and then fine sand, and then coarse sand, and then grit, stones, up to boulders as large . . . as mighty trees on the hill tops." The hurricane velocity winds turn the ground upside down, large areas of land crack and are thrown upward, and buildings are destroyed, according to the text, when "worlds clash with worlds."[5]

From the other side of the world, the *Annals of Cuauhtitlan* in Mexico describes a cosmic cataclysm accompanied by a hail of stones. At one such epoch it was said the sky "rained not water but fire and red-hot stones."

The similarity goes even further. In the book of Exodus Moses, the Hebrew patriarch, recites that the "fire ran along the ground" (Exo. 9:23). The Ipuwer Papyrus speaks thusly: "Gates, columns, and walls are consumed by fire. The sky is in confusion."[6] The fire almost "exterminated mankind," says the eye witness.

The Midrashim, in several texts, says that naphtha, and hot stones, were poured down upon Egypt. "The Egyptians refused to let the Israelites go, and He poured out naphtha over them, burning blains." Says *The Wisdom of Solomon* in the

4. Ipuwer Papyrus 9:2-3; 3:14; 6:1; 6:3; 5:12.

5. Warren, *Buddhism in Translations,* p. 328.

6. Ipuwer 2:10; 7:1; 11:11; 12:6.

Apocrypha, the Egyptians were "pursued with strange rains and hails and showers inexorable, and utterly consumed with fire: for what was most marvelous of all, in the water which quencheth all things the fire wrought yet more mightily." Burning rivers of petroleum would account for such fires as the ancients described.

The period of the Exodus of ancient Israel out of Egypt was a period of world consuming, world-engulfing macro-cataclysm. The "miracles" the Bible relates as occurring in Egypt, the terrible plagues that smote that hapless land, were not fictitious Jewish legends or ancient fables. They were actual historical events—a part of a much larger, universal age-ending epochal cosmic conflagration and worldwide upheaval, experienced by nations around the globe.

The philosopher Philo in the century after Christ in his *On the Eternity of the World* asks the question, "And what does natural history tell us?"

He answers his own question: "Destructions of things on earth, destructions not of all at once but of a very large number, are attributed by it to two principal causes, the tremendous onslaughts of fire and water. These two visitations, we are told, descend in turns after very long cycles of years. When the agent is the conflagration, a stream of heaven-sent fire pours out from above and spreads over many places and overruns great regions of the inhabited earth."

Even the plague of darkness is corroborated elsewhere in ancient historical records. Moses described it thus: "And there was a thick darkness in all the land of Egypt three days. They saw not one another, neither rose any from his place for three days" (Exo.10:22).

Rabbinic sources disclose: "On the fourth, fifth, and sixth days, the darkness was so dense that they could not stir from their place." They add: "The darkness was of such a nature that it could not be dispelled by artificial means. The light of the fire was either extinguished by the violence of storm, or else it was made invisible and swallowed up in the density of the darkness. . . . Nothing could be discerned. . . . None was able to speak or to hear, nor could anyone venture to take food, but they lay themselves down . . . their outward senses in a trance. Thus they remained, overwhelmed by the affliction."

The Jewish historian Josephus adds that "their eyes were blinded by it and their breath choked." It was not an ordinary, earthy kind of darkness.

A shrine of black granite at el-Arish, on the border between Egypt and Palestine, contains a lengthy hieroglyphic inscription which translates: "The land was in great affliction. Evil fell on this earth. . . . There was a great upheaval in the residence. . . . Nobody could leave the palace during nine days, and during these nine days of upheaval there was such a tempest that neither men nor gods could see the faces of those beside them."[7]

Why do the accounts vary between three, seven and nine days? There could be many explanations. Perhaps the period of *total* darkness in the section of Egypt where the Israelites dwelt was three days, but other portions of the land experienced a protracted period of darkness. There can be little doubt that the Egyptian source refers to the same catastrophic event, because the text of the shrine continues, saying that after the hurricane and the darkness, the pharoah pursued the "evil-doers" to "the place called Pi-Khiroti." In Exodus 14:9 we read the Hebraic version: "But the Egyptians pursued after them, all the horses and chariots of Pharaoh . . . and overtook them encamping by the sea, beside Pi-ha-khiroth."

The parallel continues. According to the shrine: "Now when the Majesty fought with the evil-doers in this pool, the place of the whirlpool, the evil-doers prevailed not over his Majesty. His Majesty leapt into the place of the whirlpool." Exodus 15:19 adds: "For the horse of Pharoah went in with his chariots and with his horsemen into the sea, and the Lord brought again the waters of the sea upon them."

Was this phenomenon of the darkness limited to the environs of ancient Egypt? Or was it again world-wide in scope?

Nations throughout the earth, in the northern and southern latitudes and other regions have traditions hoary with age about

7. F. L. Griffith, *The Antiquities of Tel-el-Yahudiyeh and Miscellaneous Work in Lower Egypt in 1887-88.*

a cosmic cataclysm in which the sun did not shine. Other sections of the globe have traditions of a lengthy day. Sudanese tribes refer in their legends to a time when the night seemingly would never end.[8] The *Kalevala* of the Finns speaks of a time when stones of iron fell from the sky and the sun and moon disappeared; after a period of darkness, a new sun and moon were positioned anew in the sky.

Caius Julius Solinus says that "following the deluge which is reported to have occurred in the days of Ogyges, a heavy night spread over the globe."[9] One translator of his work puts it this way: "a heavy night spread over the globe for nine consecutive days." Others say "nine consecutive months."

The Iranian book *Anugita* reveals that a threefold day and threefold night concluded one of the world ages. The book *Bundahis* in *Pahlavi Texts* speaks of the world being dark at midday as though it were deepest night and says the cause of this prodigy was a war between the stars and the planets.

Even in remote China during the reign of the Emperor Yahou the sun did not set for ten days, and a similar legend in ancient India or eastern Iran declares the sun remained ten days in the sky.

Colossal earthquakes also occurred during the horror which was visited upon the world during the time of the Exodus of Israel out of Egyptian bondage. Titanic earth groanings and quakings rent and sundered the planet. The eye witness Ipuwer recited: "The towns are destroyed. Upper Egypt has become waste. . . . All is ruin." He laments, "The residence is overturned in a minute."[10]

This was the tenth plague upon Egypt. Moses records: "And Pharaoh rose up in the night, he, and all his servants, and all the Egyptians; and there was a great cry in Egypt; for there was not a house where there was not one dead" (Exodus 12:30). The angel of the Lord "passed over the houses of the children of

8. L. Frobenius, *Dichten und Denken im Sudan.*

9. Solinus, *Polyhistor.*

10. Papyrus Ipuwer 2:11; 3:13.

Israel in Egypt, when he smote the Egyptians, and delivered our houses" (Exodus 12:27).

The word "smote," *nogaf* in Hebrew, means a very violent blow, such as goring by the horns of an ox. Notice that the *houses* of the Egyptians were smitten, but none of the houses of the Israelites were touched. The first-born of the Egyptians all died in the massive earthquake; but the Israelites all survived.

The fact that this tenth plague involved a tremendous earthquake should be obvious from many passages. John, who parallels the plagues of Egypt in Revelation, chapter 16, also mentions an earthquake as the final plague. Eusebius, the early Church historian, also confirms this, quoting Artapanus who described the last night before the Exodus thusly: There was "hail and earthquake by night, so that those who fled from the earthquake were killed by the hail, and those who sought shelter from the hail were destroyed by the earthquake. And at that time all the houses fell in, and most of the temples."[11]

St. Jerome wrote in a letter that "in the night in which the Exodus took place, all the temples of Egypt were destroyed either by an earthshock or by the thunderbolt."

The passage of the children of Israel through the midst of the towering waters of the Red Sea, illustrated so profoundly in the motion picture classic *The Ten Commandments,* occurred immediately after the awesome plagues upon the land of Egypt. The period of darkness continued (Exodus 10:21). That was the last day of darkness. During this passage, the *Koran* states, the waters stood up "like mountains." The commentator Rashi, going by the grammatical structure of the sentence in Exodus, explained: "The water of all oceans and seas was divided." The Scriptures state that the waters mounted up to the heavens (Psa. 104:6-8; 107: 25-26). David wrote of this event centuries later: "He divided the sea, and caused them to pass through; and he made the waters to stand as a heap" (Psa. 78:12-13).

Did cosmic disturbances play havoc with the seas and tides around the world—or was this merely a local event?

The Chinese annals mention that in the days of Emperor

11. Eusebius, *Preparation for the Gospel,* book IX, xxvii.

Yahou when the sun did not go down for ten days, and the world was in flames, the waters themselves "overtopped the great heights, threatening the heavens with their floods." The early peoples of Peru, on the other side of the world, tell of a tradition that for five days and five nights the sun was not in the sky, and the ocean left the shore and with a terrible noise broke over the entire continent.

"The earth was plunged in darkness for a long time," say legends of the Choctaw Indians of Oklahoma. Finally a light appeared in the north, "but it was mountain-high waves, rapidly coming nearer."[12]

Notice how in each of these tales two common elements appear in sequence: a lengthy prolonged darkness (in Asia, protracted daylight), followed by mountainous-high waves, and violence in the seas.

Geologic evidence of gigantic boulders being tossed like playthings, and hurled around by these tremendous waves, is also found in many places in the world. Large boulders and rocks, of totally different mineral composition than local rocks but similar to formations many miles distant, have been found. Sometimes an erratic boulder of granite perches on a high dolerite ridge, weighing as much as ten thousand tons. The Madison boulder near Conway, New Hampshire, 90 feet by 40 feet by 38 feet weighs almost that much. It is totally unlike the bedrock beneathe it, so geologists call it "erratic."

Although great ice sheets in the ice ages may have moved some of these boulders out of position, there is evidence that many of these boulders were moved within the past 6,000 years. Tremendous ocean waves were the logical cause of these erratics.

What, then, actually happened about the middle of the second millennium before Christ? What agents triggered the massive global destruction, havoc, and chaos?

Whatever it was, deep marks were left upon the entire ancient world. Civilizations toppled. Ancient legends were born of fierce struggles for supremacy between Marduk and Tiamat, the

12. H.S. Bellamy, *Moons, Myths and Man.*

dragon; between Isis and Seth; between Vishnu and the serpent or Krishna and the serpent; between Ormuzd and Ahriman; and between Zeus and Typhon.

Typhon was that old dragon of ancient legend who "out-topped all the mountains, and his head often brushed the stars. One of his hands reached out to the west and the other to the east, and from them projected a hundred dragons' heads. From the thighs downward he had huge coils of vipers which . . . emitted a long hissing. . . . His body was all winged . . . and fire flashed from his eyes. Such and so great was Typhon when, hurling kindled rocks, he made for the very heaven with hissing and shouts, spouting a great jet of fire from his mouth."

Zeus pursued Typhon "rushing at heaven." Then, "Zeus pelted Typhon at a distance with thunderbolts, and at close quarters struck him down with an adamantine sickle, and as he fled pursued him closely as far as Mount Casius, which overhangs Syria. There, seeing the monster sore wounded, he grappled with him. But Typhon twined about him and gripped him in his coils. . . . Having recovered his strength Zeus suddenly from heaven riding in a chariot of winged horses, pelted Typhon with thunderbolts. . . . So being again pursued he (Typhon) came to Thrace and in fighting at Mount Haemus he heaved whole mountains . . . a stream of blood gushed out on the mountain, and they say that from that circumstance the mountain was called Haemus (bloody). And when he started to flee through the Sicilian sea, Zeus cast Mount Etna in Sicily upon him. That is a huge mountain, from which down to this day they say that blasts of fire issue from the thunderbolts that were thrown."

The Egyptian shore of the Red Sea was called Typhonia.[13] According to Strabo, the Aramaeans or Syrians (he called them the Arimi) were terrified witnesses of this titanic struggle for supremacy. And Typhon, "who, they add, was a dragon, when struck by the bolts of lightning, fled in search of a descent underground . . ."

Who is Typhon, or Tiamat, the dragon of mythology? What

13. Strabo, *The Geography.*

kind of ancient classic struggle were the ancients actually beholding with eyes bulging with terror?

In Pliny's *Natural History* we read: "A terrible comet was seen by the people of Ethiopia and Egypt, to which Typhon, the king of that period, gave his name; it had a fiery appearance and was twisted like a coil, and it was very grim to behold: it was not really a star so much as what might be called a ball of fire."

A disastrous comet? But a wicked king also bore this name. Since Typhon was buried at the bottom of the sea, and the Pharoah of the Exodus was also buried in the midst of the Red Sea, they are probably one and the same.

But what about the fiery comet?

Rockenbach, who wrote *De cometis tractatus novus methodicus* in 1602—he was professor of Greek, mathematics and law and dean of philosophy at Frankfort—used the most trustworthy and the most ancient of the early writers for his source material. He asserted:

"In the year of the world two thousand four hundred and fifty three—as many trustworthy authors, on the basis of many conjectures, have determined—a comet appeared which Pliny also mentioned in his second book. It was fiery, of irregular circular form, with a wrapped head; it was in the shape of a globe and was of terrible aspect. It is said that King Typhon ruled at that time in Egypt. . . . Certain (authorities) assert that the comet was seen in Syria, Babylonia, India, in the sign of Capricorn, in the form of a disc, at the time when the children of Israel advanced from Egypt toward the Promised Land, led on their way by the pillar of cloud during the day and by the pillar of fire at night."

This comet's color was bloody. It caused destruction in rising and in setting—many plagues, evils, and hunger. The Roman astrologer Campester believed that should the comet Typhon meet the earth again, in four days the world would be destroyed.

Another ancient historian, Samuel Bochart of the seventeenth century, in *Hierozoicon* also identifies the appearance of the comet Typhon with the Exodus period. He maintains that the plagues upon Egypt resemble the calamities Typhon brought in his train.

Many of the descriptive Psalms of the Old Testament become much more meaningful when we understand that they were literally true, not mere poetic license. David the Psalmist wrote:

"Then the earth shook and trembled; the foundations also of the hills moved and were shaken. . . . He bowed the heavens also and came down . . . he did fly upon the wings of the wind. . . . At the brightness that was before him his thick clouds passed, hail stones and coals of fire. The Lord also thundered in the heavens, and the Highest gave his voice; hail stones and coals of fire . . . and he shot out lightnings. . . . . Then the channels of waters were seen, and the foundations of the world were discovered" (Psalm 18:7–15).

"The voice of the Lord divideth the flames of fire. The voice of the Lord shaketh the wilderness; the Lord shaketh the wilderness of Kadesh" (Psa. 29:4-8).

"The kingdoms were moved; he uttered his voice, the earth melted" (Psa. 46:6).

"The waters saw thee; they were afraid: the depths also were troubled . . . the skies sent out a sound: thine arrows also went abroad. The voice of thy thunder was in the heaven; thy lightnings lightened the universe: the earth trembled and shook" (Psa. 77:16-19).

"Clouds and darkness are round about him . . . a fire goeth before him and burneth up his enemies round about. . . . His lightnings enlightened the world: the earth saw, and trembled" (Psa. 97:2-4).

"The earth trembled, and the heavens dropped . . . the mountains melted" (Song of Deborah, Judges 5:4-5).

"The earth shook, the heavens also dropped at the presence of God: even Sinai itself was moved" (Psa. 68:8).

Did the heavens actually drop? What was meant? Many references to the sky falling down are found in legends around the world. In the *Kalevala* of the Finns the support of the sky gave way. The Lapps pray today that the sky will not lose its support and collapse. The Eskimos of Greenland are also afraid the sky may lose its support and fall down and kill human beings, preceeded by a darkening of the sun and moon[14].

Primitive tribes in Africa also tell about the sky falling in times long ago. According to the Ovaherero tribesmen, many years ago "the Greats of the sky" let the sky fall on mankind, and only a few remained alive. The Wanyoro in Unyoro relate that the god Kagra threw the firmament upon the earth to destroy mankind.

The Cashinaua, aborigines of western Brazil, narrate the tradition: "The lightnings flashed and the thunders roared terribly and all were afraid. Then the heaven burst and the fragments fell down and killed everything and everybody. Heaven and earth changed places. Nothing that had life was left upon the earth."[15]

During this cosmic encounter of the worst kind, violent volcanoes erupted and spewed out lava. The Scriptures relate: "The mountains shake with the swelling . . . the earth melted" (Psa. 46:3-6). The Psalmist declared: "Clouds and darkness . . . fire . . . the earth saw and trembled. The hills melted like wax" (Psa. 97:2-5). Again: "He looketh on the earth, and it trembleth: he toucheth the hills, and they smoke" (Psa. 104:32). "The earth trembled . . . the mountains melted . . . even that Sinai" (Song of Deborah, Judges 5:4-5).

Even rivers dried up. "He rebuketh the sea, and maketh it dry, and drieth up all the rivers . . . The mountains quake at him, and the hills melt, and the earth is burned . . . yea, the world, and all that dwell therein" (Nahum 1:4-5).

Even these events were corroborated around the world in the memory of man.

Says the *Zend-Avesta,* "The sea boiled, all the shores of the ocean boiled, all the middle of it boiled." Indian tribes in British Columbia noted: "Great clouds appeared . . . such a great heat came, that finally the water boiled. People jumped into the streams and lakes to cool themselves, and died."[16]

---

14. Olrik, *Ragnarok.*

15. Bellamy, *Moons, Myths and Man.*

16. "Kaska Tales," *Journal of American Folk-lore,* collected by J. A. Teit.

Other tribes on the North American coast of the Pacific agreed: "It grew very hot . . . many animals jumped into the water to save themselves, but the water began to boil."[17] The Southern Utes in Colorado mention in their legends that the rivers once boiled.

The sacred *Popol-Vuh* of the Mayans tells of the time when the god "rolled mountains" and "great and small mountains moved and shaked."

This excruciating heat wave in the cosmic orogeny of the middle of the second millennium B.C. is also predicted to occur once again by the apostle John in the 16th chapter of the book of Revelation.

Obviously, ancient historical records show that something strange happened approximately four thousand, five hundred years ago. Something hard to explain. Something we cannot deny.

An author of the first century after Christ, called Pseudo-Philo, writing about the events at the Exodus, said: "The mountain (Sinai) burned with fire and the earth shook and the hills were removed and the mountains overthrown; the depths of fire shone forth and thunderings and lightenings were multiplied, and winds and tempests made a roaring: the stars were gathered together (collided)."[18] This author added, referring to the verse in Psalm 18 where "He bowed the heavens," that the Lord actually "impeded the stars." He asserted: "The earth was stirred from her foundation, and the mountains and the rocks trembled in their fastenings, and the clouds lifted up their waves against the flame of the fire that it should not consume the world . . . and all the waves of the sea came together."

What we see, with painstaking clarity, is that in the midst of the second millenium B.C. a cosmic catastrophe occurred which shook the planet earth to its foundations. It was witnessed by nations around the globe, and it terrified them and shattered their societies. It was accompanied by sky-high tidal waves;

17. Thompson, *Tales of the North American Indians.*

18. *The Biblical Antiquities of Philo.*

volcanic outpourings; tremendous earthquakes; meteor showers; murky, turgid darkness; upheavals of every description on land, in the sea, and in the air.

Why don't history books mention this? But there is much, much more to the story. We have only begun to unravel the amazing truth.

Chapter Three

The Universal Flood

Another great cosmic upheaval which rocked the planet earth and annihilated almost every living thing upon the planet, was the tremendous deluge of the days of Noah.

In recent years a motion picture attempted to demonstrate the reality of the Flood and the Ark. Climbers have scaled the slopes of Mount Ararat in eastern Armenian Turkey, to approximately the 13,000 foot mark, where they have found a frozen ice-locked lake, and within it they have discovered pieces of timber—ancient coal black oak. Various laboratories have analyzed the wood and have dated it as very, very ancient. Perhaps it is not the wood from Noah's ark, as some of the radioactive datings obtained have indicated the wood is too recent for that. But the mystery of the boat in the lake in the high reaches of Mount Ararat remains. Why have tremendous quantities of wood been found high above the timber line? How did it get there?

From time to time human sitings of the remains of what is believed to be the Ark have been made. Flavius Josephus in his epochal book *Antiquities of the Jews* declared:

"Now all the writers of barbarian histories make mention of this flood, and of this ark; among whom is Berosus the Chaldean. For when he is describing the circumstances of the flood, he goes on thus: 'It is said there is still some part of this ship in Armenia, at the mountain of the Cordyaeans; and that some people carry off pieces of the bitumen, which they take away, and use chiefly as amulets for the averting of mischiefs.'

Hieronymus the Egyptian also, who wrote the Phoenician Antiquities, and Mnaseas, and a great many more, make mention of the same. Nay, Nicolaus of Damascus, in his ninety-sixth book, hath a particular relation about them; where he speaks thus: 'There is a great mountain in Armenia, over Minyas, called Baris, upon which it is reported that many who fled at the time of the Deluge were saved; and that one who was carried in an ark came on shore upon the top of it; and that the remains of the timber were a great while preserved. This might be the man about whom Moses the legislator of the Jews wrote' ".

According to the Biblical account, God told Noah: "Make thee an ark of gopher wood; rooms shalt thou make in the ark, and shalt pitch it within and without with pitch. And this is the fashion which thou shalt make it of: The length of the ark shall be three hundred cubits, the breadth of it fifty cubits, and the height of it thirty cubits" (Genesis 6:14-15).

The standard cubit, was about 18 inches, making the Ark 450 feet long, 75 feet wide and 45 feet high. Using this cubit, the volume of the Ark would have been 1,396,000 cubic feet with a carrying capacity of 522 standard sized railroad stock cars. Only in modern times have ships of such massive size been built.

Aboard such a ship the patriarch Noah could have easily carried 35,000 different species of vertebrate land-dwelling animals. If the average size of the animals was the size of a sheep, there would have been plenty of room upon the Ark. A standard two-decked stock car carries about 240 sheep. Only 146 stock cars would have been needed to carry 35,000 individual animals, or 292 standard size stock cars to carry pairs of 35,000 species.

But did the deluge really occur?

According to the book of Genesis, it rained upon the earth forty days and nights, and the fountains of the great deep were broken up. "In the six hundredth year of Noah's life, in the second month, on the seventeenth day of the month, on that day the fountains of the great abyss all burst, and the sluices of heaven were opened" (Genesis 7:11, *Moffatt*).

The account continues: "The deluge covered the earth for forty days. The waters swelled and rose high on the earth, and the barge floated on the surface of the waters; the waters swelled mightily on the earth, till every high mountain under heaven was covered—the waters swelling twenty-two feet higher, till the mountains were covered, and every living creature perished, bird, beast, and animal, every reptile that crawls on earth, and every man. For a hundred and fifty days the waters swelled over the earth" (Genesis 7:17-24, *Moffatt*).

Not until one year later, on the seventeenth day of the second month, did the waters dry from off the earth (Gen. 8:14). At that time Noah and his family—his wife, their three sons, and their three wives, numbering eight individuals—left the ark and set about to make a new life for themselves.

Did the Deluge really happen? What kind of cosmic disturbance would have created such a stupendous global event?

Stories of a universal deluge of waters abound all over the earth, in the primitive legends of countless races and peoples. The ancient Sumerians had extensive legends about a great flood which came upon the earth. The hero of the Sumerian legend was an old man by the name of Xisouthros, also called Ziusudra. According to their legend, he was warned by the diety that "a flood will sweep over the cult-centers; To destroy the seed of mankind . . ." The stone tablet containing the story, found at Nippur, continues: "All the windstorms, exceedingly powerful, attacked as one, at the same time, the flood sweeps over the cult-centers. After, for seven days and seven nights, the flood has swept over the land, and the huge boat had been tossed about by the windstorms on the great waters . . ."

Old Babylonian traditions tell how one Utnapishtim was commanded by a diety, "Tear down this house, build a ship! . . . Aboard the ship take thou the seed of all living things. The ship that thou shalt build, Her dimensions shall be to measure. Equal shall be her width and her length."

Other legends from around the globe tell a similar story. A very old Aztec flood legend, translated from the *Codex Chimalpopoca*, states: "The waters and the sky drew near each other . . . But before the flood began, Titlachahuan had warned the man Nota and his wife Nena, saying, 'Make no more pulque, but hollow a great cypress into which you shall enter in the month Tozoztli. The waters shall near the sky.' They entered, and when Titlachahuian had shut them in he said to the man, 'Thou shalt eat but a single ear of maize, and thy wife but one also.' And when they had each eaten one ear of maize, they prepared to go forth, for the water was tranquil."

The Papagos of northwestern Mexico relate that Montezuma escaped from a great flood, having been warned of its coming by a coyote. He hollowed out a boat for himself to escape the flood waters.

The Toltecs also had an extensive flood literature. The historian Ixtlilxochitl wrote: "It is found in the histories of the Toltecs that this age and the first world, as they call it, lasted 1,716 years; that men were destroyed by tremendous rains and lightning from the sky, and even all the land, without the exception of anything, and the highest mountains were covered by and submerged in water fifteen cubits (caxtolmolatli); and here they add other fables of how men came to multiply from the few who escaped from this destruction in a 'toptlipetlocali,' which nearly signifies a closed chest; and how, after men had multiplied, they erected a very high 'zacuali,' which is today a tower of great height, in order to take refuge in it should the second world (age) be destroyed."

The Kolushes of Alaska have a tradition that the father of the Indian tribes formerly lived toward the rising sun. Warned in a dream that a deluge would desolate the earth, he built a raft and saved himself, family, and all animals, floating for several months upon the water.

A flood legend in India, half way around the world, is found in the *Rig Veda.* A fish tells Manu if he protects the fish, and returns him to the ocean when of full size, he will likewise protect Manu from a great deluge which will sweep away all creatures.

A Hawaiian flood legend is remarkably similar to the Hebrew story, though apparently of totally independent origin. The natives of Hawaii say that the earth had become careless of worship and very wicked. Only one righteous man remained,—a man named Nu-u. He made a great canoe with a house on it and sailed, stocked with food, taking plants and animals on board.

The flood waters arose and destroyed all mankind except Nu-u and his family.

Other flood traditions come from the Incas, the Leeward islanders, the Fiji Islands, the Voguls in the Ural Mountains, the Laplanders, Norwegians, the Welsh, Lithuanians, Assyrians and Greeks. In the Fijiian legend, a great rain took place which submerged the islands, but before the highest mountains were covered two large double canoes appeared. Rokova, the god of carpenters, and Rokola, his head workman, were in them. Those saved in the canoes were eight in number.

The story of the deluge of Noah has its parallel in a Chinese tradition about a universal flood in prehistoric times, in the days of Fo-hi, who alone of all the country was saved.

Such a devastating flood must have had an enormous effect on the earth. Whether we like to think of it or not, the earth may have been affected in many ways. Even its diurnal rotation and position of its axis of rotation may have been affected.

In Tractate Sanhedrin of the Talmud we read: "Seven days before the deluge, the Holy One changed the primeval order and the sun rose in the west and set in the east" (108b). *Tevel* is the Hebrew name for the world in which the sun rose in the west. *Arabot* is the name of the sky where the rising point was in the west.

The *Koran* speaks of the Lord of "two easts and of two wests." Averrhoes, an Arab philosopher of the twelfth century, tells about the eastward and westward movements of the sun.

Even the Eskimos of Greenland told missionaries that in an ancient time the earth turned over and the people who lived then became antipodes.[1]

Seler, perplexed by the statement of the old Mexican sources that the sun moved toward the east, exclaimed: "The traveling toward the east and the disappearance in the east. . . . must be understood literally. . . . However, one cannot imagine the sun as wandering eastward: the sun and the entire firmament of the fixed stars travel westward." Nevertheless, the ancient peoples of Mexico called the sun that moves toward the east Teotl Lix-

1. Orlik, *Ragnarok.*

co. They symbolized the changing direction of the sun's movement as a heavenly ball game with attendent upheavals and earthquakes.

It is also noteworthy that in the city of Ugarit, also known as Ras Shamra, in Palestine, a poem was found dedicated to the planet goddess Anat who "Massacred the population of the Levant" and who also "exchanged the two dawns and the position of the stars"[2].

Bellamy, in *Moons, Myths and Man* points out: "The Chinese say that it is only since a new order of things had come about that the stars move from east to west." He adds: "The signs of the Chinese zodiac have the strange peculiarity of proceeding in a retrograde direction, that is, against the course of the sun."

Statements of the sun setting in the east are also found among the ancient Greek classical authors, particularly in the works of Plato. In *Timaeus* Plato describes a collision of the earth with "a tempest of winds," with "alien fire from without," or waters of "the immense flood which foamed in and streamed out," with the earth engaging in all motions, "forwards and backwards, and again to right and to left, and upwards and downwards, wandering every way in all the six directions."

Plato speaks of the earth, represented as possessing a soul, as suffering a "violent shaking of the revolutions of the Soul," "a total blocking of the course of the same," and which "produced all manner of twistings, and caused in their circles fractures and disruptures of every possible kind, with the result that, as they barely held together one with another, they moved indeed but more irrationally, being at one time reversed, at another oblique, and again upside down."

Have the directions east and west been reversed? According to a short fragment of a historical drama by Sophocles (*Atreus*) the sun rises in the east only since its course was reversed: "Zeus . . . changed the course of the sun, causing it to rise in the east and not in the west."

2. C. Virolleaud, *Mission de Ras Shamra.*

Euripides wrote in *Electra,* "Then in his anger arose Zeus, turning the stars' feet back on the fire-fretted way; yea, and the sun's car splendour-burning, and the misty eyes of the morning grey. And the flash of his chariot-wheels back-flying flushed crimson the face of the fading day. . . . The sun . . . turned backward . . . with the scourge of his wrath in affliction repaying mortals."

Seneca, in *Thyestes,* reveals the reaction of the people living through such traumatic events. He has them asking, in terror: "Have we of all mankind been deemed deserving that heaven, its poles uptorn, should overwhelm us? In our time has the last day come?"

Ironically, or so it would seem to most Egyptologists, in the tomb of Senmut, the architect of Queen Hatshepsut, a panel on the ceiling shows the vault of heaven depicted, with the signs of the zodiac and other constellations in a reversed orientation of the southern sky. In this panel, which was a venerated chart apparently from several centuries earlier, in the Orion-Sirius group, Orion appears west of Sirius instead of east. A. Pogo, in "The Astronomical Ceiling Decoration in the Tomb of Senmut," wrote candidly: "A characteristic feature of the Senmut ceiling is the astronomically objectionable orientation of the southern panel." He continues: "The orientation of the southern panel is such that the person in the tomb looking at it has to lift his head and fact north, not south." Says Pogo, "With the reversed orientation of the south panel, Orion, the most conspicuous constellation of the southern sky, appeared to be moving eastward, i.e., in the wrong direction."

Apparently, the southern panel shows the sky over Egypt as it was before the heavens reversed north and south, east and west.

Such a contention is, of course, contrary to the established beliefs of astronomers. But the words of the ancients are demanding, loud, strident, and clear. They unanimously and with one voice shout that the sun once rose in the west and set in the east! As impossible as this seems to be to believe, and we shake our heads in incredulity, the inscriptions do not leave any room for misunderstanding. Harakhte is the Egyptian name for the western sun. Breasted records the inscription: "Harakhte, he *riseth* in the west."[3]

In the *Ermitage Papyrus*,[4] reference is made to a cataclysm that turned the "land upside down; happens that which never (yet) had happened."[5]

Similarly the Magical Papyrus Harris speaks of a tremendous catastrophe in which fire and water destroy the earth, and "the south becomes north, and the Earth turns over."

The priests of Egypt, when Herodotus, the "father of history," was researching his history of Egypt, asserted that within historical ages and since Egypt became a kingdom, "four times in this period (so they told me) the sun rose contrary to his wont; twice he rose where he now sets, and twice he set where he now rises."[6]

What then are we to believe?

Caius Julius Solinus, a Latin author of the third century after Christ, wrote a story about the people living on the southern borders of Egypt. He narrates: "The inhabitants of this country say that they have it from their ancestors that the sun now sets where it formerly rose."

These facts make more meaningful the observation that many of the ancient tribes of the earth equated "sun" with an "age."

The Talmud and other rabbinical sources relate of great disturbances in the solar movement at the time of the Exodus, the passage through the Red Sea, and at Mount Sinai. Other traditions connect the reversal in the direction of the sun's journey across the sky with a great deluge.

But perhaps the Scripture becomes more literally clear, in this context, when we read: "all the foundations of the earth are out of course" (Psalm 82:5).

From as far north as Finland, in the *Kalevala,* we read, "the sun occasionally steps from his accustomed path."

---

3. *Ancient Records of Egypt,* III, section 18.

4. Leningrad, 1116b recto.

5. Gardiner, *Journal of Egyptian Archaeology.*

6. *Herodotus,* book II, 142.

In *Voluspa* of the Icelanders we are told: "No knowledge she (the sun) had where her home should be, The moon knew not what was his, The stars knew not where their stations were."

In the western hemisphere, the shattered condition of the earth after an "age" ended, with prevailing gloom and darkness, and disorder, led to speculation as to where the new sun would first appear.

The Mayan legends relate that "it was not known from where the new sun would appear." "They looked in all directions, but they were unable to say where the sun would rise. Some thought it would take place in the north and their glances were turned in that direction. Others thought it would be in the south. Actually, their guesses included all directions because the dawn shone all around. Some, however, fixed their attention to the orient, and maintained that the sun would come from there It was their opinion that proved to be correct."

The Aztecs put it this way: "There had been no sun in existence (that is, visible) for many years . . . (The chiefs) began to peer through the gloom in all directions for the expected light, and to make bets as to what part of heaven he (the sun) should first appear in. Some said 'Here,' and some said "There,' but when the sun rose, they were all proved wrong, for not one of them had fixed upon the east."

Ancient memory scars persist. On the Andaman Islands the natives are fearful that someday a natural catastrophe will cause the world to turn over. And in Greenland the Eskimos fear that the earth will turn over. The people of Flanders in Belgium go further: "In Menin (Flanders) the peasants say, on seeing a comet: 'The sky is going to fall; the earth is turning over!' "

This planet has gone through turbulent, tumultuous times. Isaiah the prophet, son of Amos, who lived about 800 years before Christ, wrote:

"Behold, the Lord maketh the earth empty, and maketh it waste, and *turneth it upside down,* and scattereth abroad the inhabitants thereof. . . . The land shall be utterly emptied, and utterly spoiled: for the Lord hath spoken this word. The earth mourneth and fadeth away, the world languisheth and fadeth away, the haughty people of the earth do languish. The earth also is defiled under the inhabitants thereof; because they have transgressed the laws, changed the ordinance, broken the everlasting covenant. Therefore hath the curse devoured the earth, and they that dwell therein are desolate; therefore the inhabitants of the earth are burned, and few men left" (Isaiah 24:1-6).

The prophet laments:

"From the uttermost part of the earth have we heard songs, even glory to the righteous. But I said, My leanness, my leanness, woe unto me! the treacherous dealers have dealt treacherously. Fear, and the pit, and the snare, are upon thee, o inhabitant of the earth. And it shall come to pass, that he who fleeth from the noise of the fear shall fall into the pit; and he that cometh up out of the midst of the pit shall be taken in the snare: *for the windows from on high are open, and the foundations of the earth do shake.*"

Surely the prophet was describing a colossal destruction upon mankind. He spoke of the foundations of the earth being shaken, of the inhabitants of the earth being "burned," the earth being "utterly emptied," made "waste," and even "turned upside down."

But to leave no doubt as to the extent of the catastrophe he was describing, Isaiah continued:

"The earth is utterly broken down, the earth is clean dissolved, the earth is *moved* exceedingly" (verse 19). "The earth shall *reel to and fro* like a drunkard, and shall be removed like a cottage; and the transgression thereof shall be heavy upon it; and it shall fall, and not rise again" (verse 20).

Dramatic changes in the earth's orbit—destruction on every continent—a planet careening through space—upside down—hurled into a new orbit around the sun.

A great change of climate occurred after the flood of Noah's time. The life span of mankind was greatly reduced. Tremendous changes had been wrought in the surface of the earth. Naturally, a change in the orientation of the sun would alter the seasons. The Egyptian papyrus known as *Papyrus Anastasi IV* laments: "The winter is come as summer, the months are reversed and the hours are disordered''[7].

In the *Texts of Taoism,* we read, "The four seasons do not observe their proper times''[8].

In China, during the reign of Emperor Yahou, the emperor sent astronomers to the Valley of Obscurity and to the Sombre Residence to observe the new movements of the sun and the moon, and to investigate and inform the people "of the order of the seasons." Tradition also relates that Yahou introduced a calendar reform, bringing the seasons into accord with the observations.

Plutarch attributed the changes of the seasons to Typhon "the destructive, diseased and disorderly" who caused "abnormal seasons and temperatures''[9].

According to Plutarch: "The thickened air concealed the heaven from view, and the stars were confused with a disorderly huddle of fire and moisture and violent fluxions of winds. The sun was not fixed to an unwandering and certain course, so as to distinguish orient and occident, nor did he bring back the seasons in order''[10].

From a far distant part of the globe, among the Oraibi Indians in Arizona, the oral tradition is held that the firmament once hung low and the world was dark, and no sun, moon nor stars could be seen. The people grumbled because of the darkness and the cold. Then the god Lachito "appointed times, and seasons, and ways for the heavenly bodies''[11].

During the time of Moses, also, the seasons were changed, as the earth underwent convolutions and paroxysms of nature. It is said in rabbinical sources that in Moses' day the course of the heavenly bodies became confounded[12].

During the Exodus, God gave Moses a new calendar. Moses was told: "This month shall be unto you the beginning of mon-

7. A. Erman, *Egyptian Literature,* 1927, p. 309.
8. I, 301.
9. *Isis and Osiris,* 49.
10. *Morals.*
11. Donnelly, *Ragnarok,* p. 212.
12. Pirkei Rabbi Elieser 8; Leet Midrashim 2a; Ginzberg, *Legends,* VI, 24.

ths: it shall be the first month of the year to you" (Exo. 12:2). Why a new calendar that began in the spring, when the traditional calendar that dated back to Creation began in the fall? The beginning of the calendar was moved to a point about half a year away from the autumnal New Year. It is suspected by some, and there is evidence in the Jewish sources, that during the Exodus observation of the sky was hindered and changes occurred in the movement of the earth and moon. The calendar could not be correctly computed. The altered year, month and day required new, prolonged, unobstructed observation.

During the flood of Noah's time, and the time of Moses and the Exodus, great world ages came to an end. The four quarters of the world were displaced. The sun rose in a different location. The seasons were altered. great calamities and catastrophes overtook frightened, terrorized nations. Wind storms, fires of enormous size, violent paroxysms of wind and water, upheavals of land, earthquakes and volcanic eruptions, tremendous lava flows, combined to herald at both historic junctures "the end of the world."

How long was the year at that time? Scripture reveals that God has it within His power to establish—or to change—seasons and laws of the heavens. A statement found as a gloss on a manuscript of *Timaeus* states that a calendar of a solar year of three hundred and sixty days (not 365 and a quarter) was introduced in Egypt by the Hyksos after the fall of the Middle Kingdom (after the Exodus of Israel).

The calendar year in the days of Noah was apparently 360 days—shorter than the current year by five and one quarter days. This can not be conclusively proven; however, statements in the book of Genesis are quite clear that from the 17th day of the second month to the 17th day of the seventh month were 150 days, making each month 30 days in length. One can deduce from this that a year of 12 months was exactly 360 days in length. This 360 day year crops up often in Scripture. It is used in the book of Daniel, and the book of Revelation, in the New Testament, in terms of what scholars call the "prophetic year."

One is tempted to speculate that originally the year was 360 days in length; it became confused, and changed, due to the exacerbations of the planet earth in its turbulent history; but during the time of "restitution of all things," the year will once again, in the future, during another "end of an age," revert back to its original 360 day length.

In Midrash Rabba, on the authority of Rabbi Simon we learn that a new world order came into being with the end of the sixth world age at Mount Sinai: "There was a weakening of the creation. Hitherto world time was counted, but henceforth we count it by a different reckoning." Midrash Rabba also refers to "the greater length of time taken by some planets."

Here is indication that not only the earth was involved in astronomical abnormalities; other planets of the solar system might also have been affected.

Could the violent upheavals of the Deluge, and the period of the Exodus from Egypt and the Conquest of the Promised Land, have been largely due to the visitation of a strange comet? Was it the destructive ravages of this malevolent comet that unhinged humanity, and left a subconscious scar upon the memory banks of mankind?

In 1910 Halley's comet appeared, and the earth actually passed through the comet's tail. At that time there was mass prediction of doom, gloom and even hysteria and panic. For a month prior to the passage of the comet, newspapers played up the story about the "celestial intruder," "the awesome torch of heaven," and "the wandering monster of the sky."

At that time the industrial revolution had already changed society. The age of rationalism had dawned. Evolutionary theory propounded by Charles Darwin had shaken the citadels of religious orthodoxy and the believers in special Creation. People considered themselves as bright, intelligent, definitely non-superstitious, level-headed and shrewd.

Nevertheless, with the appearance of the comet, rationality was abandoned. Scientists widely predicted that "the towering rocks which overlook Lake Superior may be smashed to smithereens, that fire might spout from the interior of the earth and that all the world may undergo the same alarming process of annihilation."

One savant claimed the comet of 1910 would cause a new Ice

Age. Another suggested that the comet's gravitational pull would cause 13,000-foot tidal waves. He added that the tail of the comet consisted of poisonous gases and the planet might perish by asphyxiation, or hydrogen in the tail might ignite and create a universal conflagration.

Still another opined that the gases in the comet's tail might unite with nitrogen in the air and form laughing gas. "In that case, humanity would go to its death in a delirium of joy," he cheerfully suggested.

As the comet approached, panic grew. There were scattered reports of suicides. In the South there were reports of mass conversions to Christianity, more people began attending church, seeking to make amends for their sins. Miners in Wilkes-Barre, Pa., on the day of the comet's arrival refused to go into the mines.

May 18 came and went; the earth passed through the comet's tail; and nothing happened. The end of the world didn't come, after all.

But why is it that people become jumpy, nervous, their facial muscles begin to twitch, when they hear of a new comet approaching the earth? Why have millions considered comets to be dire warnings of the future—to presage death and destruction? Why have comets throughout history been considered dire messengers of God to proclaim the "end of the world"?

Is it because, in actual fact, long, long ago close encounters of the earth with comets did result in widespread devastation, chaos and catastrophe?

The legend of Phaethon may be a reference to such an ancient comet of fiery destruction. The Greek legend tells of young Phaethon who on that fatal day tried to drive the chariot of the sun. Unable to proceed against "the whirling poles," he was swept away by their "swift axis." Phaethon in Greek actually means "the blazing one"—and what better reference could one make of a comet.

The Latin poet Ovid dealt with the story of Phaethon. In his version the chariot of the sun, driven by Phaethon, moved "no longer in the same course as before." The chariot's horses "break loose from their course" and "rush aimlessly, knocking against the stars set deep in the sky and snatching the chariot along through uncharted ways." The constellations of the Bears tried to plunge into the forbidden sea. The sun's chariot was "borne along just as a ship driven before the headlong blast, whose pilot has let the useless rudder go and abandoned the ship to the gods and prayers."[13]

The legend continues: "The earth bursts into flame, the highest parts first, and splits into deep cracks, and its moisture is all dried up. The meadows are burned to white ashes; the trees are consumed, green leaves and all, and the ripe grain furnishes fuel for its own destruction. . . . Great cities perish with their walls, and the vast conflagration reduces whole nations to ashes."

How similar this description to the end-time plagues of the Book of Revelation, chapter 16! There a third of the green trees is burned up. Revelation, chapter 8, also recounts these enormous plagues, tying them in with a cometary visitation from the nether regions of outer space! We will discuss this marvelous wonder more fully in a later chapter.

Solon, a wise ruler of Athens, on his visit to Egypt questioned the priests who were well versed in the lore of antiquity. One of the priests, an old man, told him:

"There have been and there will be many and divers destructions of mankind, of which the greatest are by fire and water, and lesser ones by countless other means. For in truth the story that is told in your country as well as ours, how once upon a time Phaethon, son of Helios, yoked his father's chariot, and, because he was unable to drive it along the course taken by his father, burnt up all that was upon the earth and himself perished by a thunderbolt—that story, as it is told, has the fashion of a legend, but the truth of it lies in the occurrence of a shifting of the bodies in the heavens which move around the earth, and a destruction of the things on the earth by fierce fire, which recurs at long intervals."[14]

The Scriptures also refer to such celestial wonders.

---

13. Ovid, *Metamorphoses,* Book II.
14. Plato, *Timaeus,* 22 C-D.

In the King James Bible we read:

"God came from Teman (the south), and the Holy One from mount Paran. Selah. His glory covered the heavens . . . And his brightness was as the light; he had horns coming out of his hand: and there was the hiding of his power. Before him went the pestilence, and burning coals went forth at his feet. He stood, and measured the earth: he beheld, and drove asunder the nations; and the everlasting mountains were scattered, the perpetual hills did bow: his ways are everlasting. I saw the tents of Cushan in affliction: and the curtains of the land of Midian did tremble. Was the Lord displeased against the rivers? was thine anger against the rivers? was thy wrath against the sea, that thou didst ride upon thine horses and thy chariots of salvation? . . . Thou didst cleave the earth with rivers. The mountains saw thee, and they trembled: the overflowing of the water passed by: the deep uttered his voice, and lifted up his hands on high. The sun and moon stood still in their habitation: at the light of thine arrows they went, and at the shining of thy glittering spear. Thou didst march through the land in indignation, thou didst thresh the heathen in anger" (Habakkuk 3:3-12).

A chariot pulled by horses—"horns coming out of his hands"—such a description could easily apply to the form of a comet and its flaming tail. Is it possible that the ancients were right? That God used comets, or specially prepared comets, as agents of His divine wrath and destruction? Are comets at times harbingers of divine fury unleashed upon a froward and recalcitrant mankind, arbitrary, full of pride and ego, bent upon his own ways, heedless of the mercies of a divine Providence?

Habakkuk says the portent upon that fateful day of old had the form of a man in a chariot drawn by flaming horses, and was regarded as God's angel. When it came, the world burned, rivers dried up, the mountains were scattered, melted down like wax, trembled, and the deep ocean uttered its voice, and stirred up into a frenzy.

Could the Deluge have been caused by such a heavenly prodigy?

The story of Noah's deluge, according to many skeptics is beyond the pale of scientific acceptance. Any references to global catastrophes, they claim, are mythological and unworthy of serious consideration by educated scholars.

But tremendous globe-shaking catastrophes which destroyed much of life on earth would not be quickly forgotten, by the affected peoples of the world. The story of the Flood has survived for about 5,000 years, and is still going strong. It can be found in the traditions and legends in some form in more than 200 different cultures, past and present. These accounts are truly global in nature. Flood accounts are found in the far north, among the Eskimos, among the Siberian peoples, in Finland and Iceland. In the south, similar legends are found among the Maori of New Zealand, the Australian aborigines, and the natives at Tierra del Fuego, at the tip of South America.

Dr. Arthur C. Custance, fellow of the Canadian Royal Anthropological Institute, who has authored 52 treatises relating to ancient history, archaeology and Biblical history, has studied in detail the massive amount of cultural accounts relating to the Noachian Flood. In "Flood Traditions of the World," he points out that although the accounts often differ widely, they are in accord in four basic respects:

"1. The cause was a 'moral' one. Man brought the Flood on himself either by his disobedience or because of lack of piety and reverence. In all the Flood accounts, with the one notable exception—the Flood tradition from Egypt—the catastrophe comes as a judgment.

"2. They speak of one man who is warned of the coming catastrophe and thus saves not only himself but also his family or his friends. Forewarning is always given in some way. In the Biblical account, Noah is warned by revelation in a manner which is clear and reasonable if we allow that God is able to communicate with man.

"3. The world was depopulated except for these few survivors, from whom the present people of the world were derived. None of the flood accounts leaves one with the impression that the survivors named subsequently met any other survivors to form a new community for the repopulating of the area. They alone escaped in every case creating strong evidence for a universal flood rather than a local flood.

"4. Animals play a part either in conveying the warning, in providing the transportation to safety, or in giving information about the state of things after the Flood had subsided. Very frequently birds are mentioned in the accounts. The use of birds in antiquity and in modern times as navigational aids has been very widespread."

Lending further authenticity to the Biblical account, says Dr. Custance, is the fact that in extra-Biblical accounts the survivors always land on a local mountain. But in the Hebrew account the Ark lands far from Palestine, in a distant country. Declares Custance:

"This is an unusual circumstance because all other Flood accounts report that the Ark landed locally. In Greece, on Mount Parnassus; in India, in the Himalayas; and in America, one ancient Indian account has it landing on Keddie Peak in the Sacramento Valley. Everywhere the same—always a local mountain."

He continues: "This circumstance surely suggests that here in the Bible we have the genuine account. And it also underscores the great respect that the Hebrew people had for the Word of God and the requirement that they never tamper with it. It would surely, otherwise, have been most natural for them to land the Ark on their most famous mountain, Mount Zion."[15]

Some of the widespread accounts agree with the Biblical account that eight souls survived. A number of accounts give extraordinarily graphic details of such incidental events to the Flood as must have accompanied it. Although the Biblical account, based on the first-hand observations and records kept by Noah himself, seems matter-of-fact, and contains no embellishments, one cuneiform text tells of bodies floating about like logs in the water.[16]

Dr. Custance continues: "The great majority of these flood

---

15. Patten, *A Symposium on Creation,* pp. 9-10.

16. Barton, George, *Archaeology and the Bible,* p. 337.

accounts have in common, as we have seen, only four basic elements. All other details—the nature of the warning, the escape 'vessel,' the part played by animals, and so forth—differ in such a way that borrowing from the Biblical record is virtually excluded altogether."

"These native traditions of the flood," says Dr. Custance, "are undoubtedly recollections from the very distant past of an event which was so stupendous that it was never forgotten, even though the details themselves became blurred, with local coloring restoring what had faded.

"In a sense, therefore, all these stories are in agreement, though in fact, they are often as different in detail as it is possible to imagine. In a court of law the testimony of witnesses who both agree and disagree in this fashion is considered to be a more powerful witness to the central truth than would be complete concord, for in the nature of the case collaboration is manifestly excluded."

One of the most ancient and most remarkable corroborative testimonies to the great flood was found on a clay tablet in an ancient library excavated at Nineveh. This tablet came from the reign of Assyrian king Ashurbanipal (669-627 B.C.). The library contained 100,000 clay tablets, sealed and forgotten until the site was uncovered by archaeologists in the 1850s.

In this particular clay tablet, Ashurbanipal himself mentioned: "I have read the artistic script of Sumer on the back of Akkadian, which is hard to master. Now I take pleasure in the reading of the stones coming from before the flood."

Also first unearthed at the Nineveh site was the famous Gilgamesh flood epic. Various versions of the flood epic have since been found at other places, but the Gilgamesh Epic is still the most famous of these accounts. Like the Biblical account, the Gilgamesh epic states the flood was divinely planned. Both agree that the impending Flood was divinely revealed to the hero of the account. Both agree the Deluge was sent as punishment upon a wicked human race. Both agree the hero and his family were delivered. Both agree the hero was divinely instructed to build a huge vessel to preserve life. Both accounts indicate the physical causes of the Deluge. Both specify the duration of the

Flood, though they disagree in the length of the Flood. Both name the landing place. Both tell of sending out birds to determine the decrease of waters. Both describe acts of worship of the hero following deliverance. And both accounts speak of special blessings upon the hero after the catastrophe.

Among the most impressive accounts of the Noachian deluge are those coming down to us from the ancient Chinese. A flood of devastating force is said to have occurred around 2300 B.C. (one account says 2297 B.C.). An overflowing of the great rivers caused the flood, according to the story. Fah-Le, the Chinese hero, escaped the destruction with his wife and three children.

Other traditions about the universal Flood in China maintain that all Chinese are descendants of "Nu-wah," an ancient ancestor who became famous by surviving a great flood.

But of all the flood accounts, the Biblical account seems to be the best, the most reliable. Wrote Sir William Dawson, a historian of the nineteenth century, in *The Story of the Earth and Man* (London, 1880): "I have long thought that the narrative in Genesis 7 and 8 can be understood only on the supposition that it is a contemporary journal or log of an eye-witness incorporated by the author of Genesis in his work.

"The dates of the rising and fall of the water, the note of soundings over the hilltops when the maximum was attained, and many other details as well as the whole tone of the narrative, seem to require this supposition."

The cause of the universal flood, the specific agent which precipitated the Deluge, has never been identified conclusively. Although the Bible simply states that God brought on the flood to destroy a wicked, erring humanity, the actual cause for the subterranean deeps to break up, and for the waters of the ocean to gush over the land masses of the earth, covering them completely, has gone undetected.

Speculation, however, is rife. And most authorities seem to agree that the spark that set off the flood had to be extraterrestrial in origin. Dr. Frederick Filby in *The Flood Reconsidered* suggests that a canopy of water hung over the pre-Flood world. Many Biblical scholars assert that the pre-Flood world's atmosphere was canopied by a layer of water vapor, creating a greenhouse effect on the planet. Temperatures throughout the earth, they say, were remarkably similar, and tropical plants and life forms even thrived in the Arctic and Antarctic regions.

Support for the water vapor canopy theory comes from the book of Genesis itself, chapter 1, verses 6-7: "And God said, Let there be a firmament (expansion) is the midst of the waters, and let it divide the waters from the waters. And God made the firmament, and divided the waters which were under the firmament *from the waters which were above the firmament:* and it was so."

A canopy of water vapor around the earth would have had very important corollary effects upon life on earth. It would have moderated fluctuations in temperature change, and produced a "greenhouse" type of world. Harmful ultraviolet radiation from the sun would have been largely filtered out before it reached the earth, thus possibly enabling men to live much longer lives. The traditions of several ancient peoples, aside from the Biblical record, indicates that in a long gone era men lived for hundreds of years. Methuselah, the Bible records matter-of-factly, lived to the ripe old age of 969. The indication from Genesis is that humans matured much more slowly and were often over one hundred years old before they married and had children (Genesis 5:6, 9, 12, 15, 18, 28).

Says geographer Donald Patten, "It is proposed that the water vapor canopy was 3,000 to 5,000 feet thick, and ranged between 5,000 and 10,000 feet above sea level.

"The pre-Flood atmosphere also is suspected to have contained from 6 to 8 times as much carbon dioxide as the present atmosphere.

"Both carbon dioxide and water vapor are efficient at capturing long wave radiation, which happens to be the kind our planet's crust gives off. Hence, in the lower atmosphere, pre-Flood conditions existed in which the Earth lost very little of its long wave radiation, its heat. Indeed, it retained almost all. The temperatures of the Earth's surface, it is suspected, were warm on a pole-to-pole basis, and the oceans were similarly warm in high latitudes as well as in low latitudes.

"The Earth was lighted by diffused rather than direct light.

Short wave (ultraviolet) radiation was filtered out through the upper level ozone layer. The sun's long wave radiation (sun's heat) . . . was partly reflected off and what entered was diffused through the water vapor canopy and absorbed by the Earth's surface." This serene, balmy, zephyr world of halcyon beauty, came to an abrupt end around the middle of the third millennium before the present era.

Dr. Frederick Filby asserts that a wandering minor planet that flew by at a close distance collapsed the water vapor canopy and caused the eruptions which produced the Noachian deluge.

Geographer Donald Patten claims the gravitational pull between these two bodies could have collapsed the canopy, created tidal waves, and caused a cataclysm including volcanic eruptions and gigantic sea-bed upheavals, thus producing the Flood.

Patten also suggests that the wandering planet, like some comets, carried vast quantities of frozen gases and ice particles. Some of these were captured as electrically charged particles by the earth's atmosphere. "Any such 'seeding' of our atmosphere by solid, intensely cold particles as well as meteoric dust would obviously account for the deluge of rain observed by Noah and the vast snowfalls which covered Siberia," adds Filby.

Other theories suggest that a giant meteorite collided with the earth, jarring the crust sufficiently so that universal cataclysmic conditions were created. Assert Balsiger and Sellier in their book *In Search of Noah's Ark,* which was made into a sensationally popular motion picture of the same name: "When a huge meteorite, say up to 500 miles in diameter, hits a planet, fast-moving compressive waves move through the planet, followed by slower surface waves. They converge at a point opposite the meteorite impact, shattering land forms and leaving the area in shambles.

"Scientists are quite sure this happened when a huge meteorite collided with Mercury and created the 800 mile wide Caloris basin. The fast-moving compressive waves followed by surface waves moved through the planet shattering the land forms opposite Caloris, creating what scientists call the 'weird terrain.' Similar shattered land forms exist on the moon opposite great crater basins.

"There is little need to speculate on what such an impact would do to the Earth in Biblical times when atmosphere, continents and oceans existed. It would start an indescribable series of events that could easily have sparked the Flood" (pp. 62-63).

Whether the extra-terrestrial agent of fury and destruction was indeed a meteorite of huge, awesome dimensions, or a minor wandering planet, or a comet, remains to be proven. But the *fact* of the universal Flood within the historic memory of man is indisputable.

Chapter Four

Joshua's Long Day

Children sing songs about "Joshua at the battle of Jericho," where "the walls came a tumblin' down." Children are regaled with tales of the day Joshua made the sun stand still in the sky. Such stories indeed seem to the educated mind like proper stuff for children—just like Santa Claus, Rudolph the red-nosed reindeer, Cinderella, or Snow White and the Seven Dwarfs.

But how did the story of Joshua become incorporated into the fabric of the Bible? How did such an incredible saga become part of Scripture?

Is there any truth to the legend?

In the book of Joshua we read the account of the Conquest of Palestine. Joshua and the Israelites had captured the city of Ai, and destroyed it. The remaining Canaanite powers, filled with dread, allied themselves together. The five kings of the Amorites, the king of Jerusalem, the king of Hebron, the king of Jarmuth, the king of Lachish, and the king of Eglon gathered together their armies and marched upon Gibeon, a city which had made peace with Israel. Severely pressed on every side, the Gibeonites sent a message to Joshua, saying, "Come up to us quickly, and save us, and help us: for all the kings of the Amorites that dwell in the mountains are gathered together against us" (Joshua 10:6).

Immediately Joshua responded to the new threat. After a forced, all night march, his army came upon the Amorite enemy suddenly. We read:

"And the Lord discomfited them before Israel, and slew them with a great slaughter at Gibeon, and chased them along the way that goeth up to Beth-horon, and smote them to Azekah, and unto Makkedah. And it came to pass, as they fled from before Israel, and were in the going down to Beth-horon, that the Lord cast down *great stones* from heaven upon them unto Azekah, and they died: they were more which died with hailstones than they whom the children of Israel slew with the sword" (Joshua 10:10-11).

Prior to this battle, the walls of the fortress Jericho had fallen flat in a great earthquake, enabling Joshua and his army to put the inhabitants to the sword. The great walls of Jericho, twelve feet wide, have been excavated. They were found to have been destroyed in an earthquake. The evidence proves they collapsed at the beginning of the Hyksos period in Egypt, shortly after the close of the Middle Kingdom.

But an even greater event took place at the battle of Beth-horon. The Lord "cast down great stones from heaven" upon the Amorites so that more "died with hailstones than they whom the children of Israel slew with the sword." According to Ginzberg's *Legends,* "The hot hailstones which, at Moses' intercession, had remained suspended in the air when they were about to fall upon the Egyptians, were now cast down upon the Canaanites."

These great stones were probably part of the meteorites in the train of the comet which struck during the last days of the Egyptian Middle Kingdom. They remained in the heavens, until the days of Joshua, when they fell to earth, crashing into the valley of Beth-horon and smashing the enemies of Israel.

Later this same day, we read: "Then spake Joshua to the Lord in the day when the Lord delivered up the Amorites before the children of Israel, and he said in the sight of Israel, 'Sun, stand thou still upon Gibeon; and thou, Moon, in the valley of Ajalon.' And the sun stood still, and the moon stayed, until the people had avenged themselves upon their enemies. Is not this written in the book of Jasher? So the sun stood still in the midst of heaven, and hasted not to go down about a whole day. And there was no day like that before it or after it, that the Lord hearkened unto the voice of a man: for the Lord fought for Israel" (Joshua 10:12-14).

Was the story of Joshua mere poetic license? Or did it really happen? You would be hard put, today, to find any astronomers who would admit that the story was literal and that the events happened just as the Scriptures relate.

But consider for a moment. Such a prodigy could have occurred if the earth had 1) ceased to rotate upon its axis for about a whole day; this would have created serious disturbances around the world and would have resulted in a prolonged night in the part of the earth opposite the Middle East; 2) changed its axis of rotation. Judging from the clear description given in the book of Joshua, however, both sun and moon appeared to remain stationary, motionless, for about a whole day. This would necessitate the earth ceasing to rotate—for its diurnal rotation to be interrupted.

Nothing terrestrial could have accomplished such a feat. The cause must have been celestial.

"A departure of the earth from its regular rotation is thinkable," says Immanuel Velikovsky, "but only in the very improbable event that our planet should meet another heavenly body of sufficient mass to disrupt the eternal path of our world."

He continues: "That a comet may strike our planet is not very probable, but the idea is not absurd. The heavenly mechanism works with almost absolute precision; but unstable, their way lost, comets by the thousands, by the millions, revolve in the sky, and their interference may disturb the harmony. Some of these comets belong to our system. Periodically they return, but not at very exact intervals, owing to the perturbations caused by gravitation toward the larger planets when they fly too close to them. But innumerable other comets, often seen only through the telescope, come flying in from immeasurable spaces of the universe at very great speed, and disappear—possibly forever. Some comets are visible only for hours, some for days or weeks or even months"[1].

1. *Worlds in Collision,* p. 40.

At one occasion D.F. Arago computed that there is one chance in 280 million that a comet will hit the earth. Nevertheless, huge objects from space have in historic times collided with the earth. The *Encyclopedia Britannica* states that the number of meteorites falling in the centuries before Christ was higher than today.

The meteorite that fell in prehistoric times near Winslow, Arizona created a crater 4,500 feet across and 600 feet deep. It flung out masses of rock weighing up to 7,000 tons each, altogether displacing roughly 400 million tons of rock. The pressure of impact was greater than 1,000,000 pounds per square inch. In the blast, silica was changed into coesite and stishovite.

An even greater crater at Ries Kessell in Bavaria—15 miles across—was made by an enormous meteorite.

In *The Universe,* published by Life Nature Library, we read: "Asteroids sometimes come close enough to the earth to collide with it. Of the boulder-sized ones, which are called meteorites, about 1,500 strike each year. *Full-fledged flying mountains* are thought to strike much less frequently, perhaps once every 10,000 years on an average. When they do, the earth acts like so much soft mud and swallows them explosively into its surface. Geologists have only recently begun to recognize the 'astroblemes,' or star-wounds, which they inflict but it seems likely from the evidence unearthed so far that only the shield of the atmosphere and the healing power of vegetation, erosion and mountain-building have kept the earth from being as pock-marked as the moon"[2].

Out beyond the orbit of the planet Mars, over 3,000 odd asteroids—small chunks or islands of rock and metal—have been tracked by astronomers. Totalling less than 5 percent of the moon in mass, these wandering chunks of rock range in size from Ceres, discovered in 1800, with a diameter of 480 miles and surface area of 700,000 square miles; Pallas, 300 miles wide; Juno, 120 miles in diameter; and Vesta, 240 miles across; to the small flying mountains like Icarus, only one mile in diameter.

2. *The Universe,* p. 67.

About 30,000 sizable asteroids are believed to exist, and uncounted billions of smaller asteroids, the size of pebbles, boulders, or grains of sand.

Since most of the asteroids move in a broad band between the orbits of Mars and Jupiter, the enormous planet Jupiter affects their motions. Some asteroids are called Trojans, named after Homeric heroes who fought in the Trojan war, and are held in captivity by Jupiter, much as satellites. Occasionally Jupiter's strong gravitation pull yanks one of the asteroids on a series of orbital trips toward the sun or the outer planets. Eventually such straying asteroids are likely to be hurled by Jupiter into new erratic paths, which may bring them uncomfortably close to the earth. Eros, a rock 15 miles long, tumbling end over end, can come within 14,000,000 miles of earth. Amor, Icarus, Apollo, Adonis can pass even closer to earth. The asteroid Hermes came so close to the earth in 1937 that astronomers compared it to the fly-by of a jet; it passed within 500,000 miles of earth, only twice as far away as the moon.

Comets, those odd denizens of the icy edges of the solar system, number in the 100 billions. They orbit not only in the flattened disc of the planets, but also in a spherical halo reaching out 10 trillion miles from the solar system. Those which have been studied by astronomers reveal they are an accumulation of frozen gases and grit, a few miles in diameter. When a comet approaches the sun, "solar energy vaporizes its outer layers to form a swollen head and then drives some of this material away to form a tail of incandescence pointing out toward space"[3].

The Great Comet of 1843 had a streaming tail 500 million miles long. Halley's comet, which returns approximately every 76 years, is so brilliant that records of its observation are complete for every time but once since 240 B.C. in the annals of the Chinese and Japanese. It may have been seen in 467 B.C.

What happens when a comet approaches too near the sun? Biela's comet, first noticed hurtling in from outer space in 1772, came close to the sun and began reappearing near the sun every

3. *The Universe*, p. 69.

six and one half years. In 1846 on its swing by the sun it became two comets; after 1852 it vanished. Twenty years later astronomers were still looking for it when the whole of Europe was suddenly treated to a wild pyrotechnic shower of meteors burning up as they entered the earth's atmosphere. Says *The Universe:* "The rain of cosmic sparks increased as it moved west. By the time it reached England, people could see a hundred blazing meteors a minute. Over the Atlantic, the display gradually diminished so that New Yorkers, at midnight, saw only a luminous drizzle. Careful calculations have since proved that the meteors were really the remnants of Biela's comet, crossing the earth's orbit just in time to meet the earth."

June 30, 1908 a comet smashed into the forests along the Tunguska River in Siberia, toppling trees, knocking people off their feet and blowing out window panes 100 miles away. The pressure of the blast affected barometers in England. The pall of smoke that shot into the air affected sunsets for a week.

Long a mystery, the Tunguska explosion was finally explained by the Committee on Meteorites of the Soviet Academy of Sciences in 1960. Chairman Vassily Fesenkov announced that the explosion had definitely been caused by the head of a comet with a diameter of several miles and weighing about a million tons. Other comets ranging over the solar system weigh a million times as much.

With these facts in mind, let us try to reconstruct what happened in the days of Joshua, in the middle of the second millennium B.C.

A strong hint of the answer should be apparent when we see that immediately before the sun and moon stood still, an incredible meteor shower took place. Stones of *barad* had rained down upon the valley of Beth-horon—a tremendous deluge of massive stones and boulders rained from the sky, killing tens of thousands. "They were more which died with hailstones than they whom the children of Israel slew with the sword" (verse 11).

Interestingly, Aristotle asserted that a meteorite fell at Aegospotami when a comet was glowing in the sky. Comets have been associated with meteor showers historically.

If Joshua's comet had been of sufficient mass, it might have "played tag" with the earth. If in alignment with the sun, or opposite the sun, its gravitational force might have had tremendous influence upon the earth, its tides, and even its rotational velocity. Such an event could readily explain the "long day" of Joshua; and the comet which held the earth motionlessly captive for about a day, also held the moon in captive thraldom at the same time.

Says Immanuel Velikovsky: "If the head of a comet should pass very close to our path, so as to effect a distortion in the career of the earth, another phenomenon besides the disturbed movement of the planet would probably occur: a rain of meteorites would strike the earth and would increase to a torrent. Stones scorched by flying through the atmosphere would be hurled on home and head." As Velikovsky points out, the author of the book of Joshua was surely ignorant of any connection between the two phenomena. "As these phenomena were recorded to have occurred together, it is improbable that the records were invented"[4].

Such a torrent of stones falling from the sky in one location strongly suggest that a train of meteorites associated with a comet had struck our planet.

But a meteorite bombardment is one thing. Did the sun really "stand still" for about a day? Such an event would have been noticed around the globe.

Joshua, in his prayer of thanksgiving, declared:

"Sun and moon stood still in heaven,
and Thou didst stand in Thy wrath against our oppressors
. . .

All the princes of the earth stood up,
the kings of the nations had gathered themselves together
. . .

4. *Worlds in Collision,* p. 42.

Thou didst destroy them in Thy fury,
and Thou didst ruin them in Thy rage.

Nations raged from fear of Thee,
kingdoms tottered because of Thy wrath . . .

Thou didst pour out Thy fury upon them . . .
Thou didst terrify them in Thy wrath . . .

The earth quaked and trembled from the noise of Thy thunders.

Thou didst pursue them in Thy storm,
Thou didst consume them in the whirlwind . . .

Their carcasses were like rubbish"'[5].

A torrential rain of meteorites, a disturbance in the movement of the earth, an earthquake, a whirlwind—these catastrophic phenomena, by their very nature, should be associated together. As Immanuel Velikovsky writes: "It appears that a large comet must have passed very near to our planet and disrupted its movement; a part of the stones dispersed in the neck and tail of the comet smote the surface of our earth a shattering blow"[6].

Do the ancients testify of such a series of events, connected with a long day, or a long night?

If we allow for differences in longitude, it must have been early morning or night in the Western Hemisphere.

In the Mexican *Annals of Cuauhtitlan,* known also as the *Codex Chimalpopoca,* which scholars say contains annals of very ancient date, which may go back to more than a thousand years before the Christian era—which contains the history of the Culhuacan empire—it is written that during a cosmic catastrophe that occurred in remote antiquity the night did not end for a long time.

5. Ginzberg, *Legends,* IV, 11-12.
6. *Worlds in Collision,* p. 43.

Bernardino de Sahagun, a Spanish scholar who came to the New World a generation after Columbus, in his *Historia general de las cosas de Nueva Espana,* points out that at the time of one cosmic catastrophe the sun rose only a little way over the horizon and remained there without moving; the moon also stood still.

Traditions exist around the globe attesting to the miracle of Joshua's day—the stopping of the sun in its tracks. Although each of the traditions has a local flavor, the essential story remains the same.

In the Pacific islands, the legend of the semigod Maui is important. He is noted for three vital achievements—he fished up the land, snared the sun, and sought the fire. The Hawaiian version of the exploits of Maui tells us: "Maui's mother was much troubled by the shortness of the day, occasioned by the rapid movement of the sun; and since it was impossible to dry properly the sheets of tapa used for clothing, the hero resolved to cut off the legs of the sun, so that he could not travel fast.

"Maui now went off eastward to where the sun climbed daily out of the underworld, and as the luminary came up, the hero noosed his legs, one after the other, and tied the ropes strongly to great trees. Fairly caught, the sun could not get away, and Maui gave him a tremendous beating with his magic weapon. To save his life, the sun begged for mercy, and on promising to go more slowly ever after, was released from his bonds."[7].

The appearance of new islands took place at the same time as the catching of the sun, tying these two events of Maui's exploits together. In the midst of worldwide throes of agony, earthquake, and eruptions, such as must have accompanied the stoppage of the earth's rotation, one would have expected "new islands" to appear where formerly there were none.

The Menomini Indians, an Algonquin tribe, tell this tale: "The little boy made a noose and stretched it across the path, and when the Sun came to that point the noose caught him around the neck and began to choke him until he almost lost his breath. It became dark, and the Sun called out to the ma'nidos

7. Dixon, *Oceanic Mythology,* p. 42.

(a spirit being), 'Help me, my brothers, and cut this string before it kills me.' The ma'nidos came, but the thread had so cut into the flesh of the Sun's neck that they could not sever it. When all but one had given up, the Sun called to the Mouse to try to cut the string. The Mouse came up and gnawed at the string, but it was difficult work, because the string was hot and deeply imbedded in the Sun's neck. After working at the string a good while, however, the Mouse succeeded in cutting it, when the Sun breathed again and the darkness disappeared. If the Mouse had not succeeded, the Sun would have died"[8].

In a legend of the southern Ute Indians the cottontail rabbit is connected with a disruption in the movement of the sun across the heavens. He went to the east intending to break the sun in pieces, and waited for the sun to rise. "The sun began to rise, but seeing the cottontail, it went down again. Then it rose slowly again and did not notice the animal. He struck the sun with his club, breaking off a piece, which touched the ground and set fire to the world.

"The fire pursued Cottontail, who began to flee. He ran to a log and asked if it would save him if he got inside. 'No, I burn up entirely.' So he ran again and asked a rock with a cleft in it. 'No, I cannot save you, when I am heated I burst. . . .' At last he got to a river. The river said, 'No, I cannot save you; I'll boil and you will get boiled.' "

The fire came closer. Weeds burned and fell on the cottontail's neck. "From everywhere he saw smoke rising. He walked a little way on the hot ground and one of his legs was burned up to the knee; before that he had been longlegged. He walked on two legs, and one of them burned off."[9].

In many places on the earth, nations and primitive tribes have legends about a cosmic cataclysm in which the sun did not shine. In some areas, the local tradition says that the sun did not set for a period of time equal to several days. Tribes of the Sudan, south of Egypt, speak of a time when the night seemingly would not come to an end.

8. Thompson, *Tales of the North American Indians.*

9. R. H. Lowie, "Shoshonean Tales," *Journal of American Folk-lore,* XXXVII, 61ff.

The *Kalevala* of the Finns mentions a time when hailstones of iron fell from the sky, and the sun and moon disappeared, or were "stolen from the sky." In their stead, after a period of darkness, a new sun and new moon were placed in the sky.[10].

The manuscripts of Avila and Molina, who collected the traditions of the New World Indians, tell of a time that the sun did not appear for five days, and a cosmic collision with stars preceded the cataclysm. People and animals fled to caves in the hills.

Brasseur translated the story in *Sources de l'histoire primitive du Mexique.* The sea also rose, breaking out of its bounds, and began to rise on the Pacific coast, filling the valleys and plains around. The mountain of Ancasmarca rose, too, like a ship on the waves. "During the five days that this cataclysm lasted, the sun did not show its face and the earth remained in darkness".

The book *Anugita* of the Iranians shows that at one time a threefold day and threefold night concluded one of the world ages.[12] Also, the book *Bundahis,* speaks of a world being darkened at midday as though it were deepest night—a phenomenon caused, according to the *Bundahis,* by a war between the stars and the planets.[13]

Thus evidence that a prolonged day in the Middle East, and a prolonged night, or early morning in the Western Hemisphere, and in other parts of the world, does exist. Although one cannot state with certainty that each of these legends from around the globe must refer to the same historical event, they suggest that the account in the book of Joshua in the Old Testament is not an isolated, unheard of, unbelievable account. It stands corroborated by witnesses around the world. When we understand the nature of the event—that great cosmic forces were involved, and tremendous celestial dramas were being worked out in the heavens—then the indication that the "sun stood still in the

10. *Kalevala,* transl. J. M. Crawford, 1888, p. xiii.

11. *Sources de l'histoire primitive du Mexique,* p. 40.

12. Volume III, *The Sacred Books of the East.*

13. "The Bundahis," in *Pahlavi Texts,* transl. E. W. West, *The Sacred Books of the East,* V, 1880, pt. I, p. 17.

midst of the heaven, and hasted not to go down about a whole day" becomes readily believable.

The prophet Habakkuk, writing about this event hundreds of years later, declared: "The mountains saw thee, and they trembled: the overflowing of the water passed by: the deep uttered his voice, and lifted up his hands on high. The sun and moon stood still in their habitation: at the light of thine arrows they went, and at the shining of thy glittering spear. Thou didst march through the land in indignation, thou didst thresh the heathen in anger" (Habakkuk 3:10-12).

These colossal events were not done in a corner. They were witnessed in every nation under the sun. They became a part of the legend and folklore of nations widely scattered around the globe.

Chapter Five

Hezekiah and the Sun Dial

Another great phenomenon occurred in earth's history in the days of King Hezekiah of Judah. Hezekiah reigned over the nation of Judah, in Palestine, from approximately 726-697 B.C.

Hezekiah was one of the few "righteous" kings in ancient Judah. Most of them were guilty in the eyes of the Biblical writers of transgressing the laws of God and plunging into idolatry, notably the worship of Baal and Asteroth. When Hezekiah assumed the mantle of government from Ahaz, he immediately broke down the idols that his predecessor set up. He launched a great Reformation in all the land, re-opened and cleansed the Temple of God which Solomon had built, and restored the Temple services.

Fears of invasion were rife in the days of Hezekiah. The land was in great agitation. In the sixth year of his reign, the northern Kingdom of Israel fell. It was a time of great upheaval, confusion, and war.

Samaria, the capital of Israel, the northern kingdom, fell to the Assyrians 721-718 B.C. A three-year siege ended with the entire city and the majority of the people being carried away into captivity, with the entire population being transported into Assyria, to the cities of Halah and Habor, and to the land of Media to the east. The Scriptural writer attests: "For so it was, that the children of Israel had sinned against the Lord their God, which had brought them up out of the land of Egypt, from under the hand of Pharoah king of Egypt, and had feared other gods, and walked in the statutes of the heathen, whom the Lord cast out from before the children of Israel, and of the kings of Israel, which they had made. And the children of Israel did secretly those things that were not right against the Lord their God, and they built them high places in all their cities, from the tower of the watchmen to the fenced city. . . .And they rejected his statutes, and his covenant that he made with their fathers, and his testimonies which he testified against them; and they followed vanity, and became vain . . .And they left all the commandments of the Lord their God, and made them molten images, even two calves, and made a grove, and worshipped all the host of heaven, and served Baal. And they caused their sons and daughters to pass through the fire, and used divination and enchantments, and sold themselves to do evil in the sight of the Lord, to provoke him to anger.

"Therefore the Lord was very angry with Israel, and removed them out of his sight; there was none left but the tribe of Judah only" (II Kings 17:7-18).

Hezekiah was only 25 years of age when he began his reign. He was young, but a man of strong convictions. We read: "He removed the high places, and brake the images, and cut down the groves, and brake in pieces the brasen serpent that Moses had made: for unto those days the children of Israel did burn incense to it: and he called it Nehushtan ('a piece of brass'). He trusted in the Lord God of Israel; so that after him was none like him among all the kings of Judah, nor any that were before him. For he clave to the Lord, and departed not from following him, but kept his commandments, which the Lord commanded Moses. And the Lord was with him; and he prospered whithersoever he went forth: and he rebelled against the king of Assyria, and served him not" (II Kings 18:4-7).

In Hezekiah's sixth year, Samaria fell to the Assyrian hordes. Eight years later, Sennacherib, the king of Assyria, once again invaded the land, this time to punish Hezekiah. His armies aggressed against the cities of Judah, "and took them" (II Kings 18:13). At this point, Hezekiah temporarily lost his courage and sent a message of entreaty to the Assyrian monarch, saying, "I have offended; return from me: that which thou puttest on me will I bear" (verse 14). The Assyrian king relented, halted his invasion forces, and put the Jews to tribute demanding 300 talents of silver and 30 talents of gold in payment.

Assyrian records corroborate this Biblical account. On walls of Sennacherib's palace at Nineveh, uncovered by Layard, a sculptured relief of his encampment at Lachish bore this inscription: "Sennacherib, king of the world, sat upon his throne, and caused the spoil of Lachish to pass before him." The inscription speaks of the tribute Hezekiah sent to the tyrant as well: "Fear of my majesty overwhelmed Hezekiah. He sent tribute: 30 talents of gold, 800 talents of silver, precious stones, ivory, women of his palace, and all sorts of gifts."

Archaeological excavations confirm that Lachish suffered disaster in the time of Hezekiah. The Biblical record states that Sennacherib laid siege against Lachish with all his power during the time (II Chronicles 32:9). At Lachish, the Wellcome Archaeological Expedition found a layer of ashes from a fire of 700 B.C. Gibeah, another town assaulted by the Assyrian king (Isaiah 10:29), also suffered. William Albright, known as the dean of archaeologists in Palestine, found a layer of ashes from a fire there, dated to 700 B.C.

But the tribute levied upon the Jews only bought Hezekiah a brief breathing space. Soon the Assyrians were back again, this time attacking Jerusalem itself. "And the king of Assyria sent Tartan and Rabsaris and Rabshakeh from Lachish to king Hezekiah with a great host against Jerusalem. And they went up and came to Jerusalem. And when they were come up, they came and stood by the conduit of the upper pool, which is in the highway of the fuller's field" (II Kings 18:17).

Hezekiah was greatly troubled by the Assyrian invasion. They had indeed laid low all the surrounding nations and kingdoms and were the dominant military power in the Middle East at that time. It looked like doomsday. Jerusalem didn't stand a ghost of a chance.

In dire distress, Hezekiah "rent his clothes, and covered himself with sackcloth, and went into the house of the Lord" (II Kings 19:1). He also sent messengers to the prophet Isaiah, son of Amoz, saying: "Thus saith Hezekiah, This day is a day of trouble, and of rebuke, and blasphemy: for the children are come to the birth, and there is not strength to bring forth. It may be the Lord thy God will hear all the words of Rabshakeh, whom the king of Assyria his master hath sent to reproach the living God; and will reprove the words which the Lord thy God hath heard: wherefore lift up thy prayer for the remnant that are left" (verses 3-4).

Isaiah sent a message back to the king, saying: "Thus saith the Lord, Be not afraid of the words which thou hast heard, with which the servants of the king of Assyria have blasphemed me. Behold, I will send a *blast* upon him, and he shall hear a rumour, and shall return to his own land; and I will cause him to fall by the sword in his own land" (vs. 6-7).

History records that the attack on Jerusalem was interrupted, when Sennacherib heard a rumor that Tirhakah, king of Egypt, had come out to fight. After the brief interlude, the Assyrians resumed their assault on Jerusalem. But before they were able to stage their final attack, a most unusual thing happened. The Scriptures put it this way:

"And it came to pass that night, that the angel of the Lord went out, and smote in the camp of the Assyrians an hundred fourscore and five thousand: and when they arose early in the morning, behold, they were all dead corpses. So Sennacherib king of Assyria departed, and went and returned, and dwelt at Nineveh. And it came to pass, as he was worshipping in the house of Nisroch his god, that Adrammelech and Sharezer his sons smote him with the sword: and they escaped into the land of Armenia. And Esarhaddon his son reigned in his stead" (vs. 35-37).

Sennacherib's own account of this invasion has been found, on a clay prism which he himself had made. It is now in the Oriental Institute Museum in Chicago. It says:

"As for Hezekiah, king of Judah, who had not submitted to my yoke, 46 of his fortified cities, and smaller cities without number, with my battering rams, engines, mines, breaches and axes, I besieged and captured. 200,150 people, small and great, male and female, and horses, mules, asses, camels, oxen, sheep, without number, I took as booty. Hezekiah himself I shut up like a caged bird in Jerusalem, his royal city. I built a line of forts against him, and turned back everyone who came forth out of his city gate. His cities which I captured I gave to the king of Ashdod, king of Ekron, and king of Gaza."

In those days no king admitted a defeat. He would certainly not record a defeat on an inscription to be read by all posterity. It is noteworthy, therefore, that Sennacherib omitted Jerusalem from his list of captured cities. He specifically did not claim to have captured Jerusalem—a most remarkable confirmation of Biblical history.

But what was this sudden "plague" or "catastrophe" which overnight wiped out 185,000 trained soldiers? What was this strange "blast" which the prophet Isaiah had said would be sent upon the Assyrian forces by God Himself?

Were there great signs in the heavens, in the sun, moon and stars, when Sennacherib invaded Judah? When the Assyrian monarch overthrew the kingdom of Israel to the north?

Was the period of the lifetime of Hezekiah another of the global catastrophes such as occurred at the Noachian Deluge, the Exodus, and the Conquest of Canaan?

In the tenth chapter of Isaiah, God said He intended to use the Assyrian nation as a rod of wrath to punish the disobedient (vs. 5-12). Yet, God promised, a "remnant shall return, even the remnant of Jacob, unto the mighty God. For though thy people Israel be as the sand of the sea, yet a remnant of them shall return: the consumption decreed shall overflow with righteousness. For the Lord God of hosts shall make a consumption, even determined, in the midst of the land" (Isa. 10:21-23).

At that time, the Lord said, He would also punish the stout heart of the king of Assyria (vs. 12-19). "And the rest of the trees of his forest shall be few, that a child may write them" (vs. 19). The might, pomp, and power of Assyria was to be taken down a few notches.

The Lord said, " . . . as his rod was upon the sea, so shall he lift it up *after the manner of Egypt.* And it shall come to pass in that day, that his burden shall be taken away from off thy shoulder, and his yoke from off thy neck, and the yoke shall be destroyed because of the anointing. . . . Behold, the Lord, the Lord of hosts, shall lop the bough with terror: and the high ones of stature shall be hewn down, and the haughty shall be humbled" (vs. 26-33).

Here the fall of the Assyrians is compared with the fall of Egypt in the days of Moses. God said He would punish the Assyrians as He punished the stout heart of Pharoah, king of Egypt, centuries before. Here, then, is evidence that the times of trouble in the days of Hezekiah again involved heavenly catastrophes—tremendous upheavals so that 185,000 soldiers died in one night.

God spoke of it as a "consumption." He spoke of tremendous destruction in the land, so that few people were left alive—so few that "a child may write them."

As Hezekiah cried: "For it is a day of trouble, and of treading down, and of perplexity by the Lord God of hosts in the valley of vision, breaking down the walls, and of crying to the mountains" (Isa. 22:5).

It was the same time spoken of in Isaiah 24—a time when "the haughty people of the earth do languish," a time when "the inhabitants of the earth are burned, and few men left" (compare Isaiah 24:65 with chapter 10:19, 33-34).

What kind of destruction befell Sennacherib's vast army? *Malach,* translated as "angel," means in Hebrew "one who is sent to execute an order." Elsewhere we read that a "blast" was sent upon the Assyrian host. The death of scores of thousands of warriers could not be due to a sickness, or plague, as no plague would strike down so many so quickly. It would require several days for a contagion to spread through a large encampment of troops.

Talmudic and Midrash sources all agree on the manner in which the Assyrians met their fate. It was not a flame, but a consuming blast that fell from the sky. "Their souls were burnt, though their garments remained intact," say the ancient records[1]. The blast was accompanied by a terrific noise, say the same sources.

1. *Tractate Shabbat* 113b; *Sanhedrin* 94a; Ginzberg, *Legends,* VI, 363.

It is interesting to note that the famous passage in Herodotus which says that since Egypt became a kingdom, the sun had repeatedly changed its direction, is inserted in no other place in Herdotus' history but directly after the story of the destruction of Sennacherib's army.

Most probably some cosmic cause was the agent of death to the thousands of soldiers in Sennacherib's army. Dr. Immanuel Velikovsky suggests: "Gaseous masses reaching the atmosphere could asphyxiate all breath in certain areas"[2].

It seems clear that heavenly disturbances were responsible, or at least directly accompanied the slaying of Sennacherib's army. During those "days of perplexity," as Hezekiah called them, as far away as China, we find the notation in a book of Edouard Biot: "The year 687 B.C., in the summer, in the fourth moon, in the day sin mao (23rd of March) during the night, the fixed stars did not appear, though the night was clear. In the middle of the night stars fell like a rain"[3].

The annals of the *Bamboo Books* tell us that in the tenth year of the Emperor Kwei—referring probably to the same event, or to approximately the same date—"the five planets went out of their courses. In the night, stars fell like rain. The earth shook"[4].

The phenomenon described here was unusual—so unusual that no similar event is described in all the remainder of the Biot *Catalogue* which begins with this astounding event.

But there is even more Biblical evidence—the strongest evidence yet.

After the battle in which Sennacherib's army was annihilated by a "blast" from heaven, in one night, and Judah was saved from the threat of captivity, Hezekiah fell strangely ill—"sick unto death" (II Kings 20:1). He was told by the prophet Isaiah to "Set thine house in order; for thou shalt die, and not live."

Hezekiah wept sorely, and turned his face to the wall of his

---

2. *Worlds in Collision,* p. 234.

3. *Catalogue général des étoiles filantes et des autres météores observées en Chine après le VII siècle avant J.C.*

4. *The Chinese Classics,* III, Pt. 1, 125.

room, praying fervently, beseeching God to spare his life.

Before Isaiah had even departed from the courtyard outside, he received another message from God. God heard Hezekiah's prayer. He determined to heal him of his fatal illness and add fifteen years to his life (vs. 4-6).

Hezekiah then asked the prophet, "What shall be the sign that the Lord will heal me, and that I shall go up into the house of the Lord the third day?" (v. 8).

Isaiah responded: "This sign shalt thou have of the Lord, that the Lord will do the thing that he hath spoken: *shall the shadow go forward ten degrees, or go back ten degrees?* And Hezekiah answered, It is a light thing for the shadow to go down ten degrees: nay, but let the shadow return backward ten degrees.

"And Isaiah the prophet cried unto the Lord: and *he brought the shadow ten degrees backward, by which it had gone down in the dial of Ahaz*" (II Kings 20:9-11).

This phenomen has plagued scholars for generations. Should it be taken literally? Did God actually interfere in the rotation of the earth, causing it to stop, then go backwards ten degrees, and then to stop, and then to resume its former rotational direction and velocity?

Unbelievable! Incredible! It must have been either 1) a hallucination, or 2) an optical illusion, or 3) some strange allegory not meant to be taken literally. Or so the majority of skeptical scholars would conclude.

But is it really so marvelous that the Creator of the heavens and the earth can interrupt the rotation of the earth? Would it really be so difficult for God to perform such a miracle? Is it any harder than stopping the sun in the days of Joshua? Or parting the Red Sea in the days of Moses? Or bringing on the Deluge in the days of Noah?

China is far removed from Palestine, but again, corroborative evidence of the miracle of the sun dial of Hezekiah is found there. A Chinese historian who lived in the second century B.C., one Huai-nan-tse, reports that "when the Duke of Lu-yuang was at war against Han, during the battle the sun went down. The Duke, swinging his spear, beckoned to the sun, whereupon the sun, for his sake, came back and passed through three solar mansions."[5]

This description of a short retrograde motion by the sun corresponds with the event recorded in II Kings 20 and Isaiah 38 of the Old Testament. Although the dates of the reign of Han are not certain, the event must correspond to the sun retreating ten degrees in the days of Hezekiah. If Han reigned later, then the story described must antedate his dynasty.

In another part of China, there is a story recorded by Lu-Heng who tells us that Prince Tau of Yin was a prisoner of the king of China when the sun returned to the meridian. This was interpreted as a sign to allow the prince to return home[6]. According to the historian Appollodorus[7], "Atreus stipulated with Thyestes that Atreus should be king if the sun should go backward; and when Thyestes agreed, the sun set in the east."

Ovid also describes this event. Pheobus (the sun) broke off "in mid-career, and wresting his car about turned round his steeds to face the dawn"[8]. In *Tristia* Ovid refers to the tradition of the "horses of the sun turning aside."

The legends of Maui in the Pacific islands of Polynesia roping the sun in the heavens could also relate to this prodigy, although they more likely refer to the event which occurred in the days of Joshua, son of Nun.

Although not many people are aware of it, there is another legend among the Jews, recorded in rabbinical sources, that on the day king Ahaz was carried to his grave an equal perturbation in the sun's path took place but in the opposite direction. On that day the sun, according to the story, set early. Immanuel Velikovsky points out: "A case of two consecutive perturbations of a celestial body, where the second perturbation corrected the effect of the first, is recorded in the annals of modern observations. In 1875 Wolf's comet passed near the large planet Jupiter and was disturbed on its way. In 1922, when it again

5. Huai-nan-tse VI. iv; Forke, *The World Conception of the Chinese,* p. 86.
6. Lu-Heng, 176; Forke, *ibid.,* p. 87.
7. *The Library,* Epitome II.
8. Ovid, *The Art of Love,* i. 328ff.

passed near Jupiter, it was once more disturbed, but with an effect which corrected that of the first disturbance. No perturbation was noticed in the revolution of Jupiter; its rotation probably proceeded normally, too—there was a great difference in the masses of these two bodies"[9].

Celestial phenomena are recorded in the legends of other nations about this same period. According to tradition, Rome was founded approximately 747 B.C. Roman traditions relate that at the birth of Romulus, at the foundation of Rome, and at the death of Romulus, great commotions occurred in the heavens. The movement of the sun was altered. Latin historians tell us that at the foundation of Rome the sun was disrupted in its movement and the world was darkened.

At the death of Romulus, Plutarch asserts, "suddenly strange and unaccountable disorders with incredible changes filled the air; the light of the sun failed, and night came down upon them, not with peace and quiet, but with awful peals of thunder and furious blasts"[10].

Ovid's description is even more colorful. At the death of Romulus, the poet states, "Both the poles shook, and Atlas shifted the burden of the sky. . . . The sun vanished and rising clouds obscured the heaven . . . the sky was riven by shooting flames. The people fled and the king (Romulus) upon his father's steeds soared to the stars"[11].

Was this the same time frame we are dealing with in the case of king Hezekiah? They were contemporaries. Says the noted Church historian Augustine: "Now these days extend . . . down to Romulus king of Romans, or even to the beginning of the reign of his successor Numa Pompilius. Hezekiah king of Judah certainly reigned till then"[12].

The beginning of Romulus' life, and the founding of Rome, took place during the reign of another Judean king, Uzziah. Was the reign of Uzziah noted for any spectacular occurrence,

9. *Worlds in Collision,* p. 237.
10. Plutarch, *Lives,* "The Life of Romulus."
11. Ovid, *Fasti,* II 11. 489 ff.
12. Augustine, *The City of God,* Bk. XVIII, chap. 27.

such as we are told happened at the birth of Romulus and the founding of Rome in 747 B.C.?

King Uzziah reigned 52 years in Judah—from 787 to 735 B.C. He was 16 years old when he began to reign, "And he did that which was right in the sight of the Lord . . . And he sought God in the days of Zechariah, who had understanding in the visions of God: and as long as he sought the Lord, God made him to prosper" (II Chronicles 26:4-5).

Uzziah's armies broke down the walls of the Philistine cities of Gath, Jabneh and Ashdod. The chronicler relates: "And God helped him against the Philistines, and against the Arabians that dwelt in Gurbaal, and the Mehnims. And the Ammorites gave gifts to Uzziah: and his name spread abroad even to the entering in of Egypt; for he strengthened himself exceedingly" (vs. 7-8).

Something strange, however, happened in the days of this king. The prophet Zechariah records it, and compares it to the great catastrophe which is to occur in the future, at the Second Coming of the Messiah. Zechariah says:

"Behold, the day of the Lord cometh, and thy spoil shall be divided in the midst of thee. . . . Then shall the Lord go forth, and fight against those nations, as when he fought in the day of battle. And his feet shall stand in that day upon the mount of Olives, which is before Jerusalem on the east, and the mount of Olives shall cleave in the midst thereof toward the east and toward the west, and there shall be a very great valley; and half the mountain shall remove toward the north, and half of it toward the south.

"And ye shall flee to the valley of the mountains; for the valley of the mountains shall reach unto Azal: yea, ye shall flee, like as ye fled from before the earthquake in the days of Uzziah king of Judah: and the Lord my God shall come, and all the saints with thee" (Zech. 14:1-5).

This devastating catastrophe, which made the people flee, is called *raash* or "commotion" in Hebrew. The prophecy of Amos was made two years before the *raash* (Amos 1:1). Amos declared that fire would devour Israel's enemies, Syria, Tyre, Ammon, Moab, Philistia, "with a tempest in the day of the whirlwind" (1:14). He foretold "great tumults" upon the mountains of Israel (Amos 3:9) and that "the great houses shall have an end" (vs. 15).

Amos declared to the people of his day, "I have overthrown some of you, as God overthrew Sodom and Gomorrah, and ye were as a firebrand plucked out of the burning: yet have ye not returned unto me, saith the Lord" (4:11). He challenged Israel: "Seek him that maketh the seven stars and Orion, and turneth the shadow of death into the morning, and maketh the day dark with night: that calleth for the waters of the sea, and poureth them out upon the face of the earth: The Lord is his name" (Amos 5:8).

The Lord God swore to Amos, "Shall not the land tremble for this, and every one mourn that dwelleth therein? and it shall rise up wholly as a flood; and it shall be cast out and drowned, as by the flood of Egypt.

"And it shall come to pass in that day, saith the Lord God, that I will cause the sun to go down at noon, and I will darken the earth in the clear day" (Amos 8:8-9).

This destruction came on Israel shortly after Amos' prophecies were uttered. The great earthquake or commotion in the days of Uzziah was but the beginning. Before the end of that century was out, Israel had suffered greatly and been taken into captivity, ceasing to exist as a separate nation.

These calamities, Amos said, involved the tempestuous wind, the whirlwind, tossing seas, fire, and great burning. These cataclysms involved the very heavens themselves (Amos 8:9).

"And the Lord God of hosts is he that toucheth the land, and it shall melt . . . and it shall rise up wholy like a flood; and shall be drowned, as by the flood of Egypt" (Amos 9:5).

According to Jewish tradition, it was in anticipation of these dire prophecies and in fear of them that king Uzziah went to the Temple to burn incense. The priests opposed him vehemently, as it was not the king's appointed duty. "And Azariah the priest went in after him, and with him fourscore priests of the Lord, that were valiant men: And they withstood Uzziah the king, and said unto him, It appertaineth not unto thee, Uzziah, to burn incense unto the Lord, but to the priests the sons of Aaron, that are consecrated to burn incense: go out of the sanctuary; for thou hast trespassed; neither shall it be for thine honour from the Lord God" (II Chronicles 26:17-18).

Furious at their resistance, the king struggled to carry out his desires until the leprosy started rising in his forehead and body. According to Jewish tradition, "Suddenly the earth started to quake so violently that a great breach was torn in the Temple. On the west side of Jerusalem, half of a mountain was split off and hurled to the east"[13].

This tremendous upheaval was, in later times, used as a famous date reference point. Time was counted from the *raash* in the days of Uzziah, king of Judah (Amos 1:1; Zech. 14:5). Isaiah began to prophesy immediately after that great quake and cataclysm. This great prophet, inspired by the events he had already witnessed, foretold of coming upheavals and calamities. The events in the days of Uzziah, he declared, were mere forerunners. The catastrophe which had occurred was only a prelude. An even greater day of divine Wrath, he thundered, was still ahead.

The word *shaog,* used by Amos and Joel, is explained by the Jerusalem Talmud (Tractate Berakhot 13b) as an earthshock, in which the field of action is the entire world. Such "earthshocks" are predicted for the future—for the end of the age. Such events are predicted in the Scriptures for the end of our age, today.

These events in the days of Uzziah to Hezekiah were also recorded by the poet Seneca. In his *Thyestes* the chorus asks the sun:

"Whither, O father of the lands and skies, before whose rising thick night with all her glories flees, whither dost turn thy course and why dost blot out the day in mid-Olympus (midday)? Not yet does Vesper, twilight's messenger, summon the fires of night; not yet does thy wheel, turning its western goal, bid free thy steeds from their completed task; not yet as day fades into night has the third trump sounded; the ploughman with oxen yet unwearied stands amazed at his sup-

13. Ginzberg, *Legends,* IV, 262.

per hour's quick coming. What has driven thee from thy heavenly course? . . . Has Typhoeus (Typhon) thrown off the mountainous mass and set his body free?"

Seneca continues:

"The shadows arise, though the night is not yet ready. No stars come out; the heavens gleam not with any fires: no moon dispels the darkness' heavy pall. . . . Trembling, trembling are our hearts, sore smit with fear, lest all things fall shattered in fatal ruin and once more gods and men be overwhelmed by formless chaos; lest the lands, the encircling sea, and the stars that wander in the spangled sky, nature blot out once more."

Thyestes and his brother Atreus were two of the Argive tyrants, who also date from the eighth century before the present era. Greek tradition states that a cosmic upheaval occurred during the time of these tyrants. Wrote Archilochus, men should be prepared for anything since the day that Zeus "turned midday into night, hiding the light of the dazzling sun; and sore fear came upon men"[14].

Seneca, who writes of this time, declares:

"The Zodiac, which, making passage through the sacred stars, crosses the zones obliquely, guide and signbearer for the slow moving years, falling itself, shall see the fallen constellations."

Seneca describes the changes in each constellation's position—the Ram, Bull, the Twins, the Lion, Virgo, Libra, Scorpio, the Goat and the Great Bear (the Wain). He says: "And the Wain, which was never bathed in the sea, shall be plunged beneath the all-engulfing waves."

Seneca says clearly that the poles were changed in this cataclysm. The Great Bear had never before set beneath the horizon.

But the astonishing, truly astounding, fact is that these events happened. They are not all merely the imagination of poets around the world, who happened to stumble upon the same identical theme at the same relative time. These facts are recorded in history. They are set forth, in the Scriptures, specifically,

14. Archilochus, Fragment 74.

as matter-of-fact, straightforward documentaries. The authors of the books of Kings, Chronicles, and Isaiah stated these events in such a manner as to draw no undue attention to them. They are merely part of the ancient historical record. And they are corroborated by witnesses, with varying accounts, as far away as China, in Rome, and Greece.

But for those of us who live today, the even more astonishing fact is that similar events are to happen again!

Chapter Six

The Lost Continent of Atlantis

Perhaps more legends, tales, and stories have been told about the Lost Continent of Atlantis than almost any other subject of antiquity. Fanciful, fantastic, incredulous theories have been spawned about this ancient continent, or island.

Atlantis, also spelled Atalantis or Atalantica, generally refers to the legendary island in the Atlantic, beyond the Pillars of Hercules, which was ultimately overwhelmed by the sea. The legend of its existence persisted throughout the Middle Ages, and since Renaissance times it has been variously identified with the Americas, Scandinavia, the Canary Islands, the Bahamas, and the island of Santorini in the eastern Mediterranean.

"Atlantis—the lost civilization! Has there ever been a myth so tantalizing to man's romantic fancy? Over the years the land of the noble and artistic people who disappeared suddenly beneath the sea has been located by overactive imaginations in several places: the Bahamas, the East Indies, the North Sea, South America, Spain. The most enduring version of the legend can be traced to the Greek philosopher Plato, who described Atlantis as a sizable country and placed it beyond the 'Pillars of Hercules'—present-day Gibraltar . . . New investigations show, however, that Plato misread data in Egyptian manuscripts and multiplied both the age and the dimensions of Atlantis by a factor of ten. A drastically smaller and more recent Atlantis could have been located easily at the site of the cataclysmic 15th century B.C. Santorini explosion, and many scientists are convinced that this is the answer to the mystery." We are told, "Indeed, recent surveys have established that the size of Santorini before the explosion matches the Egyptian specifications, and excavations have turned up remains of an advanced civilization on the last rocky remnants of the island"[1].

Ronald Schiller in an article entitled "The Explosion That Changed the World," stated that approximately the 15th century B.C., Santorini exploded. The 4900 foot mountain on the beautiful island located some 70 miles north of Crete in the Aegean Sea between Greece and Turkey, "heaved, roared, then blew up in a volcanic eruption of unimaginable violence. When the fiery rain finally stopped, the central portion of the island dropped into a deep hole in the sea. The pieces that remained—called the islands of Santorini today—were buried under volcanic ash. The explosion and its aftereffects were enough to change the course of history"[2].

Schiller continues: "Archaeological evidence has long indicated that a series of catastrophic events—in fact, the cataclysm out of which Western civilization emerged—took place around the 15th century B.C."

This, of course, dates precisely to the time of the Biblical Exodus, the plagues upon the Middle Kingdom of Egypt, and the time of the crossing of the Red Sea by the Israelites—miraculous events which are the pivotal points of Biblical history.

In 1956 Professor Angelos Galanopoulos of the Athens Seismological Institute made an accidental discovery on the island of Thera, one of the remnants of Santorini. At the bottom of a mine shaft, from which volcanic ash is removed for use as cement, he found the fire-charred ruins of a stone house. Inside, were two pieces of blackened, charred wood, and the teeth of a man and a woman. Says Schiller: "Radio-carbon analysis disclosed that they had died in approximately 1400 B.C.—the 15th century B.C. And the volcanic ash that covered them was 100 feet thick; the eruption that laid it down may indeed have been the greatest in history."

1. *Reader's Digest, Marvels and Mysteries of the World Around Us,* p. 68.
2. *Ibid.*, p. 64.

The explosion that shook ancient Santorini has been compared with the eruption of famed Krakatoa in the East Indies in 1883. An entire year after the eruption of Krakatoa sunset and sunrise in both hemispheres were very colorful. The Krakatoa explosion produced a sound so loud that it was heard as far away as Japan, 3,000 miles distant—the farthest distance traveled by sound recorded in modern times.

Krakatoa cracked at its base and cold sea water rushed in, mingling with hot lava. The tremendous pressure of expanding steam and gases blew the top off the 1,460 foot mountain-island, hurling fiery columns of dust 33 miles into the air, and ejecting rocks for fifty miles around. A 600 foot crater was formed in the sea, creating enormous tidal waves. It raised tides 100 feet high that carried steamships miles inland and were felt on the eastern shore of Africa and the western shore of the Americas, as far as Alaska.

The explosion of Santorini was similar—except that it must have been many times more violent. The energy released was equivalent to the simultaneous explosion of several hundred hydrogen bombs, according to Galanopoulos. What remained of the island was buried under 100 feet of burning ash. The wind spread the Santorini ash over 80,000-square-miles, largely to the southeast. It still forms a layer of the seabed, from several inches to many feet thick.

After the volcano disgorged its contents, the empty cone dropped into its magma chamber, 1200 feet below sea level, creating a vast crater or 'caldera'. The ocean poured in, and tidal waves estimated to have been one mile high at the vortex roared outward at 200 miles per hour. The waves smashed into the coast of Crete with successive walls of water 100 feet high, engulfed the Egyptian delta less than three hours later, and drowned the ancient port of Ugarit in Syria.

"These are the calculations of the Santorini explosion's physical effects," writes Schiller. "Its historical effects may have been even more profound."[3]

The Santorini blast coincided with one of the greatest

3. *Ibid.*, p. 64.

mysteries of the ancient Middle East—the sudden disappearance of the brilliant, flourishing Minoan civilization. At that time Greece was inhabited by relatively unsophisticated Helladic tribes. The flower of civilization was the Minoan, centering in Crete, already highly advanced. They used a complex system of writing, enjoyed sports such as boxing and wrestling, used flush toilets, and air-conditioned their homes. Their pottery was superb, and their fleets ranged the oceans of the world.

But late in the middle of the second millennium B.C., the Minoan culture received its death knell. It abruptly vanished. Excavations indicate that all of the Minoan cities were wiped out at the same time. All the great palaces were destroyed, their huge building stones tossed around like matchsticks.

Says Schiller: "Until the recent geologic discoveries, the obliteration of Minoan civilization was an intriguing mystery, attributed to revolution or invasion. However, scholars, led by Professors Dragoslav Ninkovich and Bruce C. Heezen of Columbia University's Lamont-Doherty Geological Observatory, are now convinced that the destruction was caused by the eruption of Santorini—by the holocaust itself, by its aerial shock waves and by the ensuing tidal waves. The heavy fallout of volcanic ash filled Crete's fertile valleys, destroyed the crops and rendered agriculture on the island impossible for decades. Almost the entire Minoan race perished."

Was the destruction of the Minoan civilization the ancient source of the legends of Atlantis?

The name itself—Atlantis—would seem to identify it with the Atlantic Ocean. And Plato wrote that Atlantis was "beyond the Pillars of Hercules," identified with the straits of Gibraltar. What, then, about Atlantis?

According to Plato's account, the Athenian lawmaker Solon while visiting Egypt in 590 B.C. was told an intriguing story by Egyptian priests. An old priest told Solon the story of a mighty kingdom on a great island in the middle of the Atlantic Ocean that submerged and sank forever beneath its tumultuous waters.

Plato's account begins as follows:

"Let me begin by observing first of all, that nine thousand

was the sum of years which had elapsed since the war which was said to have taken place between those who dwelt outside the Pillars of Heracles and all who dwelt within them; this war I am going to describe. Of the combatants on the one side, the city of Athens was reported to have been the leader and to have fought out the war; the combatants on the other side were commanded by the kings of Atlantis, which, as I was saying, was an island greater in extent than Libya and Asia (Asia Minor), and when afterwards sunk by an earthquake, became an impassable barrier of mud to voyagers sailing from hence to any part of the ocean"[4].

Many scholars today believe that Plato erred when he gave 9,000 years as the time differential between his day and the destruction of Atlantis. Galanopoulos believes that Solon simply misread the Egyptian symbol for "100" as "1000," and therefore multiplied all figures by 10. Thus, 9,000 should have been rendered 900 years; and 800,000 square miles should have been 80,000.

Immanuel Velikovsky agrees. He points out: "Critias the younger remembered having been told that the catastrophe which befell Atlantis happened 9,000 years before. There is one zero too many here. We do not know of any vestiges of human culture aside from that of the Neolithic age, nor of any navigating nation, 9,000 years before Solon. Numbers we hear in childhood easily grow in our memory, as do dimensions. . . . Whatever the source of the error, the most probable date of the sinking of Atlantis would be in the middle of the second millennium, 900 years before Solon, when the earth twice suffered great catastrophes as a result of 'the shifting of the heavenly bodies.' These words of Plato received the least attention, though they deserved the greatest"[5].

In *Timaeus,* Plato wrote of Atlantis:

"For these histories tell of a mighty power which unprovoked made an expedition against the whole of Europe and Asia, and to which your city (Athens) put an end. This power came forth

4. *Critias,* 108.
5. *Worlds in Collision,* pp. 147-148.

out of the Atlantic Ocean, for in those days the Atlantic was navigable; and there was an island situated in front of the straits which are by you called the Pillars of Heracles; the island was larger than Libya and Asia put together, and was the way to other islands, and from these you might pass to the whole of the opposite continent which surrounded the true ocean; for this sea which is within the Straits of Heracles is only a harbour, having a narrow entrance, but that other is a real sea, and the surrounding land may be most truly called a boundless continent"[6].

Carefully note the geographical position, and facts, recorded here. Clearly, Plato, and the Egyptians in the days of Solon, had knowledge that the Mediterranean was merely a small sea, whereas the ocean outside the Pillars of Hercules was a true ocean; and they knew that beyond that ocean, the Atlantic, was another continent—the "New World" which Columbus only *re*-discovered in 1492.

Note that between these two continents was the large island called Atlantis, and several more islands. It is my belief that these "other islands" refer to the islands of the Carribean Sea—Cuba, Puerto Rico, Santo Domingo, and the others—the very same islands which Columbus sailed to when he departed from Spain aboard the *Nina,* the *Pinta,* and the *Santa Maria.* What could be more logical? The prevailing winds in the days of Solon would have been the same as existed in the days of Columbus. Sailors departing from the straits of Gibraltar to cross the Atlantic, and Columbus who sailed from Spain, would very likely have arrived at approximately the same spot in the New World. Columbus first set foot on an island in the Carribean, and Solon mentioned such islands as existing, and added, "from these you might pass to the whole of the opposite continent."

This passage, then, places Atlantis between the islands of the Carribean and the straits of Gibraltar. Could the Bahamas be the remnants of this once mighty island empire?

Geological studies indicate that the Bahamas were once united as one large island, and pottery remains from beneath the

6. *Timaeus,* 24, 25.

shallow seas surrounding the Bahamas have been uncovered, as well as Roman coins. Several years ago I visited with Dr. Joseph Mahan in Atlanta, Georgia, an expert in ancient Indian ethnology of the southeastern Indians of the United States. He showed me samples of pottery uncovered from the waters around the Bahamas, and told me of Indian legends, including that of the Yuchis, stating they had migrated to the area of Florida and Georgia from the region of the Bahamas. According to their legends, the island sank beneath the sea and they fled for their lives.

These same Yuchis later migrated to the Oklahoma territory, where they eventually settled down. Amazingly enough, they show strong evidence that they had contact with the Old World in historic times. They have a custom which is unique among the American Indians. They are racially and linguistically different from their neighbors. Every year on the fifteenth day of the sacred month of harvest, in the fall, they make a pilgrimmage. For eight days they live in "booths" with roofs open to the sky, covered with branches and leaves and foliage. During this festival, they dance around the sacred fire, and called upon the name of God.

The Hebrews have the virtually identical custom, in many respects. In the harvest season in the fall, on the 15th day of the sacred month of harvest (the seventh month), they celebrate the "festival of booths" for eight days. During this time they live in temporary booths, covered with branches, leaves, fronds. This festival goes back to the time of Moses and the Exodus from ancient Egypt (Leviticus 23).

How is it that two totally separate peoples evolved the identical custom? Dr. Cyrus Gordon, of Brandeis University in Boston, was privileged to sit in on one of the fall harvest festivals of American Indians, and listened to their chants, songs, and sacred ceremonies. An expert in Hebrew, Minoan, and many Middle Eastern languages, he was dumstruck. As he listened, he exclaimed to his companion, "My God! They are speaking the Hebrew names for God!" Dr. Joe Mahan, who related the above story to me, laughed. He is a strong believer in cultural contacts between the Indians and the East, long before

Columbus. He showed me a small tablet containing cuneiform writing of the Babylonians. "This," he said, "was found not long ago by a woman digging in her flower bed, here in Georgia. The inscription appears to be genuine. There is no reason not to believe it is authentic."

More and more, scholars are coming to admit that peoples from the Middle East reached the New World long before Columbus or the Vikings. One stone, found at Fort Benning, Georgia, has unusual markings all over it. I saw the stone myself, and took photographs of it. Professor Stanislav Segert, professor of Semitic languages at the University of Prague, has identified the markings on the stone as a script of the second millennium before Christ, from the Minoan civilization on the island of Crete!

In *Quest of the White God,* Pierre Honore points out similarities between the ancient Minoan writing and the script of the ancient Mayas. Independently of him, other scholars have noted striking similarities between Aztec glyphs from Mexico, and Cretan glyphs on the Phaistos Disc from the island of Crete in the Mediterranean.

In addition to these remarkable discoveries, Dr. Cyrus Gordon told me that Jews were in America in ancient times. The inscription on the stone, he asserts, is in the writing style of Canaan, the promised land of the Hebrews. Concludes Gordon, whom I interviewed at his old, New England style home in the suburbs of Boston:

"There is no doubt that these findings, and others, reflect Bronze Age transatlantic communication between the Mediterranean and the New World around the middle of the second millennium B.C."

In 1968 Manfred Metcalf was looking for slabs to build a barbeque pit. Several strange-looking, flat rocks caught his eye; he picked up a large flat piece of sandstone about nine inches long, brushed it off, and noticed odd markings on it. Metcalf gave the stone to Dr. Joseph B. Mahan, Jr., Director of Education and Research at the nearby Columbus Museum of Arts and Crafts at Columbus, Georgia. Mahan sent a copy of the stone to

Cyrus Gordon in May of 1968. Gordon shocked the world with his report:

"After studying the inscription, it was apparent to me that the affinities of the script were with the Aegean syllabary, whose two best known forms are Minoan Linear A, and Mycenaean Linear B. The double-axe in the lower left corner is of course reminiscent of Minoan civilization. The single vertical lines remind us of the vertical lines standing each for the numeral '1' in the Aegean syllabary; while the little circles stand for '100.' "

Concluded Gordon: "We therefore have American inscriptional contacts with the Aegean of the Bronze Age, near the south, west and north shores of the Gulf of Mexico. This can hardly be accidental; ancient Aegean writing near three different sectors of the Gulf reflects Bronze Age transatlantic communication between the Mediterranean and the New World around the middle of the second millennium B.C."[7].

Gordon offers the exciting thought, "The Aegean analogues to Mayan writing, to the Aztec glyphs, and to the Metcalf Stone inspire the hope that the deciphered scripts of the Mediterranean may provide keys for unlocking the forgotten systems of writing in the New World. A generation capable of landing men on the moon, may also be able to place pre-Columbian Americas within the framework of world history"[8].

Further proof that transatlantic travel and communication existed in the Bronze Age, the middle of the second millennium B.C., and in the days of the ancient Phoenicians, comes to us from South America.

In 1872 a slave belonging to a plantation owner by the name of Joaquim Alves de Costa, found a broken stone tablet in the tropical rain forests of Brazil's Paraiba state. Baffled by the strange markings on the stone, Costa's son who was a draftsman made a copy of it and sent it to the Brazilian Emperor's Council of State. The stone came to the attention of Ladislau

7. *Manuscripts,* a quarterly publication of the Manuscript Society, summer of 1969.

8. *Ibid.*, p. 166.

Netto, director of the national museum. He was convinced of the inscription's authenticity and made a crude translation of it.

Contemporary scholars scoffed. The very thought of Phoenicians reaching Brazil thousands of years before Columbus was viewed with disdain. Few scholars over the next 80 years took the stone at all seriously.

In 1966 Dr. Jules Piccus, professor of romance languages at the University of Massachusetts, bought an old scrapbook at a rummage sale containing a letter written by Netto in 1874, which contained his translations of the markings on the stone and a tracing of the original copy he had received from Costa's son. Intrigued, Dr. Piccus brought the material to the attention of Cyrus H. Gordon. Dr. Gordon, the head of the Department of Mediterranean Studies at Brandeis and an expert in ancient Semitic languages, as well as author of some 13 books, was amazed. He compared the Paraiba inscription with the latest work on Phoenician writings. He discovered that it contained nuances and quirks of Phoenician style that could not have been known to a 19th century forger. The writings had to be genuine!

Gordon translated the inscription as follows:

"We are Sidonian Canaanites from the city of the Mercantile King. We were cast up on this distant shore, a land of mountains. We sacrificed a youth to the celestial gods and goddesses in the nineteenth year of our mighty King Hiram and embarked from Ezion-geber into the Red Sea. We voyaged with ten ships and were at sea together for two years around Africa. Then we were separated by the hand of Baal and were no longer with our companions. So we have come here, twelve men and three women, into New Shore. Am I, the Admiral, a man who would flee? Nay! May the celestial gods and goddesses favor us well!"

Cyrus Gordon believes the king mentioned in the script can be identified as Hiram III who reigned 553-533 B.C. The inscription seems to verify an unusual statement found in the Old Testament. An ancient Biblical chronicler wrote: "And king Solomon made a navy of ships in Ezion-geber, which is beside Eloth, on the shore of the Red sea, in the land of Edom. And Hiram sent in the navy his servants, shipmen that had knowledge of the sea, with the servants of Solomon. And they came to Ophir, and fetched from thence gold, four hundred and twenty talents, and brought it to king Solomon" (I Kings 9:26-28).

In the days of Solomon there was an alliance between Hiram, the king of Tyre and the Phoenicians, and the Hebrews. Hiram and Solomon were not only allies, but very friendly toward each other (II Chronicles 2:2-12). Israelites and Phoenicians worked together to build the Temple in Jerusalem (vs. 13-18). This alliance included shipping together, although the Phoenicians jealously guarded their knowledge of the sea and navigational secrets from other nations. We read in II Chronicles, 8 beginning verse 8:

"Then went Solomon to Ezion-geber, and to Eloth, at the sea side in the land of Edom. And Huram sent him by the hands of his servant's ships, and servants that had knowledge of the sea; and they went with the servants of Solomon to Ophir, and took thence four hundred and fifty talents of gold, and brought them to king Solomon" (vs. 17-18).

In the middle of the second millennium B.C., and even to the time of Solomon, about 900 B.C., then, oceanic travel by maritime powers in the ancient world was common. It appears to have been fairly routine. Thus it is not surprising that the Egyptians in the days of Solon knew about the New World.

Other evidence comes from the investigations of Dr. Alexander von Wuthenau, whom I interviewed at his home in Mexico City. His living room was filled to overflowing with terra cotta pottery figures and objects d' art. In his book *The Art of Terra Cotta Pottery in Pre-Columbian Central and South America,* Dr. Von Wuthenau published scores of photographs of these art objects. He tells of his astonishment, when he first noted that in the earliest, lower levels of each excavation he encountered—not typical Indian heads—but heads of Mongolians, Chinese, Japanese, Tartars, Negroes, and "all kinds of white people, especially Semitic Types with and without beards" (p. 49).

Von Wuthenau observed that a head from Guerrero, Mexico,

was remarkably similar to the Egyptian god Bes. Similar images have been found at almost all Phoenician excavation sites around the Mediterranean.

At Acapulco, Von Wuthenau found that early Semitic peoples lived in considerable numbers. "The curious points about these essentially primitive figures are that, first, there is an emphasis on markedly Semitic-Hebrew features", he declared (p. 86). Female figures found in the region are also markedly Caucasian, with delicate eyebrows, small mouths and opulent coiffures.

Cyrus Gordon, who has studied the collection, points out: "In the private collection of Alexander von Wuthenau is a Mayan head, larger than life-size, portraying a pensive, bearded Semite. The dolichosephalic ("long-headed") type fits the Near East well. He resembles certain European Jews, but he is more like many Yemenite Jews"[9].

Near Tampico, the early Huastecan culture reveals portrait heads with a predominant Semitic, white element, but also Negroid features appear. At Veracruz, meanwhile, a figurine of a female dancer possesses the features just like those of a Frenchwoman of Brittany! She wears a headdress reminiscent of Phoenician fashion. Also at Veracruz a figure with a false beard, styled like an Egyptian beard, also had a snake-like protrusion on the forehead.

Again and again, figures with definite Semitic features have been found. A sample of Maya ceramic painting shows a lady with a flower who has an undeniable Negroid character. The figure has an affinity with Egyptian painting, says Wuthenau. yet it was not found along the Nile, but in Central America!

On the Pacific coast of Ecuador, also, evidence for the presence of early Hebrews has been found. A figurine of a lovely girl was found who wore a headdress with a remarkable Phoenician affinity. Other Ecuadorian heads show definite Semitic features. Clearly, the Semites penetrated a large part of the American continent in "prehistoric" times!

---

9. *Before Columbus: Links Between the Old World and Ancient America*, p. 26.

It is a fascinating fact that wherever the ancient Phoenicians went, they modelled human figures in clay. Often a mask connected with the cult of Humbaba, guardian of the forest of Lebanon, is found at excavations of ancient Phoenician sites. If found in Mexico, such masks would immediately be classified as an ancient Indian fire god.

Similarities also exist between Etruscan art and Meso-American terra cotta faces. Egyptian terra cottas of Africa are similar in certain techniques to Veracruz clay sculptures.

A stone was discovered in Campeche, Mexico, which portrays the side view of a scowling man wearing a large Mayan earring. The earring, archaeologists were astonished to learn, contains the Star of David in its design. Also it contains a lantern-like object which illustrates an ancient Phoenician anchor. The combination of sailing ship and Star of David is also found in a figure on a Jewish tomb at Beit-Shearim, Israel, dating from the second or third century B.C.

Indeed, we are forced to conclude that the world of the second millennium B.C., and the time of Solomon and Hiram, was a world where oceanic travel was common, at least among the maritime powers of the day.

This fact explains many cultural parallels between Central America and the Mediterranean world. It helps explain why pyramids are known in both Egypt and early Mexico. The Mixtec indians squeezed royal purple dye out of the snail *Purpura patula* of the Pacific Ocean, much as the Phoenicians extracted the dye from the snails *Murex truncatus* and *Murex brandaris* in the Mediterranean. Obviously this knowledge was communicated across the Atlantic.

Reed rafts were used by the ancient Egyptians. They were also used by ancient Indian tribes from the coast of California to Chile. Like the peoples of the Middle East, the early Americans worshipped the sun, built giant stone statues, huge pyramids, wrote in hieroglyphics, performed cranial surgery and mummified the dead.

Steward and Faron in *Native Peoples of South America*, explain: "There are a number of cultural elements so strikingly alike in the two hemispheres that the possibility of their transoceanic spread to America must be seriously considered"[10]. Indeed, it has now been thoroughly established!

But what happened to this ancient legacy? What caused the transoceanic traffic to cease, and the knowledge to become lost for several millennia?

Diodorus of Sicily, in the first century before the present era, wrote: "For there lies out in the deep off Libya (Africa) an island of considerable size, and situated as it is in the ocean it is distant from Libya a voyage of a number of days to the west. Its land is fruitful, much of it being mountainous and not a little being a level plain of surpassing beauty. Through it flow navigable rivers"[11].

Diodorus adds: "In ancient times this island remained undiscovered because of its distance from the entire inhabited world." He told of the Phoenicians who voyaged beyond the Pillars of Hercules and how they "were driven by strong winds a great distance out into the ocean. And after being storm-tossed for many days they were carried ashore on the island we mentioned above"[12].

Dr. Cyrus Gordon believes that the Minoans, who dominated Crete and the Aegean in the Middle Bronze Age were related to the Phoenicians linguistically and in their nautical way of life. He suggests "In the Bronze Age the great network of merchant mariners was not limited to the Mediterranean or other inland seas. It was oceanic and intercontinental"[13].

In the past century, several Brazilians have found inscriptions on rocks along the Amazon river. Over a period of 50 years, four men, including two who were scientists, uncovered inscriptions which they independently concluded were Phoenician in origin.

The first man, Francisco Pinto, in 1872 found over 20 caves deep in the Brazilian jungle and uncovered about 250 strange in-

10. p. 41.
11. 5, 19, 1-5.
12. 20, 1-4.
13. *Before Columbus, op. cit.*, p. 46.

scriptions upon the rocks. He thought they were Phoenician, and Brazil's Director of History and Geography corroborated his suspicions. A German philologist who studied the markings in 1911 felt they were genuine.

In the 1880s, Ernest Ronan, a French scientist, combed the jungles and found several more inscribed stones. In the 1920s a scholar by the name of Bernardo da Silva discovered many more inscriptions along the Amazon.

It makes good sense. It explains why the Mayans,who considered Quetzalcoatl as the bringer of their arts and laws, depicted him as being unusually blond[14].

When the Spaniards discovered the New World in the early sixteenth century, perhaps fifty million inhabitants lived in the Western Hemisphere, speaking over 900 languages. Such linguistic diversity has long puzzled scholars, and logically attests to a diversity of origins. Carleton S. Coon reported that the conquistadores "commented on Montezuma's light skin, but did not remark that this ruler rarely exposed himself to the bright sun." Coon adds: "George Catlin, in his portraits of the Mandan Indians, depicted some of them as blond. . . . Another case of allegedly abberrant Indians is that of the Pomo, Hupa, and neighboring tribes in north-central California whose beard growth seems to have been Caucasoid when they were first seen"[15].

Another mystery to ethnologists is the existence of a white skinned, red-bearded tribe recently discovered by builders of Brazil's Trans-Amazon Highway. Called the Lower Assurinis because they live south of the route of the highway, they have ear lobes (which is uncharacteristic of other tribes), and their language differs from traditional dialects in the region.

Sir Walter Raleigh in his *History of the World* mentioned that the Indians he encountered used many Welsh words long before the Welsh were known to have come to America.

Amazingly enough, worldwide cultural contacts must have occurred long, long ago. Pyramids have been found not only in

14. Crow, *The Epic of Latin America,* p. 20.
15. Coon, *The Living Races of Man,* p. 154.

ancient Egypt and Mexico, but in central America, in Peru and far away on the island of Rapa Iti in the South Pacific!

Reed rafts were not only common among the ancient Egyptians, and known from the California coast to Tehuantepec, and from Ecuador to the Araucanians of Chile, but were also known among the Maori of New Zealand and used by the early inhabitants of Easter Island!'[16].

But something happened which caused this golden period of intercontinental commerce and communication to cease. For a time the Atlantic became impassable. What happened?

Destruction rained on the earth. The island of Santorini in the eastern Mediterranean blew up. Incredible plagues struck Egypt, including stones from the sky. The waters of the Red Sea stood on end, allowing the children of Israel to pass over dryshod. And the island of Atlantis fell into the sea.

Plato writes:

"Now in this island of Atlantis there was a great and wonderful empire which had rule over the whole island and several others, and over parts of the continent, and, furthermore, the men of Atlantis had subjected the parts of Libya within the columns of Heracles as far as Egypt, and of Europe as far as Tyrrhenia. This vast power, gathered into one, endeavoured to subdue at a blow our country and yours and the whole of the region within the straits; and then Solon, your country shone forth, in the excellence of her virtue and strength, among all mankind. She was pre-eminent in courage and military skill, and was the leader of the Hellenes. And when the rest fell off from her, being compelled to stand alone, after having undergone the very extremity of danger, she defeated and triumphed over the invaders, and preserved from slavery those who were not yet subjugated, and generously liberated all the rest of us who dwell within the pillars.

"But afterwards there occurred violent earthquakes and floods; and in a single day and night of misfortune all your warlike men in a body sank into the earth, and the island of Atlantis in like manner disappeared in the depths of the sea. For

16. *Archaeology of Easter Island,* p. 535.

which reason the sea in those parts is impassable and impenetrable, because there is a shoal of mud in the way; and this was caused by the subsidence of the island"[17].

Before its submergence beneath the sea, this island kingdom of Atlantis, Plato tells us in *Critias,* was divided into ten portions, each ruled by one of the ten sons of the founder, whom he called Poseidon; the firstborn was king over all the rest, and was named Atlas. One of the sons named was Gadeirus. It is interesting to note that in Biblical antiquity, the patriarch Jacob had ten sons by his wife Leah, her handmaid, and Rachel's handmaid, and one of them was named "Gad." Could it be that Poseidon was another name for Jacob, whose name was changed by God to "Israel," meaning "A prince of God," or "champion of God" (Genesis 32:24-30).

Regardless of who the ancestors of the Atlanteans were, Plato records:

"Now Atlas had a numerous and honourable family, and they retained the kingdom, the eldest son handing it on to his eldest for many generations; and they had such an amount of wealth as was never before possessed by kings and potentates, and is not likely ever to be again, and they were furnished with everything which they needed, both in the city and country. For because of the greatness of their empire many things were brought to them from foreign countries, and the island itself provided most of what was required by them for the uses of life."

Atlantis was, according to the descriptions given in Plato's *Critias,* a land of surpassing achievement. It was rich in metals, mineral resources, abundant in wildlife, animals, and flourishing fruits and vegetables. The civilization of the Atlanteans was also admirable, with great architecture, canals for ocean-going triremes, vast harbors, docks, and an elaborate ornamental Temple, "a marvel to behold for size and for beauty."

But, the account continues, the Atlanteans grew proud, ignoble, and became debased in nature. Avarice grew among them,

17. *Timaeus,* 24-25.

and they became unable to bear their good fortune. Human nature got the upper hand, and they became full of avarice and unrighteous power. We are told that when this honorable race fell into a woeful plight, Zeus himself called a council together to determine how to destroy—punish—them.

Did such an island paradise exist somewhere between the Old and New Worlds in the middle of the second millennium before the present era?

Immanuel Velikovsky notes: "Modern scholars, finding some affinity between American, Egyptian and Phoenician cultures, think that Atlantis may have been the intermediary link. There is much probability in these speculations. Crete, a maritime base of Carian navigators, may disclose some information about Atlantis as soon as the Cretan scripts are satisfactorily deciphered."[18]

The destruction of this mighty island people, in one day and one night, as the island was swallowed up of the sea, certainly fits the traumatic cosmic catastrophes which were inflicted upon the world 900 years before the time of Solon. Only time, and further research and archaeological excavation wil finally establish precisely where Atlantis existed.

Someday the entire story will be known; of that, I am sure.

18. *Worlds in Collision,* p. 147.

Chapter Seven

Maps of the Ancient Sea Kings

In the temples and tombs of the ancient world, and in their magnificent edifices, built at the dawn of human history, an incredible, unbelievable story is told.

Dr. Thor Heyerdahl, who crossed the Atlantic Ocean successfully in his reed boat *Ra II* several years ago, proving that the ancient Egyptians could have easily done the same thing, declared:

"Like the ancient peoples of the Old World, Indians of the Americas worshipped the sun, built pyramids, and giant stone statutes, married brother to sister in royal families, wrote in hieroglyphics, performed cranial surgery, and mummified the dead."

How could this be, unless these peoples were acquainted and had contact culturally?

Ancient peoples around the world were noted for their incredible architectural abilities. The Temple built by Solomon at Jerusalem was a wonder of the ancient world. The Scriptural chronicler states: "And the house, when it was in building, was built of stone made ready before it was brought thither: so that there was neither hammer nor axe nor any tool of iron heard in the house, while it was in building" (I Kings 6:7).

It was resplendent with gold. The Temple was "exceedingly magnifical, of fame and of glory throughout all countries" (I Chronicles 22:5).

David, the king, prepared for the Temple 100,000 talents of

gold and 1,000,000 talents of silver. On today's market, gold is valued at almost $200 per ounce, and soon it may be worth more than that. On this basis, the value of the gold David supplied for the Temple of God in Jerusalem was between 40 and 50 billion dollars, today!

The Temple was built of great stones, cedar beams, and boards, overlaid within with gold (I Kgs. 6:14-22; 7:9-12). To construct this impressive building, Solomon hired 30,000 men of Israel and 150,000 men of Hiram, king of Tyre, to hew the timber, cut the huge stones, and carry the work of construction forward (I Kgs. 5:13-16; II Chron. 2:17-18; 8:7-9). Actual construction, even with this labor force, required seven years (I Kgs. 6:38). Wages alone, based on today's pay scale, might have topped the $10 billion mark.

Every part of this magnificent building was carefully, painstakingly prepared at some distance from the building site, and then transported to Jerusalem for final installation. When each timber and stone were laid, it fit perfectly.

This example of architecture from the ancient world should not surprise us, however. Building skills were found the world over.

In South America, the Incas built incredible roads across the entire Empire, some of them stretching for thousands of miles. These roads were fifteen feet across and paved with precisely fitted stones. In places, the Incas had to tunnel through stone mountains, or cross 10,000 foot chasms, using fiber suspension bridges, or carve their roadways across the face of 5,000 foot cliffs in the rugged Andes.

Says Carleton Beals about the Inca skills: "Incan building skills created memorable Cuzco in the Andes—Massive palaces, temples, arsenals, granaries, and schools built around two main squares. In some buildings enormous blocks, sixteen by twenty four by thirty six, weighing tons, of various shapes, were fitted glove-tight."[1]

Edward Dahlberg relates: "No North American has equaled the Inca architect. Without knowledge of mortar or cement, the

1. *Nomads and Empire Builders,* p. 99.

titanic rocks of his temples were joined together with such miraculous skill that the walls of the edifices were as seamless as the coat of Christ."[2]

Among the other notable achievements of the ancients are the huge stone statues—the awesome monolithic heads—of Easter Island, 2,000 miles west of Peru.

Impressive as the stone heads of Easter Island are, Thor Heyerdahl in his book *Aku-Aku* shows convincingly how the statues were cut out of the rock, transported on rollers to their final resting sites, and lifted into place. There was certainly nothing miraculous about it. There is in fact great similarity between the cyclopean block construction in ancient Peru and Easter Island.

The earliest inhabitants of Easter Island reached the island about 386 A.D. According to their tradition, the followers of Hotu-Matua came "from the east by steering for the setting sun."

The Maoris on the other hand "claim to have left Mexico (for Peru) 3,400 years ago, (or about the middle of the second millennium B.C.) and to have left Peru for the West over 1,500 years ago, arriving in New Zealand about 1,250 years ago."[3]

The Maoris call Easter Island, with which they are most familiar, *Pito-o-te-Whenua,* or "The Navel of the Earth." Easter Islanders also call it *Te Pito o te Henua* or "Navel of the World" in their most ancient legends.[4] It is no coincidence that the Maori traditions correspond so closely with the arrival of the first settlers of Easter Island, in the South Pacific.

The connection between Easter Island and the original inhabitants of Peru is strongly attested. "The tooling and fitting of cyclopean blocks are exactly the same in Cuzco and in Easter Island."[5] The author continues: "The cyclopean work of the burial platforms is exactly the same as that of Cuzco and the adjacent regions of the Andes. The colossal blocks are tooled and cut so as to fit each other."

2. *The Gold of Ophir,* p. 28.
3. *Maori Symbolism,* p. xxviii.
4. Heyerdahl, *Aku-Aku,* p. 29.
5. *Archaeology of Easter Island,* p. 498.

Another striking similarity between the Easter Islanders, the Maoris, and the Peruvians of antiquity, was the use of reed boats.[6] The Easter Islanders drew illustrations of reed boats with masts and sails and also cultivated the Peruvian *totora* reed in crater lakes—a plant not indigenous to the island but obviously imported from Peru.

Although modern theory suggests that all these peoples came from Malaysia and sailed eastward instead of westward from Peru, we also have the similarity of features and blood types to establish otherwise. The red haired strain on Easter Island—still visible today among certain of the inhabitants—and the huge statues with red topknots—reminds us of the fact that when the Spaniards discovered the Inca Empire in Peru, they noticed that members of the royal Inca family were tall, had whiter skin than the Spaniards, and certain ones had *red hair!* Microscopic analysis of the red hair found among some of the mummies of ancient Indians along the Pacific coast of South America reveal it is a Nordic hair type, says Thor Heyerdahl.[7]

The Incas told the Spaniards that the white-skinned red heads among them were the last descendants of the *Virachochas*—a divine race of white men with beards. Inca legend tells us that before the reign of the first Sun King, the sun-god Con-Ticci Viracocha left his kingdom in Peru and sailed to the west with all his subjects. Legends from Easter Island speak vividly of large vessels used for long voyages by their ancestors—great ships that could carry 400 passengers!

The evidence of blood type is also incontrovertible. Studies show that native tribes of Polynesia lack the B factor in their blood, as did the American Indians. But B-type blood is dominant among the peoples of Southeast Asia, from India and China to the Melanesians and Micronesians. In blood type, then, we find the Maoris and Easter Islanders more closely in affinity with the ancient peoples of North and South America.

Peter H. Buck in *An Introduction to Polynesian An-*

6. *Ibid.*, p. 535.
7. *Aku-Aku*, p. 356-357.

thropology (1945) noted that the features of the Polynesians "indicate a major Caucasoid origin" (p. 11).

Thus, we find that the impressive, colossal statues of the Easter Islanders closely resemble the amazing cyclopean statuary found in ancient Peru. Strange theories that visitors from outer space, such as have been proposed by Eric von Daniken and others, have no merit whatsoever.

These huge statues, however, bespeak a fact which has not been generally recognized in the scholarly world. Cyclopean statues point to the existence, in very ancient times, of a worldwide communication and cultural contact.

One of the most impressive cultural similarities found throughout much of the ancient world are the world's oldest known solar observatories.

Ancient solar observatories were known in the South Pacific. Thor Heyerdahl found the ruins of an ancient temple on Easter Island. The stones, cut in the classic pre-Inca style, included a series of stones placed in rows, and round about on the stones were carvings of large circular eyes like sun symbols. In the middle of the whole system was a strange complex of holes bored in the rock.

On December 21, 1955, the day of the summer solstice in the Southern Hemisphere, an archaeologist thrust a rod into one of the holes. Heyerdahl reports, "When the sun rose over the crater rim on the opposite side of the giant caldron, a sharp shadow from the rod fell right into the hole." They had "discovered the first ceremonial solar observatory known in Polynesia."[8]

The holes of the rocks at Orongo were oriented to the sun. In other parts of the island it was found that mighty Inca-style walls were oriented to right angles to the sun at summer solstice. Reported Heyerdahl, "The Incas and their predecessors in Peru were sun worshipers, and once again these new observations recalled to our minds the old cultures of South America."

8. *Aku-Aku,* p. 220.

The early Easter Islanders also made solar observations and oriented religious edifices accordingly.[9]

Thor Heyerdahl and his party proved conclusively by means of pottery, masonry, boat-building, statuary, and similarity of foods, that the original Easter Islanders—called the "long ears"—were light-skinned with a predominance of red hair among them, and migrated to Easter Island from pre-Inca Peru.

They originally worshiped the solar deity under the name Makemake, the supreme deity who created the earth, sun, moon, stars and man. Makemake was more than a sun god, but it is possible that celestial activities were his domain.[10] Sun worship is virtually absent in Polynesia. However, there is evidence among the Maori and people of eastern Polynesia that the sun was deified as Tane and that Ra, the sun god, was the tutelary god of Borabora.

The Maoris, also, made use of ancient solar observatories. "At Kerikeri, in the Bay of Islands, New Zealand, there is a miniature Stonehenge, the blocks standing about 7 feet out of the ground; and near Atiamuri, north of Taupo, there are other great monumental blocks—some fifty of these still standing erect."[11]

Interestingly, ancient Maori traditions relate that since antiquity the Maoris have observed ceremonial and dietary laws very similar to those of the ancient Hebrews. They kept the seventh day as a day of rest. Every 7 times 7 years—or 49 years—they observed a Jubilee Year similar to that of the ancient Hebrews.[12]

The Maoris, like the Hebrews, had a "sacred month" given over to Harvest thanksgiving, corresponding to the Hebrew month of Tishri and the Festival of Tabernacles.

Such similarities must be more than mere coincidence. Like the Yuchi Indians of North America, the Maoris, at some very early stage of history, must have come in contact with archaic Hebraic influence!

---

9. *Ibid.*, p. 376.
10. *Archaeology of Easter Island*, p. 254.
11. *Maori Symbolism*, p. 137.
12. *Ibid.*, p. 79.

How was this contact achieved? Did Hebrews contact the Maoris when they were still in Mexico, in the first and second millennium B.C.?

Was the ancient world covered by a global cultural continuity, indicating a globe-girdling civilization?

In his book *Maps of the Ancient Sea Kings,* Charles H. Hapgood tells of the *Piri Re' is* map of 1513 A.D. Studies of this map show that it correctly gives latitudes and longitudes along the coasts of Africa and Europe, indicating that the original mapmaker must have found the correct relative longitude across Africa and across the Atlantic to Brazil. This amazing map gives an accurate profile of the coast of South America to the Amazon, provides an amazing outline of the Yucatan Peninsula in Mexico (supposedly not yet discovered!), and—incredibly enough—shows a part of the coast of the Antarctic Continent which was not discovered, supposedly, until 1818!

This map does not stand alone. A world map drawn by Oronteus Finaeus in 1531 gives a truly authentic map of Antarctica, indicating the coasts were probably ice-free when the original map was drawn (of which Oronteus Finaeus' map was a latter copy). The Oronteus Finaeus map was strikingly similar to modern maps of the Antarctic. How could this be?

Another fascinating map is the map of Hadji Ahmed of 1559. It is evident that the cartographer had some extraordinary source maps at his disposal. Says Hapgood: "The shapes of North and South America have a *surprisingly modern look;* the western coasts are especially interesting. They seem to be about *two centuries ahead* of the cartography of the time. . . . The shape of what is now the *United States is about perfect.*"[13]

Another map of the Middle Ages, the Reinel Chart of 1510—a Portuguese map of the Indian Ocean—provides a striking example of the knowledge of the ancients. Studying the identifiable geographical localities and working out from them, Hapgood was astounded to find that "this map apparently shows the coat of *Australia* . . . The map also appeared to show some of the Caroline Islands of the Pacific. Latitudes and

13. *Maps of the Ancient Sea Kings,* p. 99.

longitudes on this map are remarkably good, although Australia is shown too far north."[14]

How can such remarkable accuracy be explained on the basis of almost total ignorance of the earth during that time? Obviously, at an earlier period of earth's history, sea-faring nations must have travelled around the world and accurately mapped the major continents, and fragments and copies of their ancient maps survived into the Middle Ages and were copied again.

Concludes Hapgood: "The evidence presented by the ancient maps appears to suggest the existence in remote times . . . of a true civilization, of a comparatively advanced sort, which either was localized in one area but had worldwide commerce, or was, in a real sense, a worldwide culture."[15]

How advanced was this ancient culture? Says Hapgood, "In astronomy, nautical science, mapmaking and possibly shipbuilding, it was perhaps more advanced than any state of culture before the 18th Century of the Christian Era." He continues:

"It was in the 18th Century that we first developed a practical means of finding longitude. It was in the 18th Century that we first accurately measured the circumference of the earth. Not until the 19th Century did we begin to send out ships for purposes of whaling or exploration into the Arctic or Antarctic Seas. *The maps indicate that some ancient people may have done all these things.*"[16] What ancient society could have been responsible?

Hapgood says such mapmaking would indicate *economic* motivations and vast economic resources. Further, organized government is indicated, since the mapping of a continent such as Antarctica implies much organization, many expeditions, and the compilation of many local observations and maps into a general map under central supervision. He adds that it is unlikely that navigation and mapmaking were the only sciences developed by this ancient people.

14. *Ibid.*, p. 134.
15. *Ibid.*, p. 193.
16. *Ibid.*

Who could they have been?

Mariano Edward Rivero and John James von Tschudi in *Peruvian Antiquities* (1857) point out that after the most thorough examination and minute comparison, the religious rites of the American Indians plainly present many points of agreement with those of the Hebrew people.[17]

Continue these authors: "Like the Jews, the Indians offer their firstfruits, they keep their new moons, and the feast of expiations at the end of September or in the beginning of October; they divide the year into four seasons, corresponding with the Jewish festivals. . . . In some parts of North America circumcision is practised . . . There is also much analogy between the Hebrews and Indians in that which concerns various rites and customs; such as the ceremonies of purification, the use of the bath . . . fasting, and the manner of prayer. The Indians likewise abstain from the blood of animals, as also from fish without scales; they consider divers quadrupeds unclean, also certain birds and reptiles, and they are accustomed to offer as a holocaust the firstlings of the flock"[18].

Surely, all these parallels are not mere coincidence!

Say Rivero and von Tschudi: "But that which most tends to fortify the opinion as to the Hebrew origin of the American tribes, is a species of ark, seemingly like that of the Old Testament; this the Indians take with them to war; it is never permitted to touch the ground, but rests upon stones or pieces of wood, it being deemed sacrilegious and unlawful to open it or look into it. The American priests scrupulously guard their sanctuary, and the High Priest carries on his breast a white shell adorned with precious stones, which recalls the Urim of the Jewish High Priest: of whom we are also reminded by a band of white plumes on his forehead"[19].

Say these two reputable scientists of the last century, "The use of Hebrew words was not uncommon in the religious performances of the North American Indians, and Adair assures us

17. *Peruvian Antiquities*, p. 9.
18. *Ibid.*
19. pp. 9-10.

that they called an accused or guilty person *haksit canaha,* 'a sinner of Canaan;' and to him who was inattentive to religious worship, they said, *Tschi haksit canaha,* 'You resemble a sinner of Canaan' "[20].

Though such evidence does not prove by any means that the Indians were Jews or Israelites, it does show that long before Columbus, Hebrews had reached the New World and had left their imprint upon its inhabitants! Such incredible parallels are beyond the remotest possibilities of having developed purely by "chance"!

Why should it seem strange that peoples of the ancient world—in particular Phoenicians and Hebrews—reached the New World and travelled to South America, and even crossed the Pacific? Is it really so incredible? The trouble is, most of us of the present generation have been brainwashed to think that the ancients were merely superstitious savages, terrified of sailing out to sea lest they fall off the edge of the earth.

But it is well known that the ancient Phoenicians roamed the Mediterranean Sea and had reached the Pillars of Hercules (Straits of Gibralter) by 1200 B.C. They developed the keel, streamlined their ships, covered the decks, and improved the sail. Their ships were probably from 80-100 feet long and used a single square sail besides oars. Their ships could average 100 miles in a day's time (24 hours). They were busy traders. Commerce was their principal aim. Tyre and Sidon, their home ports, were cities of immense wealth.

Did ancient Phoenicians reach the New World? Strange as it may sound, there is *Biblical evidence* supporting the conclusions of modern archaeologists!

God told Ezekiel, "And say to Tyre, O you who dwell at the entrance to the sea, who are *merchants of the peoples of many islands and coastlands. . .* The inhabitants of Sidon and [the island] of Arvad were your oarsmen; your skilled wise men, O Tyre, were in you, they were your pilots. The old men of Gebal [a city north of Sidon] and its skilled and wise men in you were your calkers; all the ships of the sea with their mariners were in

20. *Ibid.*

you to deal in your merchandise and trading" (Exek. 27:3, 8-9).

In the days of Ezekiel, 600 B.C., the Phoenicians were already masters of the seas, skillful at navigation, captains of farflung commerce. But did they reach the New World?

Continues Ezekiel, "Your rowers have brought you out into great and deep waters; the east wind has broken and wrecked you in the heart of the seas . . . When your wares came forth from the seas, you met the desire, the demand and the necessity of many people; you enriched the kings of the earth with your abundant wealth and merchandise. Now you are shattered by the seas, in the depths of the waters; your merchandise and all your crew have gone down with you" (vs. 26, 33-34, *Amplified Version*).

Consider the impact of these verses. Ezekiel was speaking of a maritime power which virtually disappeared from the face of the earth. They vanished! But before their destruction came, they were the earth's great sea captains, merchants, and sailors. Their ships plied the oceans. Many nations and kingdoms—not just a few around the Mediterranean—were enriched by their trade. Says Ezekiel, the "kings of the earth" shared in the commerce and revenue!

The Phoenicians were extremely secretive about their trading routes and guarded against revealing them to other nations. Greeks and other nations regarded them as "liars." Very possibly the Phoenicians invented weird tales of sea serpents and horrible sea monsters to keep other nations from probing the waters beyond the Pillars of Hercules. They were determined to keep their trade routes secret.

History reveals that Phoenicians circumnavigated Africa in the sixth century B.C., anticipating Vasco da Gama by 2,000 years. They sailed to the British Isles as early as 1,000 B.C. A pot full of Phoenician coins was found in 1749 on the island of Coryo, the westernmost island of the Azores in the Atlantic. The coins were dated from 330-320 B.C.

The Phoenicians no doubt had a long and important contact with the Scandinavian countries, shown by the amazing similiarity in ship design of the Viking and Phoenician ships.

Did the Phoenicians and early Hebrews have colonies in the New World?

It is significant that the Hebrew tribe of Dan, one of the twelve tribes of Israel, placed their name everywhere they migrated, naming every place after their father Dan. Originally Dan occupied a strip of coast along the Mediterranean (Josh. 19:47). When they conquered the city of Leshem, they renamed it "Dan". When they conquered Kirjath-jearim, they called it "Mahaneh-dan" (Judg. 18:11-12). And Laish also they captured and renamed "Dan" (v. 29).

The Biblical record tells us a striking fact about the Danites. "Dan abode in ships" (Judg. 5:17). The Danites were sea men—renowned navigators.

Moses spoke of the Danites as being like lions, and said they would "leap from Bashan" (Deut. 33:22). History reveals that they sailed far and wide, throughout the Mediterranean, leaving their name *Dan* wherever they went.

Did the Danites sail as far as the New World? Remember, the Danites were white—Caucasian. Could it be that the Man*dan* Indians are descended in part from that tribe of Israel?

The Mayas claim their kingdom was founded by a great eastern ruler called Votan or *Oden* or *Dan* by various tribes—a white man who came from the *east*. Was this king the *Dan*ish king W*oden* or *Odin*, king of *Dan*mark who reigned from 1040-999 B.C.? Just as this king gave his name to Denmark—*Dan*mark—did he also give his name to the "forest of *Dan*" in the land of the Quiche Indians?

The legend that Odin travelled to the New World about 1,000 B.C. is in itself significant. As we have seen, there is historical, Biblical evidence that the ancient Hebrews, about 1,000 B.C., engaged in great oceanic commercial voyages. That was the time of King Solomon of Israel.

We read in the Biblical record that king Solomon "exceeded all the kings of the earth for riches and for wisdom" (I Kings 10:23). In one year he received *44 tons* of gold from overseas through his commercial enterprises. Silver was as common as stones, in his day (vs. 17). Where did all this wealth come from?

Says the chronicler of ancient Israel:

"And king Solomon made a *navy of ships in Eziongeber,* which is beside Eloth, on the shore of the Red sea, in the land of Edom. And Hiram sent in the navy his servants, shipmen that had knowledge of the sea, with the servants of Solomon. And they came to *Ophir,* and fetched from thence gold, four hundred and twenty talents, and brought it to king Solomon" (I Kings 9:26-28).

We also read in the Bible:

"For the king had at sea a navy of Tharshish with the navy of Hiram: *once in three years* came the navy of Tharshish, bringing gold, and silver, ivory, and apes, and peacocks" (I Kings 10:22).

Is it not significant that Ferdinand Magellan circumnavigated the globe, requiring three years—from 1519-1522? Is it not meaningful that Sir Francis Drake, the first Englishman to circumnavigate the world, took three years to do so (1577-80)?

Also interesting is the fact that the Quichua word for the sun, *Inti,* may very likely be derived from the Sanscrit root *Indh,* meaning "to shine, burn, or flame" and which corresponds to the East India word *Indra,* also meaning "the sun"[21].

It is also significant that the pre-Incas worshipped the invisible, Creator God, the Supreme Being, by the appellative *Con,* very similar to the Hebrew *Cohen,* the word for "priest," from the root *Kahan* meaning "to meditate in religious services, to officiate as a priest."

Declare Rivero and von Tschudi: "It cannot be denied, that the above tradition of the creation of the world, by the invisible and omnipotent *Con,* the primitive happy state of men, their corruption by sin, the destruction of the earth, and its regeneration, *bears a distinct analogy to the Mosaic chronicle* of the earliest epoch of the history of the human race . . ."[22].

In the book of Isaiah we read the enigmatic statement: "I will make a man more precious than fine gold; even a man than the *golden wedge of Ophir*" (Isa. 13:12). Where was the legendary "Ophir"? What was this "golden wedge"?

The Hebrew word for "wedge" is *leshonah* and refers to a

21. *Peruvian Antiquities,* p. 96.
22. *Peruvian Antiquities,* p. 149.

"tongue," an instrument of some kind. The *wedge* of gold was, then, a bar or instrument of gold—literally, a "tongue of gold."

What could this "tongue" of gold have been? The gold of Ophir was not a scarce commodity since Solomon received 44 tons of it in a single year. Could it be that Isaiah was referring to a particular instrument of gold—something famous in Ophir?

The Inca Empire was famous for the quantity and quality of the gold it produced. The Incas of modern Peru have a tradition that their earliest king was *Pirua Paccari Manco.* In modern Quichua *Pirua* means a granary or storehouse. The first dynasty of kings, called the *Pirua dynasty,* included the first eighteen kings in the king list. One of the commonest titles of the early kings was Capac which means "Rich."

One of the first kings was Manco Capac who founded the city of Cuzco ("Navel" in the special language of the Incas). Manco Capac is generally regarded as the progenitor of the Incas. Legends of the Incas tell us that he got rid of his three brothers and led the people of Cuzco. We read, "He took with him *a golden staff.* When the soil was so fertile that its whole length sank into the rich mould, there was to be the final resting place"[23].

Another story calls this golden staff a "sceptre of gold" about a yard long and two fingers thick[24]. Could this have been the "golden wedge" or "tongue" of *Ophir?.*

John Crow relates a tradition of the ancient Incas. It is the story of "the *Golden Wedge,* according to which the Sun, wearied of the crude, barbaric ways of the uncivilized Indians, sent two of his children, a son and a daughter, to lift them from their primitive life. Placed on the earth near the banks of Lake Titicaca, these two children of the Sun were given a golden wedge which they were to carry with them wherever they wandered; and on the spot where this wedge sank without effort into the ground and disappered they were told to found their mother city. When the divine pair reached the vicinity of Cuzco,

23. Markham, *The Incas of Peru,* p. 50, 53.
24. Markham, *Royal Commentaries of the Yncas,* p. 64.

their talisman slid into the earth and vanished from sight"[25].

Declare Rivero and von Tschudi about ancient Inca tradition: " . . . the merciful Father, the Sun, placed two of his children on the lake of Titicaca, and told them 'that they might go where they wished, and wheresoever they pleased; they might stop to eat and sleep; commanded them to place in the ground a small wedge of gold, which he gave them, informing them that where that wedge should sink at one blow, and go into the earth, there the Sun wished them to stop, and make their residence and court. Arrived at the valley of Cuzco, after having vainly tried, through all the roads where they had travelled, to sink the wedge, they found themselves on the ridge of Huanancauri, and there endeavored anew to sink the small wedge, which went in with so much facility at the first blow, that they saw it no more.' "[26]

Was this mysterious talisman—this "golden wedge"—the same thing mentioned by the prophet Isaiah—the "golden wedge of Ophir"?

There is a close resemblance between the *Pirua* dynasty and the Hebrew word *Ophir.* In Hebrew, *Ophir* ("ph" can be pronounced either as an "f" or a "p") was the name of a place rich in gold (I Kings 9:28); sometimes the term *Ophir* was used for gold (Job 22:24).

Ancient Peru would certainly fit the Biblical description of Ophir. It was famous for its gold. In the Temple of the Sun in Cuzco was a fantastic display of wealth. The four inside walls were covered with paper-thin sheets of gold. A giant golden figure of the Sun hung suspended over the main altar. A huge silver room was dedicated to the Moon. Surrounding the Temple of the Sun and several chapels was a huge stone wall, covered with a cornice or crest of gold a yard wide. Inside the Temple were decorations of gold and silver flowers, plants and animals. The Spaniards sacked the Temple and seized all the gold and silver ornaments.

From 1492 to 1600 about two billion pesos' worth of gold and

25. *The Epic of Latin America,* p. 25.
26. *Peruvian Antiquities,* p. 43.

silver flowed out of Spain's New World colonies—at least three times the entire European supply of these precious metals up to that time. The total production of gold and silver in the Spanish colonies between 1492 and 1800 has been estimated at six billion dollars.

Historian Fernando Montesinos visited Peru from 1629-1642, a century after the conquest by the Spaniards. He travelled fifteen years through the country collecting material for a history of Peru. Montesinos wrote *Ophir de Espana, Memorias Historiales y Politicas del Peru.* He believed Peru was the Ophir of Solomon. He contended that Peru was first settled by Ophir, the grandson of Noah (Gen. 10:29).

Montesinos has been ridiculed and derided by historians. But since the early settlers of Peru were white-skinned and red bearded; since there was abundant gold in the region; since the name of the *Pirua* dynasty may correspond to the Hebrew *Ophir*; since the voyages of Solomon's fleet took about three years to complete; and since the "golden wedge" of Ophir could very well correspond to the "golden wedge" of Manco Capac—it seems more likely that Peru was the ancient Ophir of the Bible!

When we examine all the evidence, the picture comes clear. Yes, ancient Semites—early Hebrews—sailed to the Western Hemisphere long before Columbus. The Phoenician inscriptions, coins, and the terra cotta statuettes found in Central and South America are not mere "interpretations" of scholars. They are fact. There was global navigation, commerce and communication in the Bronze Age. The great cyclopean buildings, worldwide pyramids, stone statues, and ancient astronomical observatories are legacies of that ancient civilization.

The blowgun, found in Malaysia and South America is further proof of such global contacts. It consists of a long tube constructed of two half tubes carefully worked and fitted inside a larger sheath. An 8-10 inch poisoned dart, its butt wrapped with lint to fit snugly in the bore of the gun, can be shot up to 100 feet with deadly accuracy. It is very doubtful that such a weapon would have been developed independently in two isolated cultures.

Consider, also, the Panpipes—a musical instrument found both in Southeast Asia, Oceania, and South America. The scale of certain Panpipes from Oceania and South America was found to be identical. Both Southeast Asia and South America had the identical custom of playing the Panpipes in joined, complementary pairs. Was this a mere "accident"?

Other implements common to both the Andes and Asia were star-headed war clubs, fishhooks of special shapes, tie-dyed cloth, litters, umbrellas, irrigation farming, ceramics, coiled and twilled basketry, metallurgy, mound construction, and terraced farmlands.

Admit scientists Steward and Faron, "There are a number of cultural elements *so strikingly alike* in the two hemispheres that the possibility of their transoceanic spread to America must be seriously considered"[27].

A number of domesticated plants were used by the peoples of Southeast Asia *and* American Indians prior to the voyages of Columbus. Virtually all scientists now admit that the probable explanation for the distribution of these plants "is that *human beings* carried them from one place to another"[28].

These plants include maize, coconuts, certain beans, sweet potatoes, and especially cotton. The bottle gourd (*Lagenaria siceraria*) is a native of the Old World, but has been found in many pre-Columbian archaeological sites in America, including Peru.

Cotton, also, tells an interesting story. In the Old World, wild and domesticated species have 13 large chromosomes. Wild species of American cotton have 13 small chromosomes. However, cultivated American species and wild Hawaiian species have 13 large and 13 small chromosomes, producing a total of 26 chromosomes. How could this be? The 26 chromosome American domesticated variety is "almost certainly a cross between the Old World domesticated cotton and the new World wild form."

Continue Steward and Faron:

27. *Native Peoples of South America,* p. 41.
28. Steward and Faron, *Native Peoples of South America,* p. 38.

"The simplest historical interpretation is that 13-chromosome cotton was first domesticated in the Old World, where it appeared during the *Bronze Age* and spread very widely. The domesticated was introduced to the New World, where it crossed with the 13-chromosome wild variety, producing the 26-chromosome domesticate"[29].

But what do all these surprising similarities signify? What do they mean?

First, they disprove the long-cherished theory that the Indians were the first people to reach the New World. These new startling facts show that thousands of years ago, early Phoenicians and Hebrews reached the New World and settled there. Also, early Orientals and Negroes reached the new World long prior to the time of Columbus.

The very predominance of terra cottas with white, Semitic features conclusively shows that early whites were a predominant group in the New World. Such artifacts would not be found in such incredible numbers if one or two stray, storm-tossed white voyagers from the Old World shipwrecked on the coast of the Americas. The terra cotta artifacts themselves tell an eloquent story, which becomes all the more significant when added to the other evidence!

In the light of all these astonishing discoveries in recent decades, then, let us reconstruct what actually happened.

At one time, in the middle of the second millennium before the present era, during the reign of Solomon, king of Israel, and later, there were periods of transoceanic travel and communication between the Old and New Worlds. There was distinct cross-cultural fertilization. Around the globe—in North America, Central America, South America, and in far away Easter Island and New Zealand—there was early contact with ancient Hebrew peoples. The unbelievable cultural similarities cannot be dismissed out of hand. They are real. They will not go away.

But at some point, this amazing knowledge of the ancients was lost. The world plunged into darkness. The navigational

29. *Ibid.*, p. 39.

knowledge and expertise of the sailors of old became lost to mankind.

What caused this sudden black-out of knowledge? What indeed, could explain it but the incredible accounts of cosmic upheaval and catastrophe which pour in from lands around the world—cosmic cataclysms in the middle of the second millennium B.C., in which Atlantis perished—and another series of catastrophes in the years between Uzziah and Hezekiah, kings of Judah, in the eighth century before the present era.

Chapter Eight

The Great Pyramid at Gizeh

Thus far in this book we have alluded to several major catastrophes which occurred within the memory of mankind. Catastrophes which shook the globe which spins beneath our feet. Cataclysms which had an awesome effect upon mankind and left indelible records in the various ancient histories, legends, myths, and chronicles of the human race.

But what agent caused these several episodic upheavals and violent paroxysms of nature? What was the major, underlying cause?

Was it terrestrial? Or extra-terrestrial? Some might suppose that the cause was the earth being visited by beings from another planet—or superbeings from another galaxy. Such supositions may seem ingenious, or merely imaginative speculations. But what does history reveal? What evidence is there, and what does the evidence say?

We have referred to *cosmic* violence, several times, and have mentioned specifically meteorites and comets as having a part in the maelstroms which afflicted ancient nations. Can we be more precise than that?

Yes, we can. A hint as to the ultimate answers lies both in the ancient records of mankind, and also within the mystery of the Great Pyramid of Cheops, at Gizeh, in the Valley of the Nile.

In order to understand, we need to find out when the Great Pyramid was built, why it was built, its great purpose, and, hopefully, by whom.

For ages men have been awestruck at the size and scope of the Great Pyramid of Cheops, or Khufu. Much myth and legend has surfaced about the Great Pyramid, and several investigators have studied it at great length. Many theories have been proposed by scientists who have explored and probed the Great Pyramid over the past two thousand years. But the mystery of the Great Pyramid still baffles the world. Why was it built? When? By whom? For what enigmatic purpose?

The Great Pyramid of Cheops rises 486 feet into the Egyptian sky. It was regarded as one of the seven wonders of the ancient world. Over the centuries and millennia its marble casing stones have been stripped away and plundered by marauding tribesmen and nomadic Arabs. But even today the giant colossus still stands, causing wonderment and admiration in the eyes of the modern beholder.

Nearly all of the pyramids of Egypt were built over a period of one thousand years. The Pyramid Age of Egypt begins with the IIIrd Dynasty and ends with the VIth Dynasty. During this time the kings and many of their queens were buried in tombs with a pyramidal superstructure. These pyramids were built on the edge of the desert west of the Nile in the vicinity of Memphis. Tradition has it that Menes, the first dynastic ruler of Egypt, dyked the Nile and reclaimed the land upon which Memphis was built. Menes, or Cush, was the first Egyptian king to unite both Upper and Lower Egypt under one government.

During the first dynastic period in Egypt both kings and nobles were buried in tombs built of brick. With the IIIrd Dynasty stone began to be used. Manetho, the Egyptian historian of antiquity, credits Imhotep, the architect of Zozer, with inventing the art of building with stone. As if to confirm this, his name was found on the pedestal of a statue outside the tomb of Zozer when it was excavated. Later generations of Egyptians regarded Imhotep as a magician, astronomer, and the father of medicine. Zozer was buried in a monumental step pyramid.

Toward the close of year 18 of Zozer the climax of a seven years' famine occurred. "No other seven years' famine is ever reported during the entire history of the Pharoahs," declares

Dr. Herman L. Hoeh. "This is the Biblical seven-years' famine under Joseph. It is at the right time"[1].

This calamity is mentioned in an inscription on the rocks of the island of Sehel, at the First Cataract of the Nile. G. Ernest Writht, in *Biblical Archaeology,* records it thus:

"Year 18 . . . I was in distress on the Great Throne, and those who are in the palace were in Heart's affliction from a very great evil, since the Nile had not come in my time for a space of seven years. Grain was scant, fruits were dried up, and everything which they eat was short. . . . The infant was wailing; the youth was waiting; the heart of the old man was in sorrow. . . . The courtiers were in need. The temples were shut up. . . . Everything was found empty"[2].

This was the time of the Biblical patriarch Joseph, who had been sold into slavery by his brothers. Joseph himself appears in Dynasty III and Dynasty IV of Manetho, under the name Suphis (or Souphis, or Saophis). Joseph, in Hebrew, is not pronounced with a "J" sound at all, but with a "Y" sound. Asserts H.L. Hoeh, "In Manetho's Egyptian transcription of the name only the consonants "s" and "ph" appear—hence the Greek Souphis or its variant forms. Eratosthenes wrote that the Egyptians had designated Suphis as a 'money-getter' or 'trafficker' "[3].

The step pyramid that Imhotep built paved the way for the massive true pyramids which followed. The most celebrated are the pyramids of Gizeh, immortalizing Khufu (Cheops), Khafre, and Menkaure of the Fourth Dynasty.

The Great Pyramid built for Khufu was constructed of more than two million stone blocks, most of them weighing about two and a half tons. The ancient Egyptians had to be inventive engineers, because they had only the simplest tools to work with. They did not yet possess the secret of the wheel. They had to cut hard rock with the simplest of copper and stone tools, transport massive blocks weighing tons without block and

1. Hoeh, *Compendium of World History,* p. 63.
2. Pritchard, *Ancient Near Eastern Texts,* p. 31.
3. See Fragment 17, *Manetho,* by W. G. Waddell, p. 219.

tackle or carts or draft animals. Some of the blocks were granite and posed special problems. Dolerite hammers had to be used to chip rough gutters in quarry walls. Workers then fitted wooden wedges into the slots, soaked with water, and when the wood expanded it cracked and split off chunks of rock, which were then hammered into rough blocks.

In laying the foundation of the Great Pyramid, the architects directed them to cut steplike terraces into the sides of the hill. These terraces had to be absolutely level to assure that the Pyramid would be level. Water was poured into trenches around the base of the Pyramid-to-be, and using the water level as a standard of measurement, they were able to make the entire 13 acre building site so level that the southeast corner of the Pyramid stands only one half inch higher than the northwest corner.

The Greek historian Herodotus declares that 100,000 slaves took part in building the Great Pyramid of Cheops. Writes I.E.S. Edwards: "The Pyramid of Cheops, or the Great Pyramid, marks the apogee of pyramid-building in respect of both size and quality. No exact computation of the amount of hewn stone contained in it is possible, because the centre of its core consists of a nucleus of rock, the size of which cannot be precisely determined. It has, however, been estimated that, when complete, the core of local stone and the outer facing of Tura limestone were composed of about 2,300,000 separate blocks, each averaging some 2½ tons in weight and reaching a maximum of 15 tons.

"Many attempts have been made by writers on the Great Pyramid to illustrate its size by comparison with other famous buildings. It has, for instance, been calculated that the Houses of Parliament and St. Paul's Cathedral could be grouped inside the area of its base and still leave considerable space unoccupied"[4].

It has also been reckoned that if the Pyramid were sawn into blocks one foot square and each block laid end to end, they would extend over a distance equal to two thirds of the earth's

4. *The Pyramids of Egypt,* p. 82.

girth at the Equator. From a fresh survey taken by J. H. Cole of the Survey Department of the Egyptian Government in 1925 it was found that the Pyramid measured at the base 755.43 feet on the north, 756.08 feet on the south, 755.88 feet on the east, and 755.77 feet on the west.

Says Edwards: "Each side was oriented almost exactly in line with true north and south or east and west . . . As the accuracy of this orientation implies, the four corners were almost perfect right angles . . . "[5].

The Great Pyramid was completed within the reign of Cheops. The construction was so perfect that Sir Flinders Petrie, who spent two years excavating at the site, observed that the joints in the casing of the Great Pyramid measured only one-fiftieth of an inch in thickness!

The amazing orientation of the Great Pyramid on the north-south axis and east-west axis could only have been achieved with the aid of one or more of the celestial bodies, since the magnetic compass was unknown to the ancient Egyptians.

Why was the Great Pyramid built? Arab writers from early times associated the pyramids with the Biblical narrative of the Flood. According to their traditions, the pyramids were built as a result of a dream to serve as repositories of knowledge, to protect all the science and wisdom of the Egyptians which otherwise would be lost.

Julius Honorius who lived before the fifth century quoted a legend that the pyramids were Joseph's granaries which had been used for storing corn during the years of plenty, a legend which was still going strong in the Middle Ages.

Writes Peter Tompkins in *Secrets of the Great Pyramid:* "The most ancient tradition about the Great Pyramid is that it was erected to memorialize a tremendous cataclysm in the planetary system which affected the globe with fire and flooding"[6].

He continues: "Arab authors recount that the pyramids were built before the deluge by a king who had a vision that the world

5. *Ibid.*. p. 83.
6. p. 217.

would be turned upside down, and that the stars would fall from the sky. According to these Arab sources, the king placed in the Pyramids accounts of all he had learned from the wisest men of the times, including the secrets of astronomy, complete with tables of the stars, geometry, and physics, treatises on precious stones, and certain machines, including celestial spheres and terrestial globes."

The "deluge" referred to here must have been a cataclysm which followed the universal flood of Noah's time, as history is clear that the IIIrd and IVth Dynasties of Egypt were this side of the Flood.

The earliest Jewish reports—other than the vague reference in the Bible to 'pillars of stone'—is in Josephus, who says the Sethites were inventors of a wisdom which dealt with celestial bodies and their order in the heavens, and that to preserve their wisdom for all mankind they built two monuments—one brick, the other stone—the stone one being extant in Egypt in Josephus' time.

Arab historians such as Ibrahim ben Ebn Wasuff Shah say that the Gizah pyramids were built by an antediluvian king called Surid or Saurid, who saw in a dream a huge planet falling to earth at the time when the Lyre was in the Constellation of cancer.

Another Arab legend recounted by ibn-Batuta, who wrote 730 years after the Hegira, says that Hermes Trismegistos—the Enoch of the Bible—"having ascertained from the appearance of the stars that the deluge would take place, built the pyramids to contain books of science and knowledge and other matters worth preserving from oblivion and ruin."

As to the purpose of the Great Pyramid, Peter Tompkins in the introduction to his book *Secrets of the Great Pyramid,* writes: "The Great Pyramid, like most of the great temples of antiquity, was designed on the basis of a hermetic geometry known only to a restricted group of initiates, mere traces of which percolated to the Classical and Alexandrian Greeks.

"These and other recent discoveries have made it possible to reanalyze the entire history of the Great Pyramid with a whole new set of references: the results are explosive. The common—and indeed authoritative—assumption that the Pyramid was just another tomb built to memorialize some vainglorious Pharaoh is proved to be false" (xiv).

Tompkins points out that it is now known that an advanced science existed 2-3,000 years before Christ. It is now realized that Hipparchus, Pythagoras and other Greeks who were thought to have invented mathematics on this planet merely picked up fragments of an arcane science that was evolved by "remote and unknown predecessors."

Adds Tompkins: "Like Stonehenge and other megalithic calendars, the Pyramid has been shown to be an almanac by means of which the length of the year including its awkward .2422 fraction of a day could be measured as accurately as with a modern telescope. It has been shown to be a theodolite, or instrument for the surveyor, of great precision and simplicity, virtually indestructible. It is still a compass so finely oriented that modern compasses are adjusted to it, not vice versa.

"It has also been established that the Great Pyramid is a carefully located geodetic marker, or fixed landmark, on which the geography of the ancient world was brilliantly constructed; that it served as a celestial observatory from which maps and tables of the stellar hemisphere could be accurately drawn; and that it incorporates in its sides and angles the means for creating a highly sophisticated map projection of the northern hemisphere. It is, in fact, a scale model of the hemisphere, correctly incorporating the geographical degrees of latitude and longitude."

Tompkins goes even further:

"The Pyramid may well be the repository of an ancient and possibly universal system of weights and measures, the model for the most sensible system of linear and temporal measurements available on earth, based on the polar axis of rotation, a system first postulated in modern times a century ago by the British astronomer Sir John Herschel, whose accuracy is now confirmed by the mensuration of orbiting satellites."

Says Tompkins:

"Whoever built the Great Pyramid, it is now quite clear, knew the precise circumference of the planet, and the length of the year to several decimals—data which were not rediscovered till the seventeenth century. Its architects may well have known the mean length of the earth's orbit round the sun, the specific density of the planet, the 26,000-year cycle of the equinoxes, the acceleration of gravity and the speed of light"[7].

This seems incredible—even preposterous. But Tompkins backs up his arguments with strong evidence from the Great Pyramid itself.

There is substantial evidence that the Great Pyramid was used by the ancient Egyptians as an astronomical observatory. Richard Anthony Proctor at the turn of the century suggested that the ancients needed a true meridian on the solid earth from which to extrapolate a meridian across the heavenly vault, so they could detect the precise moment when stars, sun, planets and moon transited this meridian as they moved through the heavens.

Arab historians repeatedly declared that the Pyramid had originally been designed as an astronomical observatory. Proctor showed how the Pyramid would have made an excellent observatory, the greatest instrument for observing the heavens before the advent of the modern great telescope. Proctor claimed that the Descending Passage of the Pyramid originally sighted the North Star, which he identified with alpha Draconis at that time. The Grand Gallery also could have been used to observe the stars circling in the southern sky.

Astonishingly enough, Peter Kolosimo in *Terra Senza Tempo*[8] (published in 1969 in Milan, Italy) claims that the Russians have uncovered some fascinating secrets of ancient Egyptian archaeology. He points out that they found astronomical maps of surprising accuracy showing the position of the stars as they were many thousands of years ago. Reportedly, the Russians also dug up many objects, some as yet unidentified, including crystal lenses, of great precision, perfectly spherical, which very possibly were used as telescopes! Asserts Kolosimo, similar lenses have been found in Iraq and even central Australia. Even

7. *Ibid.*, xiv-xv.
8. p. 87.

more amazing is the fact that they can only be ground today with a special abrasive made of oxide of cerium which can only be produced electrically.

Peter Tompkins attempted to verify these data with Soviet academicians, without any tangible result. But it seems out of the question that Kolosimo manufactured such an incredible story out of whole cloth. In view of the many other astonishing things uncovered relative to the Egyptians of antiquity, these discoveries seem to fit with the entire picture scientists are beginning to draw about the science of the Egyptians during the time of the Great Pyramid.

We might know much more about the Pyramids, especially the Great Pyramid, had it not been for the fact that in the Middle Ages due to the influence of the Church world learning came to be despised and denigrated. Christianized Egyptians were even forbidden access to the ancient temples which were either seized or razed to the ground by the Catholics. Thousands of statues and inscriptions were disfigured. In 389 A.D. the great library of Alexandria, Egypt, was burned to the ground and destroyed by a mob of indignant Christians on the orders of Emperor Theodosius. All that was ancient was considered pagan, and therefore sinful. Mathematicians and astronomers were persecuted and sometimes hounded to death by the established Church.

The secrets of the Great Pyramid, meanwhile, remained undiscovered. The first real attempt to excavate the Great Pyramid was made by the Arabs under Al Mamun, an enlightened Arab chief. Eventually they tunneled into the vast structure and discovered many chambers and narrow passageways, but often their attempts were thwarted by huge granite plugs impeding their progress. They finally uncovered what was called the "King's Chamber," but there was no true sarcophagus or burial coffin—no evidence any king of Egypt had ever been entombed. This fact indicates that the purpose of the Great Pyramid was not to house the body of an ancient Pharaoh, unlike the other pyramids of Egypt.

Later superstitions had it that the Great Pyramid was haunted by ghosts. Arabs claimed that at noon and sunset it was haunted by a naked woman who seduced people into her power and then drove them insane. There were stories that it was filled with serpents.

It remained, however, to our present 20th century before many of the riddles of the Great Pyramid became known and revealed.

In his book *A History of Egyptian Archaeology* Fred Gladstone Bratton states, "Of the Seven Wonders of the Ancient World, the Giza Pyramids alone have survived the ravages of time and the destructive hand of man. *They are still the most massive and impressive buildings in the world today.*

"As with astronomical measurements where the scientist has to resort to comparisons in order to demonstrate the immensity of the universe, so it is with the Pyramid of Cheops. No other building in history has called for so much study of construction, dimensions, and purpose as this pile of thirty million cubic feet of limestone. It has been estimated that the Great Pyramid . . . is large enough to accommodate St. Paul's Cathedral, Westminster Abbey, St. Peter's in Rome, and the Cathedrals of Milan and Florence."

This author continues, "By using one of the celestial bodies, the Cheops builders were able to orient the Pyramid to the four cardinal points, the errors being only in the following fractions of one degree: north side, 2' 28" south of west; south side, 1' 57" south of west; east side, 5' 30" west of north; west side, 2' 30" west of north. The four corners were almost perfect right angles with the following measurements: 90° 3' 2"; north-west, 90° 59' 58"; south-east, 89° 56' 37"; and south-west, 90° 0' 33"."[9]

Archaeologist Flinders Petrie calculated that 100,000 men were used in transporting the blocks to the base of the Pyramid, and some 4,000 in its actual construction. The precision is such that Petrie said any errors in the angles and degrees "can be covered with one's thumb."

Eight centuries ago Abd al-Latif observed that the stone blocks were fitted together so well that a knife cannot be in-

9. *Ibid.*, p. 88.

serted in the joints—a truly remarkable evidence of precision engineering and sheer architectural genius!

In his book *The Pyramids,* Ahmed Fakhry declares, "The Great Pyramid of Giza represents the culminative effort of the pyramid builders. Not only is it the largest monument of its kind ever constructed, but for excellence of workmanship, accuracy of planning, and beauty of proportion, it remains the chief of the Seven Wonders of the World"[10].

Said Fakhry of the Great Pyramid, "Even equipped with modern tools and instruments, and profiting from nearly five thousand years of experience, architects and engineers today might well quail if called upon to erect a duplicate".

In 1798 the French conquered Egypt. Napoleon Bonaparte took with him 35,000 soldiers and 175 savants, learned antiquarians and men versed in science. One of these Edme-Francois Jomard was to make some exciting discoveries about the Great Pyramid. He found that the apothem or slant height of the Pyramid was 184.722 meters (since the outer casing was entirely missing, this figure was really an approximate), but it led to some serious thinking. Diodorus Siculus and Strabo had written that the apothem of the Pyramid was one stadium long—one stadium being 600 Greek feet. Jomard learned from reading the classics that a stadium of 600 feet was considered 1/600th of a geographical degree. Dividing the geographical degree at the mean latitude of Egypt by 600, Jomard came up with 184.712 meters, within 10 centimeters of the Great Pyramid's apothem.

Jomard wondered if the ancient Egyptians had worked out their basic units of measurement from the size of the earth, and then built this knowledge into the Pyramid.

Jomard found that several Greek authors reported that the perimeter of the base of the Pyramid was intended to measure half a minute of longitude. In other words, 480 times the base of the Pyramid was equal to a geographical degree.

This time Jomard found that a half a minute of

10. p. 99.

longitude—230.8 meters—was within 10 centimeters of his measured length of the base of the Pyramid!

Since Herodotus had said 400 cubits equalled a stadium of 600 feet, Jomard divided the apothem by 400 and obtained a cubit of .4618 meters, the common cubit of the modern Egyptians! Multiplying this figure by 500 (since the Greeks said the base of the Pyramid was 500 cubits), he got 230.90 meters—the exact figure which he also obtained from measuring the base.

Jomard also suggested that the King's Chamber was not a tomb but a metric monument designed to perpetuate a system of measures. He was convinced that the builders of the Great Pyramid had the astronomical knowledge to measure a geographical degree and therefore knew the true circumference of the earth! He pointed out that all the ancient writers had named Egypt as the birthplace of the science of geometry, but his classically indoctrinated colleagues rejected the idea.

In the middle of the 19th century Mathematician and amateur astronomer John Taylor studied measurements others had brought back to England of the Great Pyramid. In his calculations he discovered that the Pyramid was of a unique structure—the sides sloped at 51° 51' not the 60° of an equilateral triangle, and each face's area was equal to the square of the height of the Pyramid. He found if he divided the perimeter by twice the height, he obtained a value of 3.144, remarkably close to the value of *pi.* The height of the Pyramid to its perimeter had the same value as the radius of a circle to its circumference. Taylor concluded that the builders of the Pyramid intended to represent the circumference of the earth by the perimeter of the Pyramid, and the height of the Pyramid to represent the distance from the center of the earth to the pole. Asserted Taylor: "It was to make a record of the measure of the Earth that it was built."

Taylor concluded: "They knew the Earth was a sphere; and by observing the motion of the heavenly bodies over the earth's surface, had ascertained its circumference, and were desirous of

11. *Ibid.*, pp. 120-121.

leaving behind them a record of the circumference as correct and imperishable as it was possible for them to construct."

Coincidentally, Taylor found that dividing the base by 25 inches gave a figure of 366, very close to the number of days in a year. If he measured the perimeter in inches, and divided the result by 100, it gave 366. At that same time independently Sir John Herschel, British astronomer, said the British inch was a hair's breath too short and recommended it be lengthened a little so that 500,000,000 inches would exactly equal the distance from pole to pole in the earth. Astonishingly enough, the inch he came up with—exactly one five hundred millionth of the polar axis of the earth—was the very same inch that Taylor found fit the Great Pyramid in multiples of 366!

Remarkably enough, the International Geophysical Year 1957-58 geodetic research with orbiting satellites obtained a figure of 3949.89 miles for the polar radius of the earth, which, divided by 10,000,000 British inches, gave a figure of 25.02614284—exactly the length of Taylor's and Sir Isaac Newton's "sacred cubit" correct to the third decimal point!

Says Tompkins: "To Taylor the inference was clear: the ancient Egyptians must have had a system of measurements based on the true spherical dimensions of the planet, which used a unit which was within a thousandth part of being equal to a British inch"[12].

Taylor also found that the cubic capacity of the granite coffer found in the King's Chamber in the Pyramid was almost exactly four times a standard measure for grain in Britain—a quarter, or eight bushels.

The first really scientific measurements of the Pyramid with modern equipment was done by Piazzi Smyth in the late nineteenth century. Smyth found the Pyramid was placed on the latitude of 29° 58' 51" and concluded finally that originally the builders had placed the Pyramid right on the latitude of 30°, but it had been gradually displaced due to a gradual shifting of latitude which occurs.

Smyth believed the Pyramid was oriented by using the

12. *Secrets of the Great Pyramid,* p. 74.

Descending Passage to observe a polar star. Smyth calculated that the circumpolar star alpha Draconis could have been seen in the 1° opening of the Descending Passage 2123 B.C., also at 3440 B.C. Smyth determined that in 2170 B.C. at the equinox, alpha Draconis would have been visible down the Descending Passage and another star, Alcyone of the Pleiades, would have been crossing the meridian in the vertical plane of the Grand Gallery of the Pyramid.

Smyth's other observations and measurements confirmed in great detail the theories of Taylor. However, he found that his results produced an astounding value for *pi* in the Great Pyramid's proportions—the value of 3.14159!

Smyth also found, in recomputing the height of the Great Pyramid, that Taylor's figure was 6 inches too short, and that the Pyramid rose 10 units of height for ever 9 units of width. Multiplying the height by 10 to the ninth power, he came up with 91,840,000—an excellent figure for the radius of the earth's orbit around the sun in miles! Was this mere chance?

Another extraordinary number found by students of the Pyramid was the sum of the diagonals of the base, which were computed to be 25,826.68 pyramid inches—a very close approximation of the number of solar years in a "great year"—that is, the length of years it takes for the earth to make a complete gyration in its wobble which causes precession of the equinoxes. Was this just coincidence?

According to David Davidson, the builders of the Great Pyramid must have been deeply familiar with the working of natural law. He claimed it was evident that if you know the earth's distance from the sun and the length of the sidereal year in seconds, you can figure the rate at which the earth is falling toward the sun; you can figure out from this the specific gravity of the earth, the sun, the earth and moon combined, and even the speed of light.

Says Tompkins: "To Davidson the mathematics of the Pyramid indicate that the former civilization was more highly skilled in the science of gravitational astronomy—and therefore in the mathematical basis of the mechanical arts and sciences—than modern civilization"[13].

Davidson concluded that it has "taken man thousands of years to discover by experiment what he knew originally by a surer and simpler method." Davidson surmised that the Pyramid was built to immortalize the science of that time and preserve it for another civilization far into the future. It was created to be a sort of "time capsule," a record of the science and mathematics of its day, to be preserved as long as the Great Pyramid itself should last.

Unfortunately for Davidson and other scientific investigators of the Pyramid, the efforts of lesser men who attempted to read prophetic interpretations into the interior passageways of the Pyramid brought much scorn, ridicule and reproach upon the entire subject of the Great Pyramid, and antagonized the scientific world.

In our own twentieth century, Professor Stecchini of Harvard has demonstrated that the ancient Egyptians indeed were highly developed and advanced in astronomy, mathematics, geography and geodesy. He has found from studying hieroglyphics hitherto neglected that from the earliest dynasties the Egyptians could measure latitude to within a few hundred feet, and longitude also—as Tompkins says, "a feat which was not repeated on this planet until the eighteenth century of our era."

These ancient texts fully vindicated the findings of Jomard. Indeed, the Egyptians of antiquity did know the precise circumference of the earth. They knew the length of their own country almost to the very cubit! "To do so the Egyptians must have been able to make astronomical observations with almost the exactness afforded by the modern telescope and chronometer"[14].

Furthermore, measurements by J. H. Cole in 1925 showed that the ancient Egyptians knew that a degree of latitude is shortest at the equator and lengthens as it approaches the pole—in other words, they knew the earth is flattened out and

13. p. 133.
14. Tompkins, p. 176.

has a bulge at the equator. Says Tompkins: "These cold facts should settle one whole facet of the mystery of the Great Pyramid. Clearly the ancient Egyptians knew the shape of the earth to a degree not confirmed till the eighteenth century when it was established that Newton was correct in his theory that the planet was somewhat flattened at the poles, and they knew the size of the earth to a degree not matched till the middle of the nineteenth century"[15]

Who built this impressive edifice?

Manetho wrote that Khufu or Cheops was "of a different race" than the Egyptians[16]. Herodotus declared that the builders of the Great Pyramid were shepherds[17]. The Egyptians considered themselves sophisticated, cultured, and looked down upon shepherds. But early in Egyptian history, in the days of the Biblical patriarchs Jacob and his sons, the Hebrews settled in Egypt and were shepherds (Genesis 46:31-34).

In later times the Israelites in Egypt were given the task of building pyramids, wrote Josephus[18].

Cheops, the builder of the Great Pyramid, was not an idolater, according to Herodotus. He "closed the temples and prohibited the Egyptians from offering sacrifices"[19]. Cheops served the God "Amen" in the older Egyptian spelling—one of the name of the Logos, or Word, who became Jesus Christ (Revelation 3:14).

According to Egyptian records, the Flood occurred before Cheops took the throne. Since Cheops was a contemporary of king Zozer, and Zozer was contemporary with Joseph of the Bible, Cheops must have lived about that same time! Historian Herman L. Hoeh dates Cheops to approximately 1726 B.C., during the beginning of the Israelite sojourn in Egypt. A noted man who helped Cheops build the Pyramid, named *Souf,* was "chief of the works of Khufu"[20]. Elsewhere he is called "Saf-

15. p. 211-212.
16. Warthen's *Arts and Antiquities of Egypt,* p. 54.
17. *Euterpe,* 128.
18. *Antiquities,* II, ix, 1.
19. *History,* II, 124.
20. Rawlinson's *Egypt,* chapter 14.

hotep," meaning "Saf the servant." He was apparently one of 12 brothers who built the Labyrinth of Ancient Egypt for Pharoah Amenemhet III[21]. "Souf," as we have seen earlier, was none other than Joseph. Joseph was given the name "*Zaph-nath-paaneah*" by Pharoah (Genesis 41:45). Today the Egyptians still call Joseph "Yousuf."

Could Cheops have been Job? Manetho writes that "He was arrogant toward the gods, but repented and wrote the Sacred Book"[22].

Cheops had another name in Egypt—Saaru of Shaaru[23]. Herman Hoeh points out that Saaru is another name for Mount Seir. Khafu, then, was a foreign king, whose domain extended from Mount Seir to Lower Egypt during and after the time of Joseph. Mount Seir was famous in antiquity as the "Land of Uz" (*Clarke's Commentary*, preface to book of Job). Uz, in fact, was descended from Seir the Horite (Genesis 36:28). The Arabs preserve a corrupt record of Cheops of Mount Seir, calling him the "wizard of Oz."

What individual who was a mighty king, who dwelt in Mount Seir, or the land of Uz, who worshipped the true God, and yet who had been arrogant and proud, was learned in the exact sciences, mathematics, astronomy, and building and engineering?

The patriarch Job!

The ancient Greeks called Job "Cheops," pronouncing the letter "ch" as if they were an "h," and pronouncing the final "b" as if it were a "p." Job, indeed, was an ancient king (Job 3:11-14; 29:21-25). Job also lived in the days of Joseph, Jacob, and Esau, Jacob's brother, for one of his friends was Eliphaz, the father of the Temanites (Job 2:11; Genesis 36:11). Eliphaz was the son of Esau, a first cousin to Joseph.

It is obvious that Job lived before the Exodus, as he still sacrificed to God for his family, although after the Exodus only the Levites were to sacrifice (Job 1:5; 42:8). The Flood was still

21. Warthen's *Antiquities*, p. 142.
22. Warthen's *Antiquities*, p. 268; Budge's *Egypt*, vol. II, p. 31.
23. Petrie's *History of Egypt*, vol. I, p. 37.

the greatest event in the memory of man during the time of Job (Job 22:17-18).

In addition, Job, the grandson of Jacob, came into Egypt with Jacob's family: "And these are the names of the children of Israel who came into Egypt, Jacob and his sons . . . And the sons of Issachar: Tola, and Phuvah and *Job,* and Shimron" (Gen. 46:13).

The tribe of Issachar, from which Job sprang, was famed in ancient Israel for its "understanding of the times"—that is, mathematical and astronomical knowledge, including the determination of the calendar.

Job may well have built the Great Pyramid, using native Egyptian labor during the three months of the year when the Nile overflowed, as a monument to commemorate what Joseph had done for Egypt and to mark the border of the territory given to Joseph's family in the land by Pharaoh. It may also stand as a monument—eternal witness—to the government of the Most High God, which is like a pyramid, Christ being the rejected capstone (Psa. 118:22), and which shines down from heaven like the rays of the sun. It may also have been built, as legends state, to be a lasting witness of the science and mathematical understanding of the peoples of that ancient time, frustrating the skeptics, and disproving the contentions of the agnostics . . . a monument to preserve the knowledge of the ancients, measurements, and mathematics, astronomy, and related sciences.

Persistent traditions of unknown authenticity tell us that the builder of the Great Pyramid was none other than the patriarch Job of the Old Testament.

According to this theory, Job was a very righteous man, and very familiar with the sciences of astronomy, geology, mathematics, physics and engineering. Evidence of this is found throughout the book of Job in the Bible.

How knowledgeable was Job?

Notice Job 38:12-14: "Hast thou commanded the morning since thy days; and caused the dayspring to know his place; that it might take hold of the ends of the earth . . . it is turned as clay to the seal . . ." Scholars have noted that this verse is very puzzling unless you take it literally—ie., the earth itself turns, as clay to the seal. The original Hebrew means "it turns itself." What more apt expression could be used to indicate the rotation of the earth upon its axis?

Did Job also know something about the law of gravity, discovered we are told by Sir Isaac Newton in the 17th century? Apparently so, because Job knew that God "hangeth the earth upon nothing" (Job 26:7). Job knew the earth did not ride about the sky upon the back of a huge tortoise.

Apparently Job also knew the earth has an axis of rotation, as God is reported to have asked him, "Where wast thou when I laid the foundations of the earth? . . . Whereupon are the foundations (sockets) thereof fastened (made to sink)?" (Job 38:4, 6). Job knew that the axis of the earth was pointed in the general direction of the North Pole Star, Polaris, allowing for the wobble which creates the precession of the equinoxes.

Job must have been a great naturalist of his day. He was even familiar with the little known fact that the sea is fed by fresh water springs. In Job 38:16 God asked him: "Have you explored the springs of the sea?" The fact is, although they usually remain undetected, submarine springs of fresh water are often found along certain types of coast line, even more commonly than are rivers. Along some shores, 20 million gallons of fresh water a day flows into the sea for every mile of shoreline from submarine springs. One such spring in the Persian Gulf creates a large area of fresh water in the midst of the sea, due to favorable limestone geology in Iran and Saudi Arabia. In Greece about 100 million cubic feet of fresh water enters the sea through such springs.

The Lord also asked Job, "Or have you walked in the recesses of the deep?" (*Amplified* Version, Job 38:16). Apparently Job even knew deep ocean trenches, or recesses, existed beneath the seas. Today bathyscapes with special cameras have explored such ocean trenches as the 35,702 foot Tonga Trench, the 36,198 foot Marianas Trench, and the 27,498 foot Puerto Rico Trench.

Studies of the ocean depth reveal it is surprisingly rugged, knifed by huge canyons bigger than the Grand Canyon. In the original Hebrew the word for "deep" is *tehown* and means "confusion," "the abyss, the great deep."

Apparently Job was even familiar with air pressure. The book of Job refers to "When he made a weight for the wind." The *Amplified* Bible makes it more plain: "When He gave to the wind weight or pressure."

As a meteorologist, Job must have been very good. He knew that rain behaved according to *laws* (Job 28:26), and he understood little known facts about lightning. He spoke of "a way for the thunderbolt" (*ibid.*). The *Amplified* says: "When he (God) made a decree for the rain, and a way for the lightning of the thunder." What was this "way"?

Inside enormous clouds exist chimney currents, columns of air rising upward with gale force. In the turbulence at the top small hailstones become positively charged, while raindrops in the lower portion are negatively charged. Below the cloud, upon the earth, meanwhile, another positive charge builds up and follows the drifting cloud. Tremendous differences of electric potential are created. Then a gaseous arc reaches down from the cloud, dangling perhaps 50 feet, building up, growing. Meanwhile, positive particles on earth streak upward fifty feet, called "St. Elmo's fire." When one of these earth "streamers" meets one of the gaseous arcs hanging down from the cloud, a path is formed—a "way"—between the thundercloud and the earth. Stating at the point of contact between negative and positive charges, a bolt of lightning hurtles through the air upward along the gaseous arc path already created. The lightning actually travels upward for the most part; the fact that it appears to shoot downward is an optical illusion.

Apparently, Job was familiar with this little understood phenomenon. He also understood the processes of erosion (Job 14:19; 28:10). He was a highly intelligent student of nature. He wrote: "But ask now the beasts and they shall teach thee; and the fowls of the air, and they shall tell thee: or speak to the earth, and it shall teach thee: and the fishes of the sea shall declare unto thee. Who knoweth not in all these that the hand of the Lord hath wrought this?" (Job 12:7-9).

Was Job also an astronomer? He must have been very

familiar with the study of the stars. God asked Job, "Can you bind the chains of (the cluster of stars called) Pleiades, or loose the cords of (the constellation) Orion?" (Job 38:31, *Amplified*). And the next verse: "Or can you guide (the stars of) the Bear with her young?"

Evidently, Job knew that the Pleiades, the stars of Orion, and the Bear (Ursa Major or the Big Dipper) travel together through space. Since the "chains" of Pleiades are mentioned, and the "cords" of Orion, Job knew that these particular groups of stars are more than just constellations in the sky—they are actually local groups of stars. The original Hebrew word translated "chains" is *ma-adannah* and means "to lace fast," bind or tie. The "cords" or "bands" of Orion is *mowshekah,* meaning something "drawing," from *mashak,* "to draw."

Says the *Larousse Encyclopedia of Astronomy:* "Usually it is found that the motions of the different stars of a constellation figure are oriented quite at random—confirming our conclusion that their apparent mutual proximity is simply an effect of perspective. But there are certain exceptions to this rule. Occasionally, velocities of the same order of magnitude, and oriented in more or less parallel directions, are observed. Such stars, without being 'near' to one another in the ordinary sense, nevertheless form a physically connected unit and are voyaging through space together. They are said to belong to the same star stream, or to form a moving cluster.

"Five of the principal stars of the Great Bear form such a moving cluster. The same thing is encountered among the stars of Orion, and with the two clusters of stars in Taurus known as the Hyades and the Pleiades"[24].

Scholars have found it very difficult to date the book of Job. But they know it is very old. Job lived in the period between the Deluge of Noah's time and the Exodus—probably at the same time as Cheops.

In fact, there is evidence that Cheops and Job are one and the same person. In the book of Job, God reprimands Job: "Where wast thou when *I* laid the foundations of the earth? declare, if

24. p. 308.

thou hast understanding. Who hath laid the *measures* thereof, if thou knowest? Or who stretched the line upon it?" (Job 38:2-5).

Apparently Job had become proud. He seemed to think highly of his own accomplishments. He laid the foundations for the greatest structure ever made by man—the Great Pyramid. He measured it, stretched the line upon it, engineered and masterminded its construction.

God had to bring Job down to size. So He challenged him: "Whereupon are the foundations (of the earth) fastened? or who laid the *corner stone thereof* . . .?"

What remains a mystery, today—the greatest mystery of all, perhaps—is not so much the incredible, amazing knowledge possessed by the ancient Egyptians, but rather the mystery of how that knowledge became lost to the world for so many centuries.

Scholars have generally given credit to the Greeks of a few centuries before Christ—Hipparchus, Pythagoras, Eratosthenes, Ptolemy—for being the founders and originators of mathematics, geometry, and astronomy. The truth, however, shows that rather they did not originate—they inherited the knowledge which they passed on. But all too often they had only a smattering of the knowledge which had been possessed by the ancient Egyptians. The vast majority of it had been lost—buried.

How did it happen?

Perhaps the ancient Arab tradition has more than a few grains of truth in it. Perhaps it was some vast, gargantuan cosmic catastrophe which caused this ancient knowledge to become buried, forgotten, and cast aside for centuries! It seems unlikely that any other cause would be sufficient to eradicate the scientific knowledge of an entire civilization. Somehow such knowledge seems to survive wars, pestilences, famines, earthquakes, and relatively minor disruptions—even invasion and captivity. But in a cosmic upheaval of immense proportions, where an entire civilization is wiped from the face of the earth, destroyed, and extinguished, it is easy to imagine the light of knowledge becoming extinguished.

We now possess definitive knowledge that a cosmic

catastrophe struck Egypt and the entire Middle East, if not the entire world, around the middle of the fifteenth century, B.C. That cataclysm was recorded in the pages of the Bible, as the time of the Exodus. In that cataclysm Atlantis perished. Entire societies were wiped out, entire nations were buried, entire civilizations such as the Minoans were destroyed.

In the wake of such an upheaval, it is no wonder that a tragic time of Dark Ages should follow, in which the torch of knowledge should be extinguished, and only a bare flicker of the light of science should remain.

Nevertheless—the story of the Great Pyramid of Cheops bears a strong witness to the worldwide civilization which we have attempted to reveal in these pages. It ties in with the knowledge of the maps of the ancient sea kings; with the fact of global commerce and transAtlantic communication in the Middle Bronze age; with the evidence of Professor Von Wuthenau in Mexico City; and with the very precise Biblical evidence.

The awesome fact that such knowledge became lost to the entire world is further proof that a worldwide, global cataclysm occurred during the middle of the second millennium before Christ!

Chapter Nine

The Tower of Babel Cataclysm

In the preceding chapter we saw that the world had achieved a height of civilization which had led to world-wide commerce, navigation, trade, and communication. In that former colossal age, magnificent buildings were erected, monumental edifices, huge temples, pyramids, and sacred buildings.

Much of this impressive achievement occurred during the period before the catastrophe of the middle of the second millennium before Christ.

Among the most famous and awe-inspiring engineering achievements of that ancient, by-gone age was the tower of Babel.

After the deluge of Noah's time, the Biblical record tells us, men began to spread abroad in the entire earth (Genesis 10:1-7). The first man in the world after the Deluge to establish a mighty kingdom was Nimrod, "the mighty hunter before the Lord" (v. 9). The Hebrew word for "before" in this verse can be rendered *against*. History and mythology both reveal the Nimrod was a mighty tyrant who ruled with force. The Biblical account states simply:

"And Cush begat Nimrod: he began to be a mighty one in the earth. He was a mighty hunter before the Lord: wherefore it is said, Even as Nimrod the mighty hunter before the Lord. And the beginning of his kingdom was Babel (Greek, Babylon), and Erech, and Accad, and Calneh, in the land of Shinar" (Genesis 10:8-10).

Adam Clarke's *Commentary* says of Nimrod: "It is very likely he was a very bad man. His name Nimrod comes from *marad,* 'he rebelled'; and the Targum on I Chron. 1:10, says: 'Nimrod began to be a mighty man in sin, a murderer of innocent men, and a rebel before the Lord.' The Jerusalem Targum says: 'He was mighty in hunting (or in prey) and in sin before God, for he was a hunter of the children of men in their languages; and he said unto them, "Depart from the religion of Shem, and cleave to the institutes of Nimrod." ' The Targum of Jonathan ben Uzziel says: 'From the foundation of the world none was ever found like Nimrod, powerful in hunting, and in rebellions against the Lord.' "

Clarke continues: "The Syriac calls him a warlike giant. The word *tsayid,* which we render hunter, signifies prey; and is applied in the Scriptures to the hunting of men by persecution, oppression, and tyranny. Hence it is likely that Nimrod, having acquired power, used it in tyranny and oppression; and by rapine and violence founded that domination which was the first distinguished by the name of a kingdom on the face of the earth."

Alexander Hislop in his work *The Two Babylons* traces the pagan mythologies of the Middle East, including that of Rome, Greece, Egypt and Palestine, back to the arch-rebel, apostate Nimrod. He was the principal instrument in creating a system of idolatry and turning men away from the worship of God. He reckoned that he himself was a "god."

Nimrod's kingdom began at Babel, which in Hebrew signifies "confusion." Out of that land he went forth into the land of Assyria, and built Nineveh. Hence Assyria is also called the "land of Nimrod" (compare Genesis 10:11 and Micah 5:6). Nineveh, the capital of Assyria in later times, is said to have had its name from Ninus, the son of Nimrod; or it may well take its name from Nimrod himself.

As Nimrod's fame grew, he attempted to unite all men to follow his form of government. He was the instigator of the building of the ancient Tower of Babel—a mighty, towering structure.

In Genesis we read the story: "And they said one to another,

Go to, let us make brick, and burn them thoroughly. And they had brick for stone, and slime had they for mortar. And they said, Go to, let us build us a city and a tower, whose top may reach unto heaven; and let us make us a name, lest we be scattered abroad upon the face of the whole earth" (Gen. 11:3-4).

The account relates that the Eternal God was displeased with their efforts, confounded their languages, and "scattered them abroad from thence upon the face of all the earth: and they left off to build the city. Therefore is the name of it called Babel; because the Lord did there confound the language of all the earth: and from thence did the Lord scatter them abroad upon the face of all the earth" (vs. 8-9).

The traditional Tower of Babel site is at Borsippa, 10 miles southeast from the center of Babylon. Sir Henry Rawlinson found in a foundation corner in Borsippa a cylinder with this inscription:

"The tower of Borsippa, which a former king erected, and completed to a height of 42 cubits, whose summit he did not finish, fell to ruins in ancient times. There was no proper care of its gutters for the water; rain and storms had washed away its brick, and the tiles of its roof were broken. The great god Marduk urged me to restore it. I did not alter its site, or change its foundation walls. At a favorable time I renewed its brick work and its roofing tiles, and I wrote my name on the cornices of the edifice. I built it anew as it had been ages before: I erected its pinnacles as it was in remote days."

Others place the site of the Tower of Babel in the center of Babylon and identify it with ruins just north of the Marduk Temple. G. Smith found an ancient tablet reading: "The building of this illustrious tower offended the gods. In a night they threw down what they had built. They scattered them abroad, and made strange their speech." What is left of this ruin is an immense hole 330 feet square which has been used as a quarry from which to take bricks.

Wherever the ancient Tower stood, as a symbol of defiance to God, it was never finished. Nevertheless, it is from that point that the chronologies of Egypt, Assyria, Babylonia and the Near East begin.

Layard the archaeologist wrote of the primitive religious system begun by Nimrod in this manner: "Of the great antiquity of this primitive worship there is abundant evidence, and that it originated among the inhabitants of the Assyrian plains, we have the united testimony of sacred and profane history."

He adds: "The zodiacal signs . . . . show unequivocally that the Greeks derived their notions and arrangements of the zodiac from the Chaldees. The identity of Nimrod with the constellation Orion is not to be rejected."[1]

Associated with Nimrod in ancient religious mythology is the Queen of heaven, one Semiramis. Writes Hislop: "The Babylonians, in their popular religion, supremely worshipped a Goddess Mother and a Son, who was represented in pictures and in images as an infant or child in his mother's arms. From Babylon, this worship of the Mother and the Child spread to the ends of the earth. In Egypt, the Mother and the Child were worshipped under the names of Isis and Osiris (also called Horus). In India, even to this day, as Isi and Iswara; in Asia, as Cybele and Deoius; in Pagan Rome, as Fortuna and Jupiter-puer, or Jupiter, the boy; in Greece, as Ceres, the Great Mother, with the babe at her breast, or as Irene, the goddess of Peace, with the boy Plutus in her arms."[2]

This son, who was sometimes called Ninus, is also sometimes called the husband of Semiramis. Osiris was represented in Egypt as at once the son and also the husband of his mother; one of his titles was "Husband of the Mother."[3] This Ninus, supposedly the son of Nimrod, is also identified with Nimrod. Says Trogus Pompeius, "Ninus, king of the Assyrians, first of all changed the contented moderation of the ancient manners, incited by a new passion, the desire of conquest. He was the first who carried on war against his neighbours, and he conquered all nations from Assyria to Lybia, as they were yet unacquainted with the arts of war."[4]

---

1. *Nineveh and its Remains,* vol. 2, p. 440.
2. *Two Babylons,* p. 20.
3. *Bunsen,* vol. 1, pp. 438, 439.
4. Justin's *Trogus Pompeius, Hist. Rom. Script.,* vol. 2, p. 615.

Diodorus Siculus adds: "Ninus, the most ancient of the Assyrian kings mentioned in history, performed great actions. Being naturally of a warlike disposition, and ambitious of glory that results from valour, he armed a considerable number of young men that were brave and vigorous like himself, trained them up a long time in laborious exercises and hardships, and by that means accustomed them to bear the fatigues of war, and to face dangers with intrepidity."[5]

Ninus (or Nimrod) is said to be the son of Bel or Belus. As "Cush begat Nimrod" (Genesis 10:8), then Bel must have been Cush. Cush, as the son of Ham, was also known as Hermes, as Hermes is just an Egyptian synonym for the "son of Ham." Hermes, or Cush, was recognized as the great original prophet of idolatry, the interpreter of the gods, and the author of the sacred religious rites of the pagans.

The name Hermes ("Her" in Chaldee is synonymous with "Ham") is significant. Her, Ham, or Khem, meant, "The burnt one," or "The hot or burning one." This name formed a foundation for covertly identifying Ham with the Sun. "Her" is also the name of "Horus" who was identified with the sun.

Ham, then, was the original Bel, or Baal, of the Babylonians. Says Hislop: "While the Greek name Belus represented both the Baal and Bel of the Chaldees, these were nevertheless two entirely distinct titles. These titles were both alike often given to the same god, but they had totally different meanings. Baal, as we have already seen, signified 'The Lord;' but Bel signified 'The Confounder.' "[6]

Semiramis was also deeply involved in the religious rites. "The Chaldean Mysteries can be traced up to the days of Semiramis, who lived only a few centuries after the flood, and who is known to have impressed upon them the image of her own depraved and polluted mind. That beautiful but abandoned queen of Babylon was not only herself a paragon of unbridled lust and licentiousness, but in the Mysteries which she had a chief hand in forming, she was worshipped as Rhea, the great

5. *Bibliotheca*, lib. 2, p. 63.
6. *The Two Babylons*, p. 26.

'Mother' of the gods, with such atrocious rites as identified her with Venus, the Mother of all impurity, and raised the very city where she had reigned to be a bad eminence among the nations, as the grand seat at once of idolatry and consecrated prostitution.'"[7]

Of these was civilization this side of the Flood largely founded. The evidence is that Semiramis was first the wife of Cush, and mother of Nimrod, and later married her hero-warrior son, and was also the mother of Ninus, or Horus, also known as Tammuz, "The Lamented One." Years later she even propositioned her son Horus, Tammuz, also called Gilgamesh in Babylonian tradition.

"When Gilgamesh had put on his tiara,
Glorious Ishtar raised an eye at the beauty of Gilgamesh:
'Come, Gilgamesh, be thou my lover:
Do but grant me of thy fruit.
Thou shalt be my husband and I will be thy wife.'
Gilgamesh opened his mouth to speak,
. . . if I take thee in marriage?
Thou art but a brazier which goes out in the cold;
A back door which does not keep out blast and windstorm;
Pitch which soils its bearers;
A waterskin which soaks through its bearer;
A shoe which pinches the foot of its owner!
Which lover didst thou love forever?
Come and I will name for thee thy lovers."[8]

The first ruler of ancient Egypt was Cush, the first husband of this wanton woman. Cush is identified with Menes, the first Pharaoh of the first Egyptian dynasty. Meni, or Mena—Menes in Greek—his name means "The Establisher." Or, "The Everlasting."[9] In other words, Menes or Cush was the first to establish himself as king in place of the Everlasting God.

7. Hislop, p. 5; see also Herodotus, *Historia,* lib. 1, cap. 199, p. 92.
8. Pritchard's *Near Eastern Texts,* p. 83-84.
9. Compare George Rawlinson, *History of Ancient Egypt,* vol. II, p. 26, and Waddell's *Manetho,* p. 215.

Athothis, Egypt's second king, was Osiris. Declares Arthur Weigall in *A History of the Pharaohs,* the tomb of Athothis at Abydos was "the sepulcre of the god Osiris, and, as such, became the shrine to which millions of pilgrims made their way."[10] Osiris, or Athothis, is identified with Nimrod.[11]

The third Egyptian king, Kenkenes, Horus, or Gilgamesh, was followed on the throne by a woman—Uenephes, Ishtar, or Isis—his own mother, Semiramis. Uenephes called herself Henneit, meaning "Neit is victorious" (Neit is the Egyptian form of the Greek Athena). She also called herself Hept, meaning "the veiled one."

Josephus, the historian of the Jews, confirms this reconstruction of early Egyptian history. He states in *Antiquities:* "All the kings from Menes, who built Memphis . . . until Solomon, where the interval was more than one thousand three hundred years."[12] Thus the earliest Egyptian dynasty was this side of the Noachian deluge.

The seventh king of this dynasty was Semempses, or Semsem—meaning the great Sem or Shem, the son of Noah. Shem is called Sem in Luke 3:36 in the New Testament. In the monuments and hieroglyphics, Shem is represented in Asian, not Egyptian dress and appears as an old man with a long beard.

This was a wicked dynasty, till the days when Shem intervened and took the kingship. Cush was the ringleader in the apostacy, to whom the name Merodach, "The great Rebel," was first applied.[13] He was a ringleader in the scheme to build the great tower and city of Babel. He was also known as Janus, "the god of gods," from whom all the other gods had their origin. He was also known as Chaos, or the god of Confusion, Chaos being one of the established forms of the name of Chus or Cush.

Nimrod, it might be interesting to note, was a black man, that is a true Negro. Plutarch records that "Osiris was black."

10. Vol. 1, p. 111.
11. *Hislop,* p. 22.
12. Book VIII, chapter VI, sec. 2.
13. *Hislop,* p. 28.

Wilkinson provides a representation of him with the unmistakeable features of the genuine Cushite or Negro. Horus, his supposed son, however, was "of a fair complexion." Thus the folly of Semiramis was manifest, and actually Horus, or Ninus or Gilgamesh was indeed illegitimate!

This age old conspiracy, however, came to a violent end. Though Scripture is silent as to how Nimrod died, there is considerable evidence that he was torn to pieces. As Hislop states: "The identity of Nimrod, however, and the Egyptian Osiris, having been established, we have thereby light as to Nimrod's death. Osiris met with a violent death, and that violent death of Osiris was the central theme of the whole idolatry of Egypt. If Osiris was Nimrod, as we have seen, that violent death which the Egyptians so pathetically deplored in their annual festivals was just the death of Nimrod . . . . A statement of Plato seems to show, that in his day the Egyptian Osiris was regarded as identical with Tammuz; and Tammuz is well known to have been the same as Adonis, the famous huntsman, for whose death Venus is fabled to have made such bitter lamentations. As the women of Egypt wept for Osiris, as the Phoenician and Assyrian women wept for Tammuz, so in Greece and Rome the women wept for Bacchus, whose name, as we have seen, means 'the bewailed,' or 'Lamented one.' "

Each of these was torn in pieces. But how did Nimrod die? Maimonides declares: "When the false prophet named Thammuz preached to a certain king that he should worship the seven stars and the twelve signs of the Zodiac, that king ordered him to be put to a terrible death."

Hislop asks: 'Who could this king be, who was so determinedly opposed to the worship of the host of heaven? . . . If Shem was at that time alive, as beyond question he was, who so likely as he? In exact accordance with this deduction, we find that one of the names of the primitive Hercules in Egypt was 'Sem'."[14]

This remarkably agrees with the Egyptian account of the death of their god Osiris. They say the enemy of their god

14. *Hislop,* p. 63.

entered into a conspiracy with seventy-two of the leading men of Egypt—the number, according to sacred and civil Egyptian law, needed to pass judgement. They condemned Osiris or Nimrod to death, put him to death, and cut his dead body into pieces, sending the different parts to seventy-two cities throughout the country as an object lesson.

The Egyptians called the slayer of Nimrod Typho, or the Evil One. Another of his most noted names was Seth, which is synonymous with Shem, both meaning "The appointed one." He was the appointed one whom God had chosen to have pre-eminence (Genesis 9:26).

It seems obvious that after the Deluge, the nations of men became very wary of the heavens. They were fearful of the stars and watched the heavenly cycles with deep misgivings. Nimrod, as he established his kingdom over the earth, also attempted to establish astrology, the worship of the stars. After his death, he became worshipped in Greece as Orion, the great and mighty hunter. Persian records tells us that it was Nimrod who was deified after his death by the name of Orion, and placed among the stars.[15]

When Nimrod died, the sorrow and lamentation were awesome. His death was considered a terrible catastrophe. The shock was intense. At that time began those weepings for Tammuz which can be traced around the world, in the annals of classical antiquity, from Ultima Thule to Japan.

Eventually it was Semiramis herself who became the great object of worship. Says Hislop: "Now the Son, even in his new reincarnation, when Nimrod was believed to have reappeared in a fairer form (i.e., resurrected and reborn as fair-skinned Horus or Gilgamesh), was exhibited merely as a child, without any very particular attraction; while the mother in whose arms he was, was set off with all the art of painting and sculpture, as invested with much of that extraordinary beauty which in reality belonged to her. The beauty of Semiramis is said on one occasion to have quelled a rising rebellion among her subjects on her sudden appearance among them; and it is recorded that the memory of

15. *Hislop,* p. 57.

the admiration excited in their minds by her appearance on that occasion was perpetuated by a statue erected in Babylon, representing her in the guise in which she had fascinated them so much. This Babylonian queen was not merely in character coincident with the Aphrodite of Greece and the Venus of Rome, but was, in point of fact, the historical original of that goddess that by the ancient world was regarded as the very embodiment of Everything attractive in female form, and the perfection of female beauty; for Sanchuniathon assures us that Aphrodite or Venus was identical with Astarte (Easter), and Astarte being interpreted, is none other than 'The woman that made towers or encompassing walls'—i.e., Semiramis. The Roman Venus, as is well known, was the Cyprian Venus, and the Venus of Cyprus—historically proved to have been derived from Babylon."[16]

This queen of heaven became the greatest and most worshipped deity of the East. Wherever her worship was introduced, it exerted a magnetic, fascinating power over the minds of men. In later years, the nations of Israel and Judah became so entranced and drunk with the worship of this idolatrous queen, that even after being taken into captivity, and sorely punished, they would not give it up.

Says Hislop, Venus or Semiramis "the queen of beauty, who assured her worshippers of salvation, while giving loose reins to every unholy passion, and every depraved and sensual appetite—no wonder that everywhere she was enthusiastically adored. Under the name of the 'Mother of the gods,' the goddess queen of Babylon became an object of almost universal worship."[17]

The "Mother of the gods" was worshipped by the Persians, the Syrians, and all the kings of Europe and Asia, with profound veneration. In the heart of Germany she was worshipped. Priests of the same goddess, known as Druids, taught her worship in ancient England. This ancient whore—this seductive prostitute—this beautiful "queen" of heaven—became the leading deity of the Orient and Europe.

16. *Two Babylons,* pp. 74-75.
17. *Two Babylons,* p. 80.

To the prophets of the Hebrews, however, the worship of this pagan sensual goddess was nothing less than an utter abomination. Jeremiah rebuked the people for giving in to this seductive worship. But the people answered him:

"As for the word that thou hast spoken unto us in the name of the Lord, we will not hearken unto thee. But we will certainly do whatsoever thing goeth forth out of our own mouth, to burn incense unto the queen of heaven, and to pour out drink offerings unto her, as we have done, we, and our fathers, our kings, and our princes, in the cities of Judah, and in the streets of Jerusalem: for then had we plenty of victuals, and were well, and saw no evil. But since we left off to burn incense to the queen of heaven, and to pour out drink offerings unto her, we have wanted all things, and have been consumed by the sword and by the famine. And when we burned incense to the queen of heaven, and poured out drink offerings unto her, did we make her cakes to worship her, and pour out drink offerings unto her, without our men?" (Jeremiah 44:16-19).

Jeremiah rebuked the people for their attitude of hostility and rebellion, saying, "So that the Lord could no longer bear, because of the evil of your doings, and because of the abominations which ye have committed; therefore is your land a desolation, and an astonishment, and a curse, without an inhabitant, as at this day. Because ye burned incense, and because ye have sinned against the Lord, and have not obeyed the voice of the Lord, nor walked in his law, nor in his statutes, nor in his testimonies; therefore this evil is happened unto you, as at this day" (vs. 22-23).

In the days of the prophet Ezekiel, the people of Israel were also recalcitrant and rebellious. The hold of pagan superstitions was so strong upon them, that they fell right into pagan rituals of worship. An angel of the Lord took Ezekiel to see the various abominations which were being committed. The prophet reported:

"He said also unto me, Turn thee yet again, and thou shalt see greater abominations that they do. Then he brought me to the door of the gate of the Lord's house which was toward the north; and, behold, there sat women weeping for Tammuz" (Ezekiel 8:13-14).

Baal and Ashtaroth were two of the principal deities of the Canaanite nations which the Israelites had displaced in Palestine. But the worship of these deities became a common practice in ancient Israel, too. Ashtaroth, Isis, Venus, Ishtar, or Easter, as her name was variously known, was none other than the harlot queen of Babylon, Semiramis. And Baal, Beltus, Bel, Bacchus, Dionysius, Osiris, Odin, Saturn, was none other than the ancient rebel-king, Nimrod, mighty hunter.

When God saw the wickedness of men on the earth before the Deluge, it grieved him to his heart, the Scriptures tell us. Wickedness prevailed on every side. Only Noah was found righteous in the earth.

Again, when wickedness was gaining a foothold after the Flood, in the days of the arch-tyrant Nimrod and his consort wife Semiramis, God intervened. At the Tower of Babel, He confounded their languages, and scattered them over the face of the earth. The Tower was destroyed in a violent catastrophe, and the nations of men were scattered, by force, into the far corners of the world. They didn't leave Babel willingly.

A Scripture in Genesis, chapter 10, the Table of Nations, has long puzzled scholars. In listing the genealogy of Shem, the chronicler relates that one of the sons of Eber was named Peleg, meaning "Division." The Scripture continues: "for in his days was the earth divided" (Gen. 19:25). This verse seems obvious enough. But what meaning may lay beneath that surface! Peleg lived during the time of the Tower of Babel.

Josephus in *Antiquities of the Jews* tells us:

"Now the multitude were very ready to follow the determination of Nimrod, and to esteem it a piece of cowardice to submit to God; and they built a tower, neither sparing any pains, nor being in any degree negligent about the work: and, by reason of the multitude of hands employed in it, it grew very high, sooner than any one could expect; but the thickness of it was so great, and it was so strongly built, that thereby its great height seemed, upon the view, to be less than it really was. It was built of burnt brick, cemented together with mortar, made of bitumen, that it might not be liable to admit water.

"When God saw that they acted so madly, he did not resolve to destroy them utterly, since they were not grown wiser by the destruction of the former sinners; but he caused a tumult among them, by producing in them divers languages, and causing that, through the multitude of those languages, they should not be able to understand one another."

Josephus then quotes the Sibyl, who also makes mention of this tower:

"When all men were of one language, some of them built a high tower, as if they would thereby ascend up to heaven, but the gods sent storms of wind and overthrew the tower, and gave every one his peculiar language; and for this reason it was that the city was called *Babylon.*"

At this juncture, a catastrophe occurred. A cosmic catastrophe struck the builders of the Tower of Babel. It did not compare with the Deluge of the preceding generation. It didn't involve water. Rather, great storms of wind caused the tower to be overthrown. To overthrow a huge, massively built tower, and to cause the builders to flee, this wind must have been more than an unusual windstorm, or even a hurricane. It was a tremendous wind.

Says Velikovsky: "The theme of a cosmic hurricane is reiterated time and again in the Hindu *Vedas* and in the Persian *Avesta,* and *diluvium venti,* the deluge of wind, is a term known from many ancient authors."[18] The term "cosmic wind" is also found in the Talmud.[19]

A wind which would sweep away a massive tower made of brick would undoubtedly sweep also giant forests and create great disturbances.

A tradition of the Maoris states that amid a stupendous catastrophe "the mighty winds, the fierce squalls, the clouds, dense, dark, fiery, wildly drifting, wildly bursting" rushed upon

18. *Worlds in Collision,* p. 68.
19. *The Babylonian Talmud,* Tractate Berakhot, 13.

the creation, in their midst was Tawhirima-tea, father of winds and storms.[20]

In a Japanese cosmological myth, the sun goddess hid herself for a long time in a heavenly cave in fear of the storm god. According to the myth, the source of light disappeared, the world grew dark, and the god of storm wreaked monstrous destruction.

The Polynesians of Takaofo Island relate, "The sky was low . . . then the winds and waterspouts and the hurricanes came, and carried up the sky to its present height."[21]

Warren, in his section on "World Cycles," in his work *Buddhism* reports on the Buddhist texts regarding a cosmic wind:

"When a world cycle is destroyed by wind," says the text, the wind turns "the ground upside down, and throws it into the sky." The havoc is so great that "areas of one hundred leagues in extent, two hundred, three hundred, five hundred leagues in extent, crack and are thrown upward by the force of the wind" and are "blown to powder in the sky and annihilated."

"And the wind throws up also into the sky the mountains which encircle the earth . . . (they) are ground to powder and destroyed," the text continues.

According to the Buddhists, the cosmic wind blows and wreaks destruction on "a hundred thousand times ten million worlds."[22]

The catastrophe that occurred in the days of the Tower of Babel was such a mighty wind.

But other destructive forces were at work.

According to the legends of the Jews, "As for the unfinished tower, a part sank into the earth, and another part was consumed by fire."[23]

Another tradition states: "As to the tower which the sons of men built, the earth opened its mouth and swallowed up one

20. Tylor, *Primitive Culture,* I, 322ff.
21. Williamson, *Religious and Cosmic Beliefs of Central Polynesia,* I, 44.
22. *Buddhism,* p. 328.
23. Louis Ginzberg, *Legends of the Jews,* vol. I, p. 180.

third part thereof, and a fire also descended from heaven and burned another third, and the other third is left to this day."[24]

The destruction of the tower of Babel, therefore, involved the earth, an earthquake; it involved fire cast down from the sky; and it involved a mighty wind.

One legend declares: "And the Lord sent a mighty wind against the tower and overthrew it upon the earth, and behold it was between Asshur and Babylon in the land of Shinar, and they called its name 'Overthrow'."[25]

This mighty wind, very likely was the Hebrew *ruwach* or "blast"—the same sort of blasting wind as occurred the night of the Exodus; the same "blast" which smote the entire army of Sennacherib in the days of Hezekiah. It could have been "shock waves from an exploding bolide, including a flash burn radiation effect or wave, not just a heavy gust of wind or rain storm."[26]

Patten asks: "How severe was the catastrophe? It was sufficiently severe to be the leading reported event in two hundred years of time. It was sufficiently severe to cause mass migrations of peoples to the four directions. To underestimate its intensity would be easy, but instead, we are inclined to equate it on a par with the Long Day of Joshua . . . "[27]

The fact that the destruction of this magnificent structure of old was due to cosmic forces, and was accomplished from the heavens, is also suggested by the evidence of Scripture. "And the Lord said . . . Go to, *let us go down,* and there confound their language . . . So the Lord scattered them abroad from thence" (Genesis 11:6-8).

Whenever the Biblical record speaks of the Eternal God coming down to earth, it is amidst a fiery display of wrath, fury, and divine judgment. Patten is probably right—the severity of the

24. *The Book of Jasher,* 9:38.
25. R. H. Charles, *The Apocrypha and Pseudepigrapha of the Old Testament,* vol. II, "The Book of Jubilees," p. 29.
26. Patten, et al., *The Long Day of Joshua and Six Other Catastrophes,* p. 283.
27. *Ibid.*

catastrophe which befell the world in the days of the Tower of Babel very likely was on a par with the destruction in the days of Joshua, the son of Nun.

This ancient Tower was intended by its architects and engineers to be the capitol building of the ruling city for the whole world under the government of Nimrod. It would have been the idolatrous and religious center of the world. With it, Nimrod intended to unite all peoples under his banner and create the world's first supergovernment over all nations.

The Tower, a Babylonian ziggurat in design, was to impress all nations with its remarkable architectural features. On the top was to be a religious temple, an observatory of the heavens, and a planetarium.

In terms of construction, the Tower of Babel, traditions tell us, was the world's first massive construction program, rivalling the Pyramids. No doubt it was to be ornamented with gold, silver, and precious metals. We are told in legend: "The iniquity and godlessness of Nimrod reached their climax in the building of the Tower of Babel. His counsellors had proposed the plan of erecting such a tower, Nimrod had agreed to it, and it was executed in Shinar by a mob of six hundred thousand men."[28]

Excavated in 1898 by Robert Koldewey, the site of the Tower of Babel astonished the archaeologist. Wrote C. W. Ceram in *Gods, Graves and Scholars:*

"Every large Babylonian city had its ziggurat, but none compared with the Tower of Babel. Fifty-eight million bricks went into the Tower's construction, and the whole land-scape was dominated by its terraced mass. The Tower of Babel was built by slaves."[29]

Says the same author: "The original Tower rose up in a series of enormous terraces. Herodotus describes a series of eight superimposed stages, each one somewhat smaller than the one below it. The uppermost terrace formed the base of a temple that looked out far over the land."[30]

---

28. Louis Ginzberg, *Legends,* vol. I, p. 179.
29. *Gods, Graves and Scholars,* p. 290.
30. *Ibid.,* p. 289.

He continues: "The base of the tower was 288 feet on a side, the total height of Tower and temple also 288 feet. The first stage was 105.6 feet in height; the second, 57.6 feet; the third, fourth, fifth and sixth, 19.2 feet each; and the Temple of Marduk 41 feet in height. The temple housed the most important god in the Babylonian pantheon. The walls of the temple were plated with gold, and decorated with enameled brickwork of a bluish hue, which glittered in the sun, greeting the traveler's eye from afar."

Herodotus states that the Tower and its artifacts required 800 talents of pure gold—worth over two hundred and forty million dollars, today. Says the Talmud, 42 years were required to build the tower, although the surrounding gates and streets were never finished. The catastrophe put an end to the years of slave labor. No one knows what happened to the 26 tons of pure gold used in decorating the massive edifice.

The monument which Nimrod intended to erect in his own honor, to bend the nations to himself, and to bring all the world into his system of idolatry, was smashed into oblivion by a cosmic catastrophe of incredible proportions. It heralded the end of an age.

Chapter Ten

Sodom and Gomorrah

Perhaps no names in all antiquity are as infamous as those of Sodom and Gomorrah. Writers, satirists, and commentators have compared the plunging immorality, pornography, and obsession with sex of the modern world with the legendary Sodom and Gomorrah—two ancient cities whose very names characterize sexual vice and inflamed passions. Sodom in fact gives its name to the practice of "sodomy" and was noted for violent crimes of homosexuality.

Josephus the ancient historian recounts the fate of these two cities of antiquity. He narrated: "About this time the Sodomites grew proud, on account of their riches and great wealth; they became unjust towards men, and impious towards God, insomuch that they did not call to mind the advantages they received from him: they hated strangers, and abused themselves with Sodomitical practices. God was therefore much displeased at them, and determined to punish them for their pride, and to overthrow their city, and to lay waste their country, until there should neither plant nor fruit grow out of it."

Josephus tells us that angels of God came to the city of the Sodomites, in the guise of young men. "Now when the Sodomites saw the young men to be of beautiful countenance, and this to an extraordinary degree, and that they took up their lodgings with Lot, they resolved themselves to enjoy these beautiful boys by force and violence; and when Lot exhorted them to sobriety, and not to offer any thing immodest to the strangers, but to have regard to their lodging in his house; and promised that if their inclinations could not be governed, he would expose his daughters to their lust, instead of these strangers; neither thus were they made ashamed.

"But God was much displeased at their impudent behaviour, so that he both smote those men with blindness, and condemned the Sodomites to universal destruction. But Lot, upon God's informing him of the future destruction of the Sodomites, went away, taking with him his wife and daughters, who were two, and still virgins; for those that were betrothed to them were above the thoughts of going, and deemed that Lot's words were trifling. God then cast a thunderbolt upon the city, and set it on fire, with its inhabitants; and laid waste the country with the like burning . . . But Lot's wife continually turning back to view the city as she went from it, and being too nicely inquisitive what would become of it, although God had forbidden her so to do, was changed into a pillar of salt; for I have seen it, and it remains at this day."[1]

Whiston, in his footnote to this passage in *Antiquities*, remarks further: "This pillar of salt was, we see here, standing in the days of Josephus, and he had seen it. That it was standing then is also attested by Clement of Rome, contemporary with Josephus; as also that it was so in the next century, is attested by Irenaeus, with the addition of an hypothesis, how it came to last so long, with all its members entire.—Whether the account that some modern travellers give be true, that it is still standing, I do not know."

The authoritative account in the Scriptures of the destruction of Sodom is brief and to the point. The author of Genesis relates: "The sun was risen upon the earth when Lot entered into Zoar. Then the Lord rained upon Sodom and upon Gomorrah brimstone and fire from the Lord out of heaven; and he overthrew those cities, and all the plain, and all the inhabitants of the cities, and that which grew upon the ground. But his wife looked back from behind him, and she became a pillar of salt" (Genesis 19:23-26).

The word *gophrith,* translated brimstone, is of very uncertain

1. *Antiquities*, I, XI, 1-4.

derivation. The plains around Sodom abounded with asphalt or bitumen pits. In Genesis 14:10 we find that the valley of Siddim or Sodom was "full of slime-pits," places where asphalt or bitumen sprang out of the ground. The Hebrew, *beeroth beeroth,* signifies a "multitude of pits."

Ancient Sodom was located in the plain or circle of the Jordan river (Gen. 13:12), an exceedingly fertile and well populated district about 2000 B.C. Scholars are now in agreement that the cities of Sodom and Gomorrah were situated in the area at the southern end of the Dead Sea, now covered with water.

Says *Unger's Bible Dictionary:* "The Biblical notices that the district of the Jordan, where these cities were located, was exceedingly fertile and well peopled (c. 2065 B.C.), but that not long afterwards was abandoned, are in full accord with archaeological evidence" (p. 1034). He cites William F. Albright.[2]

Unger continues: "Sometime around the middle of the twenty-first century B.C. this region with its cities was overwhelmed by a great conflagration (Gen. 19:23-28). The area is said to have been 'full of slimé (that is, asphalt pits)' (Gen. 14:10). Bitumen deposits are still to be found in this locality. The entire valley is on the long fault line which forms the Jordan Valley, the Dead Sea and the Arabah. An earthquake-ridden region throughout its history, geological activity was doubtless an accompanying factor in the destruction of the cities, although the Bible account records only the miraculous elements. The salt and free sulphur of this area, now a burned out region of oil and asphalt, were apparently mingled by an earthquake, causing a violent explosion. Carried up into the air red-hot, the exploding salt and sulphur literally caused a rain of fire and brimstone over the whole plain (Gen. 19:24, 28). The account of Lot's wife being turned into a pillar of salt is frequently connected with the great salt mass in the valley called by the Arabs *Jebel Usdum,* that is, 'Mountain of Sodom.' This is a hill some five miles long stretching N. and S. at the S.W. end of the Dead Sea. Somewhere under the slowly rising waters of the southern part of the lake in this general locality the 'cities of the

2. *The Archaeology of Palestine and the Bible,* p. 133ff.

plain' are probably to be found. In classical and N.T. times their ruins were still visible, not yet being covered with water (Tacitus *History* V:7; Josephus *Wars* IV:4)."

Jamieson, Fausset and Brown contend, however, that the destruction of Sodom was likely due to a volcanic eruption. "The raining down of fire and brimstone from heaven is perfectly accordant with this idea since those very substances, being raised into the air by the force of the volcano, would fall in a fiery shower on the surrounding region."[3]

R.K. Harrison verifies the dating of the catastrophe which overtook the twin cities. He asserts: "The approximate date of the catastrophe which overtook Sodom, Gomorrah, and neighboring sites may be conjectured from the evidence supplied by pottery remains discovered at Bab edh-Dhra. This festival site appears to have been frequented from about 2300 B.C. to about 1900 B.C., and the cessation of such visits may have coincided with the destruction of Sodom and the other cities of the valley, from which the worshippers apparently came on pilgrimages to the site."[4]

Peloubet's Bible Dictionary discusses the questions as to the proper identification of ancient Sodom at length. This authority concludes, "It thus appears that on the situation of Sodom no satisfactory conclusion can at present be reached. Of the catastrophe which destroyed the city and the district of Sodom we can hardly hope ever to form a satisfactory conception. Some catastrophe there undoubtedly was; but what secondary agencies, besides fire, were employed in the accomplishment of the punishment cannot be safely determined in the almost total absence of exact scientific description of the natural features of the ground round the lake. We may suppose, however, that the actual agent in the ignition and destruction of the cities had been of the nature of a tremendous thunder-storm accompanied by a discharge of meteoric stones, and that these set on fire the bitumen with which the soil was saturated, and which was used in building the city. The miserable fate of Sodom and Gomor-

3. *Commentary on the Whole Bible,* p. 29.
4. *Introduction to the Old Testament,* p. 562.

rah is held up as a warning in numerous passages of the Old and New Testaments."[5]

Peloubet alludes to the fact that the salt mountain which exists at the southern end of the Dead Sea has a tendency to split off in columnar forms or masses, presenting a rude resemblance to the human form.

Zoar, the small town to which Lot and his daughters fled for safety from the impending destruction, was very close to Sodom. All the post-Biblical references to Zoar place it at the southern end of the Dead Sea.[6]

Henry H. Halley asserts: "These cesspools of iniquity were only a few miles from Hebron, the home of Abraham, and from Jerusalem, the home of Melchizedek; yet so vile, they smelt to heaven. It had been only 400 years since the Flood, almost within the memory of men then living. Yet men had forgotten the lesson of that cataclysmic destruction of the race. And God 'rained fire and brimstone' on these two cities, to refresh men's memories, and to warn of the wrath of God that is in store for wicked men; and, perhaps, to serve as a token of the earth's final doom in a holocaust of fire."[7]

Declares Halley, there was an ancient and persistent tradition that great topographical changes took place around the south end of the Dead Sea when Sodom and Gomorrah were destroyed. Ancient writers generally thought the sites of the two great cities were buried beneath the Dead Sea.

The Dead Sea, about forty miles long and ten miles wide, is very deep at the north end, over 1000 feet in some places. The southern third, however, is nowhere deeper than 15 feet and in most places less than 10 feet. In Abraham's time the southern third of the Sea was a plain.

In 1924 Drs. W. F. Albright and M. G. Kyle directed a joint expedition of the American Schools and Xenia Seminary to the area and found at the southeast corner of the Dead Sea five Oases, made by fresh water streams. Centrally located to the

5. p. 639.
6. Peloubet, "Zoar," p. 761.
7. *Bible Handbook*, p. 100.

streams on a plain 500 feet above the level of the Dead Sea, at Bab-ed-Dra, they found the remains of a great fortified enclosure, a "high place" for religious festivals. Great quantities of potsherds, flints, and other remains dating from 2500 B.C. to 2000 B.C. were found, and evidence that the population ended abruptly about 2000 B.C. Says Halley: "This evidence that the region was densely populated and prosperous indicates that it must have been very fertile, 'like the garden of God.' That the population ceased abruptly, and that it has been a region of unmixed desolation ever since, seems to indicate that the district was destroyed by some great cataclysm which changed the soil and climate.

"The opinion of Albright and Kyle, and most archaeologists, is that Sodom and Gomorrah were located on these oases, further down the streams, and that the site is now covered by the Dead Sea."[8]

The bitumen, asphalt, or pitch—a lustrous black petroleum product which melts and burns—mentioned in the Bible account is found in vast beds on both sides of the Dead Sea, most abundantly at the south end. Great masses of it are located at the bottom of the Sea and considerable quantities have risen to the surface during earthquakes, giving off a fetid, foul stench.

M. G. Kyle in excavating the site said that a stratum of salt 150 feet thick underlies Mount Sodom, and above it lies a stratum of marl mingled with free sulphur. He suggests that at the proper time God kindled the gases, a great explosion took place, the salt and sulphur were thrown into the heavens red hot, so that it "did literally rain fire and brimstone from heaven. Lot's wife was encrusted in salt. There are many pillars of salt at the south end of the Dead Sea which have borne the name of 'Lot's Wife.' Indeed everything about the region seems to dovetail exactly with the Biblical story of Sodom and Gomorrah," writes Henry H. Halley.[9]

One wonders, in reviewing the suggested explanations of the destruction of Sodom, if perhaps they all don't have more than

8. *Ibid.*, p. 101.
9. *Ibid.*

a grain of truth. No doubt the underlying beds of sulphur, bitumen, and salt, played an important role in Sodom's fiery fate. But what triggered the cataclysmic eruption of these buried time bombs, latent with devastation, waiting to be ignited? What "spark" set off the horrorific raging inferno, so that the destruction of Sodom became a symbol of "hell"?

Volcanic eruption? Earthquake? Storm? Thunderbolt?

Asserts Jack Finegan in *Light from the Ancient Past*, "A careful survey of the literary, geological, and archeological evidence points to the conclusion that the infamous 'cities of the valley' (Genesis 19:29) were in the area which now is submerged beneath the slowly rising waters of the southern part of the Dead Sea, and that their ruin was accomplished by a great earthquake, probably accompanied by explosions, lightning, ignition of natural gas, and general conflagration."[10]

Philo of Alexandria, Egypt, who wrote in the first century A.D., was of the opinion that the conflagration which overtook Sodom and Gomorrah was the destruction by fire which he was familiar with from the Greek philosophers. He knew about the repeated destructions of the world by water and fire. To him, the destruction of Sodom was one of these. He wrote: "By reason of the constant and repeated destructions of water and fire, the later generations did not receive from the former the memory of the order and sequence of events."[11]

There are similarities between the fire that rained down on ancient Sodom and the plagues that struck ancient Egypt, at the end of the Middle Kingdom, in the days of Moses.

The eighth plague upon Egypt was "*barad* (meteorites) and *fire* mingled with the *barad*, very grievous, such as there was none like it in all the land of Egypt since it became a nation" (Exo. 9:24). There was "thunder" (loud repercussive noises) with the hail of meteorites.

The Papyrus Ipuwer describes this plague of fire: "Gates, columns, and walls are consumed by fire. The sky is in

10. P. 147; see also J. Penrose Harland in *Biblical Archaeologist* 5 (1942), pp. 17-32; 6 (1943), pp. 41-54.

11. Philo, *Moses* ii.

confusion."[12] Ipuwer stated that this horrible conflagration almost "exterminated mankind."

Says the Midrashim, in several texts, naphtha, with hot stones, poured down on the Egyptians out of the skies. "The Egyptians refused to let the Israelites go, and He poured out naphtha over them, burning blains (blisters)." The texts mention "a stream of hot naphtha." Naphtha, in Aramaic and Hebrew, is petroleum.

Says the *Wisdom of Solomon:* Egypt was "pursued with strange rains and hails and showers inexorable, and utterly consumed with fire: for what was most marvelous of all, in the water which quencheth all things the fire wrought yet more mightily." In the 105th Psalm we read: "He gave them hail for rain, and flaming fire in their land."[13]

A "rain of fire" is also mentioned by the Babylonians of ancient times.

Philo in his *On the Eternity of the World,* declared: "Destructions of things on earth, destructions not of all at once but of a very large number, are attributed by it to two principal causes, the tremendous onslaughts of fire and water. These two visitations, we are told, descend in turns after very long cycles of years. When the agent is the conflagration, a stream of heaven-sent fire pours out from above and spreads over many places and overruns great regions of the inhabited earth."[14]

The Jewish *Talmud* dates the Sodom-Gomorrah catastrophe as to the time of year. We read:

"The destruction of the cities of the plain took place at dawn of the sixteenth day of Nisan (in the spring), for the reason that there were moon and sun worshippers among the inhabitants. God said: ' . . . and if I destroy them by night, the sun worshippers will say, Were the sun here, he would prove himself our savior. I will therefore let their chastisement overtake them on

12. Papyrus Ipuwer 2:10; 7:1; 11:11; 12:6.
13. Verse 32.
14. Vol. IX, sect. 146-147.

the sixteenth day of Nisan at an hour at which the moon and the sun are both in the skies."[15]

The city of Zoar, located in the Rift Valley trench, was founded a year later than the other cities of the plain. Thus, say the *Legends of the Jews,* "it was only fifty-one years old, and therefore the measure of its sins was not so full as the measure of the sins of the neighboring cities."[16]

There had been plenty of warning of the fate of the famed cities of iniquity. "For fifty-two years God had warned the godless; He had made mountains to quake and tremble."[17]

The fires that rained down upon Sodom and the surrounding cities followed the cataclysm of the Deluge by 400 years. This fiery destruction could very probably have had a heavenly origin. In fact, if we take the Biblical account literally, it simply states:

"Then the Lord rained upon Sodom and upon Gomorrah brimstone *and fire from the Lord out of heaven*" (Genesis 19:24).

Abraham, the patriarch of the Hebrews, the next morning got out of his bed early, and climbed to a spot where he could view the entire plain of Sodom. "And he looked toward Sodom and Gomorrah, and toward all the land of the plain, and beheld, and, lo, the smoke of the country went up as the smoke of a furnace" (verse 28).

Even the next day the fires were still burning!

This ancient holocaust, like the plagues upon Egypt, could well have been triggered by a heavenly bombardment of meteorites and "fire" from the sky. Whatever the cause, it made a vivid impression upon the world, and the history of the Hebrews. Millennia later the apostle Jude referred to it as a mighty symbol of judgment: "Even as Sodom and Gomorrah, and the cities about them in like manner, giving themselves over

15. Ginzberg, *Legends of the Jews,* vol. I, p. 256.
16. *Ibid.,* p. 256.
17. p. 253.

to fornication, and going after strange flesh, are set forth for an example, suffering the vengeance of eternal fire" (Jude 7).

This "eternal" fire Jude mentions was, in the Greek language, in which he wrote, *aionion* fire, or "age-lasting fire." We may consider it a consummation of a "world age" and "world cycle," a cycle or age ended by conflagration.

According to Scripture, the Eternal God intervened, and brought about the judgment of Sodom. Later king David, in a Psalm to the Most High God, characterized the manner in which God intervenes in human matters upon the earth, when He brings judgment:

"The earth shook and trembled; the foundations also of the hills moved and were shaken, because he was wroth."

Clearly, in the days of Sodom, the Eternal was "wroth."

Continuing: "There went up a smoke out of his nostrils, and fire out of his mouth devoured: coals were kindled by it. He bowed the heavens, also, and came down: and darkness was under his feet . . . . At the brightness that was before him his thick clouds passed, hail stones and coals of fire. The Lord also thundered in the heavens, and the Highest gave his voice; hail stones and coals of fire. Yea, he sent out his arrows, and scattered them; and he shot out lightnings, and discomfited them. Then the channels of waters were seen, and the foundations of the world were discovered at thy rebuke, O Lord, at the blast of the breath of thy nostrils" (Psalm 18:7-15).

"Hail stones and coals of fire," "shot out lightnings," "thundered in the heavens," "smoke out of his nostrils"—these words could just as readily describe the fiery holocaust which overthrew the cities of Sodom and Gomorrah in the days of Abraham!

Psalm 97 also speaks of the times of the judgment of the Eternal God: "A fire goeth before him, and burneth up his enemies round about. His lightnings enlightened the world: the earth saw, and trembled. The hills melted like wax at the presence of the Lord, at the presence of the Lord of the whole earth" (verses 3-5).

Here we find a description of what occurs at the "presence" of the Lord upon the earth. But, according to Scripture, did

God himself come down to earth in the days of Sodom and Gomorrah to render Judgment?

The answer is yes. In Genesis 18 we read: "And the *Lord* appeared unto him in the plains of Mamre: and he sat in the tent door in the heat of the day; and he lift up his eyes and looked, and, lo, three men stood by him: and when he saw them, he ran to meet them from the tent door, and bowed himself toward the ground, and said, *My Lord,* if now I have found favour in thy sight, pass not away, I pray thee, from thy servant . . . " (vs. 1-3).

Verse 13 clearly identifies this personage whom Abraham was addressing as Yahveh, the Eternal (see also verses 14, 17-19).

Abraham talked with this Person. "And the Lord said, Because the cry of Sodom and Gomorrah is great, and because their sin is very grievous; I will go down now, and see whether they have done altogether according to the cry of it, which is come unto me; and if not, I will know" (verses 20-21).

The end result we all know.

The destruction of Sodom and Gomorrah was no small thing. It shook the minds and memory of man. It became firmly embedded in the collective memory of the descendants of Abraham.

Why was such a fiery destruction visited upon the inhabitants of these cities of the plain?

The wickedness and moral depravity of Sodom became proverbial (Romans 9:29). Unger points out that the ancient Sodomites (Hebrew *qadesh,* "consecrated," "devoted") derived their name from the fact that they were men "consecrated" to unnatural vice as a religious rite.

Says Unger:

"This dreadful 'consecration,' or, rather, desecration, was spread in different forms over Phoenicia, Syria, Phrygia, Assyria, Babylonia. Ashtaroth, the Greek Astarte (Easter), was its chief object. The term was especially applied to the emasculated priests of Cybele, called Galli, perhaps from the river Gallus in Bithynia, which was said to make those who drank it mad. In Deut. 23:17, the toleration of a sodomite was expressly forbidden, and the pay received by a sodomite was not to be put into the temple treasury (v. 18). 'The price of a dog' is a figurative expression used to denote the gains of a *qadesh* (sodomite), who was called *kinaidos*, by the Greeks, from the doglike manner in which he debased himself (see Rev. 22:15, where the unclean are called 'dogs')."[18]

The inhabitants of ancient Sodom were idolaters. They had given themselves over completely to follow the false religious system begun by Nimrod, Semiramis, and Cush. They worshipped the goddess Ishtar, Ashtoreth, or Venus—the original Semiramis—the goddess of sensual love, maternity and fertility. Her religious rites were characterized by licentiousness and lewd behavior.

They also worshipped Baal (Nimrod). They were addicted to this form of worship, conducted in temples and in good weather outdoors in fields and particularly on hilltops called "high places." The Baal cult included animal sacrifice, ritualistic meals, and licentious dances. Says Unger: "Near the rock altar was a sacred pillar or *massebah*, and close by the symbol of the *asherah*, both of which apparently symbolized human fertility (the male and female sexual organs). High places had chambers for sacred prostitution by male-prostitutes (*kedishim*) and sacred harlots (*kedeshoth*) (I Kings 13:23, 24; II Kings 23:7). The gaiety and licentious character of Baal worship always had a subtle attraction for the austere Hebrews bound to serve a holy God under a rigorous moral code."[19]

The worship of Nimrod was a dark and horrible system. At first he was worshiped as the "revealer of goodness and truth," but his worship was eventually made to correspond to his dark and brooding countenance. One of the names for Nimrod, under which he was worshiped, was Moloch, which originally suggested nothing of cruelty and terror. It merely meant "king," and Nimrod was the world's first "king." He was the first human being to wear a diadem or crown.

The worship of Nimrod as Moloch spread everywhere. No

18. *Unger's Bible Dictionary*, "Sodomite," p. 1035.
19. *Ibid.*, "Gods, False," pp. 412-413.

doubt that Sodom was an ancient cult center of Moloch, or Nimrod.

Says Alexander Hislop: "Greece, Rome, Egypt, Phoenicia, Assyria, and our own land under the savage Druids, at one period or other in their history, worshipped the same god and in the same way. Human victims were his most acceptable offerings; human groans and wailings were the sweetest music in his ears; human tortures were believed to delight his heart. His image bore, as the symbol of 'majesty,' a *whip,* and with whips his worshippers, at some of his festivals, were required unmercifully to scourge themselves."[20]

Sado-masochism were part of the rites of the worshippers of Moloch-Nimrod. Whips were used to bring the people to a height of frenzy. Human sacrifice, and even the sacrifice of young, innocent children, was practiced. In the worship of this detestable deity, infants were compelled to pass through or into the fire. "Palestinian excavations have uncovered evidences of infant skeletons in burial places around heathen shrines."[21]

Were such rites practised by the original inhabitants of Sodom and Gomorrah? Perhaps we cannot speak with total knowledge on this point. Nevertheless, it is evident that these worshippers of Nimrod, "consecrated" to his cult, did not restrain themselves in any manner.

Whether they engaged in human sacrifice and putting infants through the fire we do not know for a certainty. But the combined testimony of archaeology, history, and tradition tells us eloquently that these ancient peoples were given over to do iniquity. Their morals had plunged into the gutter. Righteousness was virtually unknown among them. They were *all* given over to homosexuality, bestiality, and corruption of youth. The city was so bad that God could not find even ten righteous men in it. Only Lot was spared. We find that when the two angels, disguised as men, entered Lot's house, even before they lay down to rest for the night, "the men of the city, even the men of Sodom, compassed the house round, both old and young, all the people

20. *Two Babylons,* p. 151.
21. *Unger,* p. 416.

from every quarter: And they called unto Lot, and said unto him, Where are the men which came in to thee this night? bring them out unto us, that we may know them" (Genesis 19:4-5).

All the people were involved! Young and old alike were devoted to sensual depravity. And their punishment? The greatest fiery holocaust ever to rain down upon a city and its environs!

The example of Sodom and Gomorrah cannot be quenched. The violent "hell" that swallowed up those cities, and put an end to their existence, for ever, stands as a stark reminder that wantonness and lawlessness bring their own reward.

Throughout the history of man, iniquity has brought about cosmic destruction. The Deluge—the Tower of Babel destruction—the catastrophe that claimed Sodom and Gomorrah—the Plagues upon Egypt—the cataclysm in the days of Joshua—the maelstorm which occurred in the days of Hezekiah, Uzziah, and the fall of Israel—in each case, we find that tremendous lawlessness, rebellion, and wanton, proud, wicked behavior characterized the world before divine cosmic wrath and judgment came upon them.

Peter the apostle summed up the story in his second epistle in the New Testament. He wrote:

"For if God spared not the angels that sinned, but cast them down to hell, and delivered them into chains of darkness, to be reserved unto judgment; and spared not the old world, but saved Noah the eighth person, a preacher of righteousness, bringing in the flood upon the world of the ungodly; and turning the cities of Sodom and Gomorrah into ashes condemned them with an overthrow, making them an example unto those that after should live ungodly; and delivered just Lot, vexed with the filthy conversation [conduct] of the wicked: (For that righteous man dwelling among them, in seeing and hearing, vexed his righteous soul from day to day with their unlawful deeds;) The Lord knoweth how to deliver the godly out of temptations, and to reserve the unjust unto the day of judgment to be punished: But chiefly them that walk after the flesh in the lust of uncleanness, and despise government. Presumptuous are they, selfwilled, they are not afraid to speak evil of dignities. Whereas angels, which are greater in power and might, bring not railing accusation against them before the Lord. But these, as natural brute beasts, made to be taken and destroyed, speak evil of the things that they understand not; and shall utterly perish in their own corruption; and shall receive the reward of unrighteousness, as they that count it pleasure to riot in the day time. Spots they are and blemishes, sporting themselves with their own deceivings while they feast with you; Having eyes full of adultery, and that cannot cease from sin; beguiling unstable souls: a heart they have exercised with covetous practices; cursed children: which have forsaken the right way, and are gone astray, following the way of Balaam the son of Bosor, who loved the wages of unrighteousness; but was rebuked for his iniquity: the dumb ass speaking with man's voice forbade the madness of the prophet. These are wells without water, clouds that are carried with a tempest; to whom the mist of darkness is reserved for ever" (II Peter 2:5-17).

Destruction has a cause. That cause is invariably the same. Catastrophe, cataclysm, tectonic upheaval, incredible malestroms—these events are, according to the consistent and authentic voice of Scripture, in reality the acts of judgment brought upon an errant world for its misconduct and lawless behavior.

The apostle Paul, in the book of First Corinthians, pointed out this same ironclad truth: He observed, "Moreover, brethren, I would not that ye should be ignorant, how that all our fathers were under the cloud, and all passed through the sea; and were all baptized unto Moses in the cloud and in the sea; and did all eat the same spiritual meat: and did all drink the same spiritual drink: for they drank of that spiritual Rock that followed them: and that Rock was Christ.

"But with many of them God was not well pleased: for they were overthrown in the wilderness. Now these things were our examples, to the intent we should not lust after evil things, as they also lusted. Neither be ye idolaters, as were some of them; as it is written, The people sat down to eat and drink, and rose up to play. Neither let us commit fornication, as some of them committed, and fell in one day three and twenty thousand.

Neither let us tempt Christ, as some of them also tempted, and were destroyed of serpents. Neither murmur ye, as some of them also murmured, and were destroyed of the destroyer. Now all these things happened unto them for ensamples: and they are written for our admonition, upon whom the ends of the world are come. Wherefore let him that thinketh he standeth take heed lest he fall" (I Corinthians 10:1-12).

Disobedience brings punishment. That is one of the keynotes of human experience. Idolatry leads to death. Lawlessness leads to catastrophe. Rebellion leads to cataclysm.

Before destruction rained down from heaven, the Scriptures state: "And Lot lifted up his eyes, and beheld all the plain of Jordan, that it was well watered every where, before the Lord destroyed Sodom and Gomorrah, even as the garden of the Lord, like the land of Egypt, as thou comest unto Zoar" (Genesis 13:10).

Nevertheless, the ancient record goes on: "But the men of Sodom were wicked and sinners before the Lord exceedingly" (Gen. 13:13).

Their sin was their undoing.

There are cycles in life, and cycles in the lives of nations. They begin as young struggling republics, with virtue, honor and courage highly prized among the people. But when they grow rich, and luxuriate in wealth and abundance, a change comes about. They grow fat, proud, insolent, and rebellious. They become cynical, bitter, selfish, self-centered, avaricious, boastful, disdainful, and evil. Their iniquities grow apace. Eventually they become saturated with sin, filled with lawlessness, and their judgment lingers not.

In the days of Abraham, the patriarch was given a strange vision of the future (Genesis 15:1). He was told that in the future, his seed or progeny would be afflicted for 400 years.

"And he said unto Abraham, Know of a surety that thy seed shall be a stranger in a land that is not theirs, and shall serve them; and they shall afflict them four hundred years; And also that nation, whom they shall serve, will I judge: and afterward shall they come out with great substance . . . . But in the fourth generation they shall come hither again: for *the iniquity of the Amorites is not yet full*" (Genesis 15:13-16).

The sins of the Amorites—the Canaanites—did not reach their peak until the middle of the second millennium before the present era. Their punishment did not come until the time of the Exodus!

Sodom and Gomorrah reached their peak of disobedience and corruption 4,000 years ago. Their punishment is still vividly remembered.

Chapter Eleven

Berezovka Mammoth Mystery

The prevailing theory of the earth's geological history is the theory of uniformitarianism. According to this well entrenched theory, the earth's strata has been formed by uniform, gradual processes over millions of years. What happens geologically speaking today is the same sort of geological event which happened in the ancient past. According to uniformitarianism, "the present is the key to the past."

Modern geologists tell us that uniformitarianism rejects supernatural, miraculous or incomprehensible effects as long as natural explanations of events will suffice. It seeks explanations for the earth's strata based on processes which we can observe occurring today, in the natural world around us. Uniformitarianism doctrine is the foundation of modern geological science. It is one of the pillars of investigating the ancient past. Uniformitarianism was first propounded by Charles Lyell (1797-1875) in his *Principles of Geology* (1832). The theory had previously been advanced by James Hutton and John Playfair, but Lyell's work became the backbone of geological thinking for the next century and a half.

Nobody, of course, argues with the fact that geologic processes we see occurring today also occurred millions of years ago, unless they are blinded by religious and/or superstitious dogmatism. Some people today still deny that the earth is round and will heatedly argue that despite Apollo moon flights and photographs taken from rockets and satellites, that the earth is flat!

Even Job, thousands of years ago, was familiar with the fact that water gradually wore away rocks and eroded land surfaces; that wind did the same thing. These processes, along with rain, snow, occasional storms, earthquakes, volcanic eruptions, occur on a more or less regular basis.

But can the interminal processes of day-to-day activity account for the actual geologic strata around the earth? Was the entire geologic column the result of very gradual processes going on for incalculable lengths of time?

Examination of the earth's geologic column, if we mounted the greatest thickness of each sedimentary bed of each geologic age upon each other, would reveal a massive column at least 100 miles high. The geological column has been laboriously pieced together from evidence from around the world. William Smith (1769-1839), the "Father of Stratigraphy," was the first to observe that different rock layers could be identified by the fossils they contained.

But what does a close, careful examination of this detailed fossil record—the geologic column—reveal about the earth's past?

Many geologists are coming to see that the geologic record at many places cannot be adequately explained in terms of uniformitarian theory. The facts, the rocks themselves, in twisted, convoluted strata, cry out that catastrophisms on incredible scales have indeed occurred during geologic history.

The actual record in the rocks beneath our feet confirms that global and continental catastrophes have occurred in the earth's past. Some of these, we have seen from traditions and chronicles kept by ancient nations, occurred within the memory of man. Others, as we shall see, antedated the arrival of modern man upon this earth by thousands or millions of years.

The Berezovka Mammoth mystery is a case in point.

Ivan T. Sanderson, in "The Riddle of the Quick-Frozen Mammoths," tells us that the Berezovka mammoth was found sticking headfirst out of a bank of the Berezovka River in northern Siberia about sixty years ago. It was preserved in almost perfect condition except for some portions which had been eaten by wolves. The lips, lining of the mouth, and tongue were all preserved. Portions of the mammoth's final meal were even found stuck between its teeth—sedges, grasses and buttercups which bloom in late summer!

Excavations revealed that vast herds of these enormous animals suddenly, inexplicably died. To freeze and preserve meat so well, Sanderson pointed out, it must have been frozen very rapidly. Otherwise large crystals form in the liquids of the cells, burst the cells, and the meat begins to deteriorate. The flesh of some of these quick-frozen mammoths has been eaten by trail dogs with no harmful effects. In fact, mammoth steaks were brought to London on ice and were eaten by members of the Royal Society! They also showed no ill effects.

To the north of Mount McKinley in Alaska where the Tanana River joins the Yukon vast remains of these mammoths have been found. Prospectors, searching for gold in the frozen Alaskan muck and gravel in and near riverbeds found something else—enormous deposits of frozen bodies of huge masses of prehistoric animals and trunks of prehistoric trees. The frozen bones of extinct mammoths, mastodons, super-bisons, horses have been found protruding from miles and miles of strange Alaskan muck.

This muck, composed largely of mud, silt, black organic matter, and ice, contains the remains of entire herds of now extinct woolly mammoths, woolly rhinoceroses, wild horses, giant oxen giant bison, huge prehistoric wolves, mountain lions, and the famed giant saber-tooth cat.

What caused the deaths of these millions of animals? When did it happen?

The remains of one mammoth were radio-carbon dated to about 10,000 years before the present. In the case of the Berezovka mammoth, there were no signs of violence—it simply froze to death, and many others along with it, and remained frozen until our time. In the case of other remains, found in Alaska, tons and tons of smashed, ripped up, torn and sundered bodies of animals have been unearthed, revealing incredible violence.

Twisted torsos of animals and trees, bones of mammoths, mastodons, bisons, wolves, bears, lions and cats have been found intermingled with lenses of ice and layers of peat and moss. Bones and tusks of animals have been exposed at all levels of the frozen bank at the Yukon River and its tributaries. Entire gravel bars were created out of the jumbled fragments of animal remains, and similar bone beds have been found in the frozen tundra of Siberia.

Preserved in a remarkable manner are tendons, ligaments, fragments of skin and hair, hooves and even portions of the flesh and bone. At Cripple Creek, near Fairbanks, the shoulder of a mammoth with the flesh and skin yet preserved were discovered. An Eskimo dog wandered by and ate the black and sand-impregnated meat readily.

At Rosey Creek, north of Fairbanks, miners were using a bulldozer to shove the muck into a sluice box to extract the gold. As the dozer blade scraped across the muck, it shoved aside huge piles of mammoth bones and tusks. Archaeologists on the scene reported that as the sun rose in the heavens, and warmed the earth, the stench and odor from the hundreds of tons of rotting flesh became unbearable and could be detected for miles!

Archaeologist Frank C. Hibben in *The Lost Americans* wrote of the experience: "It looks as though the middle of some cataclysmic catastrophe of ten thousand years ago the whole Alaskan world of living animals and plants was suddenly frozen in mid-motion in a grim charade."[1]

Hibben relates relative to the Rosey Creek find: "Apparently, a whole herd of mammoths had died in this place and fallen together in a jumbled mass of leg bones, tusks, and mighty skulls, to be frozen solid and preserved until this day. Only the greed of man for gold had opened up their long-frozen grave."[2]

Says Hibben, whom I interviewed at his office at the University of New Mexico, at Albuquerque: "Mammals there were in abundance, dumped in all attitudes of death. Most of them were pulled apart by some unexplained prehistoric catastrophic disturbance. Legs and torsos and heads and fragments were

1. p. 118.
2. *Ibid.*, p. 122.

found together in piles or scattered separately. But nowhere could we find any definite evidence that humans had ever walked among these trumpeting herds or had ever seen their final end."[3]

Scientific investigations into the earth's prehistoric past indicate that about 50,000 years ago the Pleistocene Wisconsin glaciation set in (the Late Wurm glaciation in Europe). There were several advances and regressions of the ice. The Tazewell advance is generally dated 20,000-17,000 years ago, although the maximum extension of ice may have been considerably later.

At the close of this Ice Age a vast Ice Cap covering half a continent and as deep as the Antarctic Ice Cap is today totally disappeared. Seemingly, within just one or two thousand years it vanished. "In any case, it was, geologically speaking, a sort of miracle," declared Dr. Charles Hapgood.[4]

Hapgood added: "There was nothing in this to suggest the painfully slow pace of usual geological history. To be blunt about it, it was a catastrophe, a cataclysm; it was a revolution."[5]

This was approximately the same time as the destructions of vast herds of mammoths, bison, mastodons, tigers, rhinos, horses, and wolves, throughout Alaska and Siberia. Hapgood clearly refers to this period as a catastrophe—a cataclysm—even a "revolution."

Something happened. Something unheard of—something almost inexplicable—something that dumfounds scientists and beggars the descriptive talents of writers. Something indeed awesome, and on an intercontinental scale. What was it?

Although it is not popular today to speak of catastrophes in geological circles "because catstrophes, so to speak, went out with the Flood," Hapgood tells us, "Yet facts are facts, and come what may, we shall have to face some quite remarkable ones as we proceed."[6]

3. *Ibid.*
4. *The Paths of the Pole,* p. 150.
5. *Ibid.*
6. *Ibid.*, pp. 152-153.

The evidence for enormous, mind-boggling catastrophes before the time of man is extensive. Scientists have found locations where remains of animals of cold and warm climate are jumbled together in caves where they all suffered death suddenly, under violent conditions. A peat bed at Puy de Dome, France, contains fossils of warm climate animals and cold climate flora.

In Hanaizumi, Japan, scientists found a conifer bed roughly dated 15,000 years ago where plant fossils of a cold climate were accompanied by several extinct animal species including fossil elephant.

This was the time of the last major glaciation of the Pleistocene Age. During that tremendous glaciation, nearly half of the continent of Europe was covered by a sheet of ice radiating from the Scandinavian highlands; much of northern Asia was covered by another sheet of ice centering in northwestern Siberia. Between them over three million square miles of land was submerged beneath the ice.

In North America, almost all of Canada and much of the northeastern United States, ranging as far south as the Ohio and Missouri rivers, was covered by 4,500,000 square miles of ice.

In the southern hemisphere there is evidence that the Antarctic ice pack was once greater, the ice descended below the present sea level in New Zealand, and Tasmania was covered with glaciers. In South America glaciers of the Andes extended to sea level in the west and into the Argentine pampas to the east. In east Africa, the glaciers of Mount Kenya were 5,400 feet below their present level.

Roughly 15 million square miles or 27 per cent of the land surface of the earth was covered by vast sheets of ice! Such a fact, by its very dimensions, speaks of an imagination-defying cataclysm which befell the earth in the middle and late Pleistocene epoch, long before the advent of modern man upon the earth.

As this ice melted, at the close of the "Great Freeze," other catastrophes occurred. Ancient Lake Missoula once covered several thousand square miles in western Montana and may have been over a mile deep, containing 500 cubic miles of water.

It was locked in a natural ice dam, but the dam broke as the ice melted, releasing tremendous torrents of water that plunged across the western portion of the state of Washington now known as the "channelled scabland." I have visited the dry falls and the scabland, and marvelled at the enormous gorge over which at one time a giant cataract plummeted. It would have made Niagara Falls and Victoria Falls combined look like a drainage ditch in comparison.

Writes William Stokes, geologist: "The erosion and deposition resulting from this flood are so extensive that many geologists have had difficulty believing such a deluge was possible."'[7]

At the close of the Pleistocene, gigantic creatures were wiped out en masse. The great dire wolf, standing six feet tall at the shoulders (how would you like to encounter him on a lonely mountain trail?); the sabertoothed cat; bears larger than the grizzly bear; giant beavers the size of black bears; buffalo that had horns extending out for six feet; large camels and pygmy camels; huge pigs and enormous dogs; a ground sloth that weighed as much as an elephant and which could reach leaves 20 feet high on trees; imperial mammoths, with 13-foot tusks, which stood with a shoulder height of 14 feet; and royal mastodons—all these were suddenly, inexplicably wiped out—exterminated—left without a single pair of descendants to carry on the species!

Edward Suess, the greatest geologist of the last century, wrote: "The earthquakes of today are but faint reminiscences of those telluric movements to which the structure of almost every mountain range bears witness." He continues, "Numerous examples of great mountain chains suggest by their structure the possibility, and even in some cases the probability, of the *occasional intervention* in the course of great geological eras of *processes of episodal disturbances of such indescribable and overwhelming violence, that the imagination refuses to follow the understanding and to complete the picture of which the outlines are furnished by observations of fact.*"[8]

7. Stokes, *Essentials of Earth History,* p. 366.
8. Seuss, *The Face of the Earth,* 398:I, 17-18.

As the Ice Age ended, something unique happened to animal life. The big animals that roamed the plains by the millions were wiped out, almost as if overnight.

Before this "Great Kill," many new animals had appeared on the earth—millions of new species, and millions of each species. It was called "The Age of New Animals." The very word "Pleistocene" actually is derived from Greek words which mean "most of the new."

But at the end of the Pleistocene, most of these new animals became extinct. Frank C. Hibben describes their demise in a chapter fittingly entitled "End of a Universe." He asserts:

"The Pleistocene period ended in death. This was no ordinary extinction of a vague geological period which fizzled to an uncertain end. This death was catastrophic and all-inclusive . . . The large animals that had given the name to the period became extinct. Their death marked the end of the era.

"But how did they die? What caused the extinction of forty million animals? This mystery forms one of the oldest detective stories in the world . . . In this particular case, the death was of such colossal proportions as to be staggering to contemplate. The antiquity adds a rare relish to the tale. Who or what killed the Pleistocene animals is a query that has not yet been answered."[9]

Pleistocene animals wandered into every corner, nook and cranny, of the New World which was not covered by glaciation. Bones of Pleistocene animals have been unearthed in the sands of Florida, from the gravels of New Jersey, found protruding from the dry terraces of Texas, and in the sticky ooze of the La Brea tar pits in Los Angeles. In Mexico and in South America their remains have been found by the thousands.

How indeed did they all die?

Hibben describes the scene thus: " . . . where we can study these animals in some detail, such as in the great bone deposits in Nebraska, we find literally thousands of these remains together. The young lie with the old, foal with dam and calf

9. *The Lost Americans,* p. 157.

with cow. Whole herds of animals were apparently killed together, overcome by some common power.

"We have already seen that the muck pits of Alaska are filled with evidences of universal death. Mingled in these frozen masses are the remains of many thousands of animals killed in their prime . . . We have gained from the muck pits of the Yukon Valley a picture of quick extinction. The evidences of violence there are as obvious as in the horror camps of Germany. Such piles of bodies of animals or men simply do not occur by any ordinary natural means."[10]

Pleistocene animals in Europe and Asia met similar grisly fates. The mammoth herds of Siberia became extinct. The European rhinoceros died out suddenly. The cave bear of Europe perished. The bison of Siberia—extinct. American camels and Asiatic elephants—extinct.

Africa alone, seems to have been spared. The modern wildlife of Africa seems more typical of the fauna which flourished before the close of the Pleistocene age.

Was the deaths and universal extinction of millions of animals around the globe according to "uniformitarian" geologic principles? Or was a massive, horrendous, cosmic catastrophe involved?

No known causes upon the earth can explain it. No seismic or geologic movements on the earth can explain why such ferocious, vast, overwhelming destruction. Says Hibben, "the consuming mystery of the death of forty million Pleistocene animals still stands."[11] One of the earliest and most attractive theories to account for the widespread extinction was catastrophism. Partisans of catastrophism hold that tremendous earthquake activity and volcanic eruptions accounted for the devastation and genocide. These great convulsions took place about 10,000 years ago.

But what would trigger such universal upheavals and cataclysms on earth? No cause within the earth itself is known, or even suspect. Could the "spark" have been extraterrestrial?

10. *Ibid.*, p. 158.
11. *Ibid.*, p. 162.

Frank C. Hibben points out: "One of the most interesting of the theories of the Pleistocene end is that which explains this ancient tragedy by worldwide earth-shaking volcanic eruptions of catastrophic violence." In Alaskan and Siberian regions, he says, this idea has considerable support from the geologic evidence because layers of volcanic ash are interspersed with the animal remains. At the time of the deaths of millions of animals volcanic eruptions took place in Alaska—eruptions of tremendous proportions. Toxic clouds of gas from these paroxysms of the earth may have contributed to the gigantic death scale.

Says Hibben:

"Throughout the Alaskan mucks, too, there is evidence of atmospheric disturbances of unparalleled violence. Mammoth and bison alike were torn and twisted as though by a cosmic hand in godly rage. In one place, we can find the foreleg and shoulder of a mammoth with portions of the flesh and the toenails and the hair still clinging to the blackened bones. Close by is the neck and skull of a bison with the vertebrae clinging together with tendons and ligaments and the chitinous covering of the horns intact. There is no mark of a knife or cutting implement. The animals were simply torn apart and scattered over the landscape like things of straw and string, even though some of them weighed several tons. Mixed with the piles of bones are trees, also twisted and torn and piled in tangled groups; and the whole is covered with the fine sifting muck, then frozen solid.

"Storms, too, accompany volcanic disturbances of the proportions indicated here. Differences in temperature and the influence of the cubic miles of ash and pumice thrown into the air by eruptions of this sort might well produce winds and blasts of inconceivable violence. If this is the explanation for the end of all this animal life, the Pleistocene period was terminated by a very exciting time, indeed."[12]

Notice again, a few of the expressions used by Dr. Frank C. Hibben to describe the mute testimony of the twisted and sundered remains of animals found in the Alaskan muck and elsewhere: *"unparalleled violence;"* "torn and twisted as

12. *The Lost Americans,* pp. 163-164.

though by a *cosmic hand* in godly rage;" "winds and blasts of *inconceivable violence.*"

Many students of the Ice Age have believed—assumed—that the temperature change during the Pleistocene followed a smooth curve, that temperatures gradually rose to a peak in each interglacial period, then gradually descended till they reached a minimum during a cold period. However, cores from the sea bottoms oppose this belief. It seems, rather, that the climatic phases were bounded by "abrupt change," state Ericson and Wollin.[13] "This is indicated by the abruptness of the faunal changes at the boundaries between the clearly defined faunal zones," they assert.[14]

In his book *Earth in Upheaval,* Immanuel Velikovsky points out that the New Siberian Islands, discovered in 1805 and 1806 have soil which is absolutely packed full of the bones of elephants and rhinoceroses in astonishing numbers. He asked how such vast herds of voracious vegetation-consuming mammoths could have survived in such a bleak country as northeast Siberia. Mammoth tusks, he observed, are dredged out of the bottom of the Arctic Ocean in nets. Sometimes arctic gales strew the shoreline of the islands with tusks.

To Charles Darwin, author of *Origin of Species,* the extinction of the woolly mammoths was a perplexing mystery. On Koltelnoi Island there are neither trees, nor shrubs nor bushes—yet the bones of elephants, rhinos, bison and horses are found in numbers which defy all calculation.

The New Siberian Islands, one thousand miles away from the muck beds of Alaska, corroborate the testimony of the Alaskan cataclysm which occurred during the Pleistocene epoch.

Georges Cuvier, the founder of vertebrate paleontology—the science of fossil bones—came out of the generation of the French Revolution and the Napoleonic Wars. He studied the finds in the gypsum formation of Montmartre in Paris and throughout Europe and concluded that even in the midst of the oldest strata of marine formations there existed other strata,

13. *The Deep and The Past*, p. 137.
14. *Ibid.*

containing remains of terrestrial and fresh-water plants and animals. He found land animals buried under heaps of marine sediment.

Curvier observed: "It has frequently happened that lands which have been laid dry, have been again covered by the waters, in consequence either of their being engulfed in the abyss, or of the sea having merely risen over them." He asserted, "These repeated irruptions and retreats of the sea have neither all been slow nor gradual; on the contrary, most of the catastrophes which have occasioned them have been sudden; and this is especially easy to be proven, with regard to the last of these catastrophes, that which, by a twofold motion, has inundated, and afterwards laid dry, our present continents, or at least a part of the land which forms them at the present day."[15]

This eminent authority on the earth of 150 years ago was a keen observer and student of natural earth processes. He declared: "The breaking to pieces, the raising up and overturning of the older strata, leave no doubt upon the mind that they have been reduced to the state in which we now see them, by the action of sudden and violent causes; and even the force of the motions excited in the mass of waters, is still attested by the heaps of debris and rounded pebbles which are in many places interposed between the solid strata. *Life, therefore, has often been disturbed on this earth by terrific events.* Numberless living beings have been the victims of these catastrophes; some, which inhabited the dry land, have been swallowed up by inundations; others, which peopled the waters, have been laid dry, the bottom of the sea having been suddenly raised; their very races have been extinguished forever, and have left no other memorial of their existence than some fragments which the naturalist can scarcely recognize."[16]

Cuvier saw the tremendous evidence of repeated catastrophes befalling life on the earth. He strove to ascertain the causes of these cataclysms. But to no avail. He was led to conclude: "Thus, we repeat, it is in vain that we search, among the powers

15. Georges Curvier, *Essay on the Theory of the Earth,* pp. 13-14.
16. *Ibid.,* p. 15.

which now act at the surface of the earth, for causes sufficient to produce the revolutions and catastrophes, the traces of which are exhibited by its crust."[17]

Cuvier did not know the causes of these vast cataclysms. He only knew that they had occurred. He lamented, "These ideas have haunted, I may almost say have tormented me during my researches among fossil bones."[18]

In a cave in Kirkdale, Yorkshire, England, eighty feet above the valley, William Buckland, professor of geology at the University of Oxford, in 1823 found teeth and bones of elephants, rhinos, hippopotami, horses, deer, tigers, bears, wolves, hyenas, foxes, hares, rabbits, as well as bones of ravens, pigeons, larks, snipe and ducks. The teeth from the tiger were larger than those from the Bengal tiger or the largest lion. It appeared that all these creatures lived in the area at one time. On the other hand, it was difficult to explain animals from cold northern latitudes being found side by side with remains from animals of tropical latitudes, such as hippopotami and crocodiles. Buckland was led to the conclusion that these remains had been washed into the cave by different tides in a general inundation of the globe—a universal deluge.

In the late thirties of the 19th century Hugh Miller studied the Old Red Sandstone in Scotland. It carried the testimony of violent death descending upon whole tribes at once—tribes of ancient species of life forms. "The earth had already become a vast sepulchre," he observed.[19]

The scene reminded Miller of the opening of Shakespeare's *The Tempest,* which began amidst the confusion and chaos of the hurricane. Said Miller, in a vast space of northern Scotland, for thousands of square miles, a vast stratum of water-rolled pebbles exists, varying in depth from a hundred feet to a hundred yards, testifying to ancient times of violent commotion. "And yet it is surely difficult to conceive how the bottom of any sea should have been so violently and so equally agitated for so

17. pp. 35-36.
18. *Ibid.,* p. 242.
19. Miller, *The Old Red Sandstone,* p. 48.

greatly extended a space . . . and for a period so prolonged that the entire area should have come to be covered with a stratum of rolled pebbles of almost every variety of ancient rock, fifteen stories' height in thickness."[20]

In the Old Red Sandstone abundant aquatic fauna are entombed. Says Miller, of the time when these formations were created, "some terrible catastrophe involved in sudden destruction the fish of an area at least a hundred miles from boundary to boundary, perhaps much more. The same platform in Orkney as at Cromarty is strewed thick with remains, which exhibit unequivocally the marks of violent death. The figures are contorted, contracted, curved; the tail in many instances is bent around to the head; the spines stick out; the fins are spread to the full, as in fish that die in convulsions . . . . The record is one of destruction at once widely spread and total."[21]

How could innumerable fish in an area perhaps 10,000 square miles in extent be annihilated at once? "Conjecture lacks footing in grappling with the enigma, and expatiates in uncertainty over all the known phenomena of death," Miller sighed.[22]

But a thousand different localities disclose the same scene of episodic violence and destruction. Fossil fish at Monte Bolca, northern Italy, perished suddenly. Their skeletons lie packed closely together one on another. Similar fossil fish deposits in the Harz Mountains, Germany, show the same violent widespread devastation, with distorted attitudes, as if they were "writhing in the agonies of death."[23]

In South America the evidence is the same. Charles Darwin, on his round the world voyage aboard the ship *Beagle* beginning in 1831 was impressed by the numerous assemblages of fossils of extinct animals. These fossils seemed to have represented a flourishing fauna which suddenly came to its end in a recent geological age.

Staggered by what he saw, Darwin wrote in his *Journal* of the

20. *Ibid.*, pp. 217-218.
21. p. 222.
22. p. 223.
23. *Buckland, Geology and Minerology*, p. 103.

voyage, January 9, 1834: "It is impossible to reflect on the changed state of the American continent without the deepest astonishment. Formerly it must have swarmed with great monsters; now we find mere pigmies, compared with the antecedent, allied races."

Intrigued, Darwin wrote of these creatures: "The greater number, if not all, of these extinct quadrupeds lived at a late period, and were the contemporaries of most of the existing sea-shells. Since they lived, no very great change in the form of the land can have taken place. What, then, has exterminated so many species and whole genera? The mind at first is irresistibly hurried into the belief of some great catastrophe; but thus to destroy animals, both large and small, in Southern Patagonia, in Brazil, on the Cordillera of Peru, in North America up to Behring's Straits, *we must shake the entire framework of the globe.*"

Darwin was befuddled. Perplexed. He had no answer. He contemplated various possibilities, discounting them one by one. He said:

"It could hardly have been a change of temperature, which at about the same time destroyed the inhabitants of tropical, temperate, and arctic latitudes on both sides of the globe." He determined that it could not have been man, as many fossil mice and other tiny quadrupeds were rendered extinct in the same catastrophe.

Darwin continued: "No one will imagine that a drought . . . could destroy every individual of every species from Southern Patagonia to Behring's Straits. What shall we say of the extinction of the horse? Did those plains fail of pasture, which have since been overrun by thousands and hundreds of thousands of the descendants of the stock introduced by the Spaniards?"

The author of *Origin of Species* concluded: "Certainly, no fact in the long history of the world is so startling as the wide and repeated exterminations of its inhabitants."[24]

24. Charles Darwin, *Journal of Researches into the Natural History and Geology of the Countries Visited During the Voyage of H.M.S. Beagle Round the World,* under the date January 9, 1834.

The Pleistocene was a time of advances and retreats of major glaciation. Louis Agassiz, a leading naturalist of the 19th century, was largely responsible for convincing the world that indeed ice ages had existed, when great ice sheets covered much of Europe. Agassiz' reputation was strengthened and his position verified when William Buckland joined forces with him in propounding the Ice Age theory.

According to Agassiz, however, both the inception and the termination of the Ice Age were catastrophic events. He thought that mammoths in Siberia were suddenly caught in the ice that spread swiftly over much of the earth. Repeated global catastrophes, he thought, were accompanied by a fall in temperature of the globe and its atmosphere. He concluded that each glacial age, of which the earth experienced several, was also terminated by renewed igneous activity in the interior of the earth. Agassiz maintained that the Alps had risen at the end of the last Ice Age, or at the end of the Pleistocene.

It is astonishing to realize, however, that during the Ice Age the areas covered by sheets of ice were not necessarily where you would expect. For example, Alaska and the low lands of northern Siberia show no sign of ancient glaciation at all. And the northern part of Greenland was never covered with ice. And the islands of the Arctic Archipelago were never glaciated.

Also surprising, ice did cover British Guiana, and Madagascar in the tropical regions of the earth. In fact, vestiges of the Ice Age in equatorial Africa were found indicating the ice had moved from the equator toward the higher latitudes of the Southern Hemisphere. In India, too, evidence of an Ice Age was uncovered—the ice had moved from the equator, and even moved uphill, from lowlands to the foothills of the Himalayas!

Says R. T. Chamberlain: "No satisfactory explanation has yet been offered for the extent and location of these extraordinary glaciers." He adds, almost as an afterthought: "Glaciers, almost unbelievable because of their location and size, certainly did not form in deserts."[25]

25. *The World and Man,* "The Origin and History of the Earth," ed. F.R. Moulton, p. 80.

Brazil, also, showed evidence of glaciation. But why the polar lands were not glaciated during the Ice Age has not been satisfactorily explained. In fact, the opposite is true. For where we would expect to find vast evidence of glaciation, we find instead evidence that forests of exotic trees, subtropical plants, and magnolias and fir trees once grew where today there is nothing but bleakness and desolation.

In the 1860s O. Heer of Zurich published his work on the fossil plants of the Arctic—he found remains of all of the above in the northern reaches of Greenland. Near Spitsbergen, which is as far north from Oslo, Norway, as Oslo is from Naples, Italy, O. Heer found 136 species of fossil plants including pines, firs, spruces, cypresses, elms, hazels, and water lilies. Spitsbergen, which lies 1000 miles within the Arctic Circle, was once as warm, balmy and tropical as the French Riviera!

The waters of the frigid Arctic Ocean once must have been at least some 30 degrees warmer, because corals, which only grow in warm water, have been found there. Large formations of coral, covered with snow, can be seen in Spitsbergen, today.

Wrote D. H. Campbell, "It is difficult to imagine any possible conditions of climate in which these plants could grow so near the pole, deprived of sunlight for many months of the year."[26]

The continent of Antarctica, too, must have once been much warmer than now. Seams of coal, and sandstone containing coniferous wood, have been found in deposits there.

What *did* happen in the Pleistocene?

Extinction—floods—Ice sheets miles thick and covering millions of square miles—volcanic eruptions—violent winds and atmospheric blasts—altered temperatures and climates . . . what caused these disturbances?

C. E. P. Brooks in *Climate Through the Ages* remarked: "So long as the axis of rotation remains in nearly its present position relative to the plane of the earth's orbit round the sun, the outer limit of the atmosphere in tropical regions must receive more of

26. Campbell, "Continental Drift and Plant Distribution," *Science*, January 16, 1942.

the sun's heat than the middle latitudes, and the middle latitudes more than the polar regions; this is an invariable law. . . . It is much more difficult to think of a cause which will raise the temperature of polar regions by some 30° F. or more, while leaving that of equatorial regions almost unchanged."[27]

Says Immanuel Velikovsky, in *Earth in Upheaval*: "The finding of warm-climate animals and plants in polar regions, coral and palms in the Arctic Circle, presents these alternatives: either these animals and plants lived there at some time in the past or they were brought there by tidal waves. In some cases the first is true, as where stumps of trees (palms) are found *in situ.* In other cases the second is true, as where, in one and the same deposit, animals and plants from sea and land, from south and north, are found in a medley. But in both cases one thing is apparent: such changes could not have occurred unless the terrestrial globe veered from its path, either because of a disturbance in the speed of rotation or because of a shift in the astronomical or geographical position of the terrestrial axis."

Declares Velikovsky, further: "In many cases it can be shown that southern plants grew in the north; either the geographical position of the pole and the latitudes or the inclination of the axis must have changed since then. In many other cases it can be shown that a marine irruption threw into one deposit living creatures from the tropics and from the Arctic; the change must have been sudden, instantaneous. We have both kinds of cases. Consequently there must have been changes in the position of the axis, and they must have been sudden."[28]

Such periods of catastrophe as we have been recounting, in this chapter, dealing with the Pleistocene Ice Age, must also be accompanied with mountain building. It would naturally seem that any catastrophe which shakes the entire framework of the globe, as Charles Darwin put it, would also uplift entire mountain ranges.

And this is exactly what we find in the Pleistocene Ice epoch.

Writes Flint in *Glacial Geology and the Pleistocene Epoch:*

27. p. 31.
28. *Earth in Upheaval,* pp. 58-59.

"Mountain uplifts amounting to many thousands of feet have occurred within the Pleistocene epoch itself."[29] This occurred with the Cordilleran mountain system in both North and South America, the Alps-Caucasus-Central Asian system, and many others.

Many of these massive uplifts occurred within the time of man—others were before modern man left his footprints in the riverbanks of the earth.

The rocks of the Alps of Switzerland have been shoved northward distances of 100 miles. The Alps used to be on the site of northern Italy. Mount Blanc was moved from its place and the Matterhorn was overturned.

Chief Mountain in Montana is a huge massif which rises several thousand feet above the adjoining Great Plains. Analysis of the fossils within its formation shows conclusively that it was upthrust and pushed over on top of much younger strata beneath. Wrote Daly in *Our Mobile Earth,* Chief Mountain "has been thrust bodily upon the much younger strata of the Great Plains, and then driven over them eastward, for a distance of at least eight miles. Indeed, the thrust may have been several times eight miles."[30]

Daly adds, "By similar thrusting, the whole Rocky Mountain Front, for hundreds of miles, has been pushed up and then out, many miles over the plains."[31]

In the Himalayas, the greatest stretch of mountains in the entire world, rising like a thousand mile wall north of India and China, there is evidence that since paleolithic times—or within the time frame of early man—mountain passes have risen 3,000 feet or more. So says Arnold Heim, Swiss geologist, "however fantastic changes so extensive may seem to a modern geologist."[32]

Arnold Heim says that paleolithic fossils, belonging to the

29. pp. 9-10.
30. pp. 223-229.
31. *Ibid.*, p. 231.
32. Arnold Heim and August Gausser, *The Throne of the Gods, An Account of the First Swiss Expedition to the Himalayas,* p. 218.

early stone age of man, have been found at an altitude of 5000 feet or more in an ancient sea bottom. The paleolithic, or Old Stone Age, corresponds in general to the time of the Pleistocene epoch.

The great Himalayan massif stands as a mute, towering testimony that the highest mountains in the world are also among the youngest.

Similar testimony comes from South America. The ruins of the ancient great city of Tiahuanaco in the Andes, near lake Titicaca, lie at an elevation of 12,500 feet. The region is so high that corn will not ripen. It is so cold upon this elevated plateau that few people live in the area—mainly hardened, tough Indians.

But at one time Tiahuanaco was a flourishing, prospering city. It was built by highly skilled masons with huge, cyclopean blocks, such as were used also in Egypt and Mesopotamia, shortly after the Noachian deluge.

Extensive investigation has shown that at one time the entire plateau was at sea level, or 12,500 feet lower than it is today. Once Tiahuanaco was at the water's edge. The beds of Titicaca and local lakes are similar chemically to the ocean.[33]

Archaeological and radio-carbon dating prove this ancient culture is about 4,000 years old—built after the Noachian deluge. This means the massive uplift of the Andes to their present height must have occurred since that time.

Charles Darwin had the opportunity to climb among the foothills of the Andes, 7000 feet high, and view the plain of Argentina below. He wrote:

"It required little geological practice to interpret the marvellous story which this scene at once unfolded; though I confess I was at first so much astonished that I could scarcely believe the plainest evidence. I saw the spot where a cluster of fine trees once waved their branches on the shores of the Atlantic, when that ocean—now driven back 700 miles—came to the foot of the Andes. . . . But again the subterranean forces exerted themselves, and now I beheld the bed of that ocean, form-

33. Posnansky, *Tiahuanacu*, p. 23.

ing a chain of mountains more than seven thousand feet in height. . . . Vast, and scarcely comprehensible as such changes must ever appear, yet they have all occurred within a period, recent when compared with the history of the Cordillera; and the Cordillera itself is absolutely modern as compared with many of the fossiliferous strata of Europe and America."[34]

Could these massive upheavals in the earth have been caused by a close encounter with another planetary body, or a comet, aeons ago?

The possibility must be considered.

Interestingly, in 1933 Melton and Schriever of the University of Oklahoma presented a theory about peculiar depressions, elliptical in shape, called "oval craters," which are thickly scattered over the coast of the Carolinas, and more thinly from New Jersey in the north to Florida in the south. They declared these depressions are scars left by a "meteoric shower or colliding comet."[35]

These depressions are numbered in the tens of thousands and may actually number half a million. Some of these "bays" are 2200 feet long, and a few reach 8000 feet. Remarkably, they are all parallel, the axis of each one being from northwest to southeast. Circling the southeastern portion of the bays are rims of earth, such as you might expect if the train of meteorites or particles of a comet struck from the northwest. The form, ellipticity, alignment, and parallelism of these fascinating bays leads to the conclusion that they must have been formed by a storm of meteorites falling in a shower, or to a large passing comet which struck from the northwest.

When did this extra-terrestrial bombardment take place? F. A. Melton and W. Schriever estimated that it occurred during the Ice Age, or Pleistocene period. They point out that the bays are filled to a large extent with sand and silt deposits which occurred while the area was covered by the sea during the terrace-

34. Darwin, *Journal*, entry of March 30, 1835.

35. Melton and Schriever, "The Carolina Bays—Are They Meteorites Scars?" *Journal of Geology*, XLI, 1933.

forming marine invasion of the Pleistocene period.[36] A very large number of meteorites have been found, they also pointed out, in the southern Appalachians, in Virginia, North and South Carolina, Alabama, Kentucky, and Tennessee.

From the ocean bottoms comes further evidence that cosmic violence has struck the earth in by-gone ages. Surveys of the ocean bottom of the Atlantic Ocean found virtually no sediment deposits in the great flat basins on either side of the Atlantic Ridge, the long chain of mountains extending approximately down the center of the Atlantic running north and south. Instead, scientists aboard the *Atlantis* found in 1949 that these ocean bottom sediments were formed from shells and skeletons of countless small sea creatures, volcanic dust and dust drifting out over the sea from the land, and "from the ashes of burned out meteorites and cosmic dust from outer space sifting constantly down upon the earth."[37]

How could cosmic dust from outer space and the ashes from burned out meteorites have made up a substantial part of the ocean sediment?

Another expedition found, in the words of H. Pettersson, director of the Oceanographic Institute at Goteborg, "evidence of great catastrophes that have altered the face of the earth."[38]

The ocean floor bears witness of repeated global violent catastrophes. Wrote Pettersson: "Climatic catastrophes, which piled thousands of feet of ice on the higher latitudes of the continents, also covered the oceans with icebergs and ice fields at lower latitudes and chilled the surface waters even down to the Equator. Volcanic catastrophes cast rains of ash over the sea." He added: "Tectonic catastrophes raised or lowered the ocean bottom hundreds and even thousands of feet, spreading huge 'tidal' waves which destroyed plant and animal life on the coastal plains."

Has the earth been showered by meteorites on a large scale?

Samples of red clay from the Pacific floor revealed a high

36. *Ibid.*, p. 56.

37. M. Ewing, "New Discoveries on the Mid-Atlantic Ridge," *National Geographic Magazine*, November 1949.

38. Pettersson, "Exploring the Ocean Floor," *Scientific American*, August 1950.

content of nickel, and radium, though the oceans are almost totally free of those elements. Red clay contains ferruginous or iron compounds within it, causing it to appear red.

Meteorites, interestingly enough, contain iron which, unlike terrestrial iron, is mixed with nickel. Nickel is very rare in most terrestrial rocks. On the other hand, it is a major component of meteorites. Thus, Pettersson concludes that the origin of the nickel on the abyssal plains of the Pacific was in meteoric dust from "the very heavy showers of meteors in the remote past. The principal difficulty of this explanation," he hastens to add, "is that it requires a rate of accretion of meteoric dust several hundred times greater than that which astronomers, who base their estimates on visual and telescopic counts of meteors, are presently prepared to admit."

Pettersson, leader of the July 1947 Swedish expedition aboard the *Albatross,* calculated: "Assuming the average nickel content of meteoric dust to be two per cent, an approximate value for the rate of accretion of cosmic dust to the whole Earth can be worked out from these data. The result is very high—about 10,000 tons per day, or over a thousand times higher than the value computed from counting the shooting stars and estimating their mass."[39]

What does this indicate? Since the normal precipitation of meteoric dust to the earth is much less than this figure, and yet the deposits are found, the logical conclusion is that catastrophic meteoric bombardments have in the past created abnormal amounts of meteoric dust and ashes. Iron and nickel deposits point back in time to great celestial showers of meteorites—possibly even large asteroids or comets—as the cause of the tectonic ruptures of the ocean floor, of lava flows beneath the sea and on land, of great seismic disturbances, volcanic eruptions, drastic change of climate on earth, raging upheavals on land and in sea causing the extinction of vast numbers of species, perhaps also shifting the polar axis of the earth, and creating the vast ice sheets of the Pleistocene.

The evidence for cosmic upheavals both during and before

39. Pettersson, *Westward Ho with the Albatross,* p. 150.

the time of man is immense. There is not a single continent on earth or a single sea which does not witness to the scars of repeated cosmic bombardments and celestial encounters of a cataclysmic kind.

Chapter Twelve

Neanderthal Man

Many forms of animal life perished at the close of the Pleistocene. It was a time of great upheaval and incredible violence as nature seemingly went on a rampage. The havoc and destruction of all wars since mankind went to war was nothing in comparison to the widespread desolation caused by the fury of the forces unleashed in the cosmic catastrophe that befell the entire globe approximately 10,000 years ago.

At that same time early humanoids perished as well. Whether or not they were "true men" has been debated by anthropologists for decades. They were *not* homo sapiens. But they were indeed humanlike in almost every way, in some cases. What is the truth about these mysterious beings? These manlike predecessors of ours upon the earth?

How do they fit into the picture of repeated global catastrophes?

In Alaska, as the remains of an Alaskan lion was being disinterred from the earth and muck, the excavators found a flint point still frozen solid in silt. The indication was that "paleo-Indians" must have been alive at that time.

Discoveries of Paleo-Indians have been made at many other sites in the New World as well. Near the small town of Clovis, New Mexico, along the bed of an old river called the Blackwater Draw fossils of animal bones of extinct species were found over a vast area. Evidence of early "man," called "Clovis man," was also unearthed along the banks of the ancient river, and huge piles of mammoth bones stretching for miles around in every direction.

Remains of Folsom man were also found, just above the Clovis layer. Whereas Clovis man had hunted mammoths with large lance points, fluted at the base, Folsom man hunted bison with shorter fluted Folsom points. Both these tribes were alive at the close of the Ice Age, about 10,000 years ago.

The first discovery of Folsom man occurred when a black cowboy noticed bones jutting from the bank of a dried stream bed in northeastern New Mexico and found a flint projectile point unlike any he had ever seen before. J. D. Figgins, director of the Colorado Museum of Natural History learned of the discovery.

In 1927 he began his own excavation of the site and found two more projectile points. September 2nd he found a point still lodged between two ribs of the skeleton of an ancient extinct bison.

In the Sandi Mountains near Albuquerque, New Mexico, Dr. Frank C. Hibben and his team were looking for more evidence of early man. While digging in a cave, where several artifacts had been unearthed, they found the bony core of the claw of a huge ground sloth which had become extinct 10,000 years ago. As they kept on digging, luck was with them. They came upon a flint point of undoubted human origin, older than the Folsom points found elsewhere. In all, nineteen projectile points were found at the site, evidence of Sandia man. These points were longer and more primitive than the Folsom points.

Radio-carbon dates for these early Hunters—Folsom, Clovis and Sandia man—range approximately from 9,000 to 13,000 years before the present.

But what happened to them?

They disappeared. Suddenly. Unexpectedly. Even as the big game animals were wiped out by the millions, so the Paleo-Indians suddenly disappeared from view. According to the dating of radio-carbon techniques, several thousand years passed before the next human cultures appeared on the scene. These later cultures lived a more sedentary existence, picked berries and nuts, and knew agriculture. They eventually became the later Pueblo and Mound Builders of the American scene. But apparently they had no connection with the Early Hunters, the Paleo-Indians, who went before.

Writes Frank C. Hibben in *The Lost Americans:*

"With the occasional torrential showers of the closing phase of the glacial period, the bare earth of the Folsom landscape was washed away by the millions of tons. Many a Folsom point and mammoth tusk must have been sluiced away in the process." He adds, "Many campsites and kill sites on high ground must have been washed away entirely. Those in the valleys and hollows were covered so deeply that many probably will never be discovered. It was as though the cosmic forces of nature had, at the end of the age of extinct mammals and ancient hunters, dragged a covering blanket over the landscape to hide all their traces. It has only been occasionally and by accident that corners of this blanket have been turned back or torn away to reveal the story of ancient man beneath."[1]

Dr. Cyrus Ray examined the cutbank of a local stream bed near Abilene, Texas, in 1929, and noticed charcoal lenses and fragments of chipped stone protruding from the sand. As he casually glanced upward, he was startled. Above him was a huge ledge of forty feet of layered sediments in the cutbank. Down where he was, he found crude implements of early man, charcoal, bits of stone, flint points, scrapers and knives. Dating of "Abilene man" indicated they lived at the very end of the Ice Age.

At Lime Creek, Nebraska, lance points and bones were found fifty feet below the surface—again, Ice Age hunters.

Evidence of the existence of Paleo-Indians has been unearthed at many sites, now, from southern Mexico, Central America, South America, southern Canada, New Mexico, California, and every corner of the Eastern United States. From 1951 to 1957 some three thousand Paleo-Indian tools were found beneath Wisconsin age sand at Ipswich, Massachusetts. Ecuador, Peru, Argentina, and Chile also bear evidence of Ice Age hunters.

1. pp. 77-78.

How they died remains one of the colossal mysteries of science.

The destructive catastrophe also raged in Europe. The Rock of Gibraltar is intersected by many crevices and fissures, filled with bones which are broken and splintered. Bones of panther, lynx, caffir-cat, hyena, wolf, bear, rhinoceros, horse, wild boar, red deer, fallow deer, ibex, ox, hare and rabbit have been found in these fissures.

Says Prestwich, "The bones are most likely broken into thousands of fragments—none are worn or rolled, nor any of them gnawed, though so many carnivores then lived on the rock." He continues, "A great and common danger such as a great flood, alone could have driven together the animals of the plains and of the crags and caves."[2]

Found among the animal bones in some of the crevices of the Rock of Gibraltar were a human molar, some flints of the Paleolithic (Old Stone Age) man, as well as broken pieces of pottery of Neolithic man.[3]

Prestwich reported that on Corsica, Sardinia, and Sicily, as in Europe itself and upon the British Isles, broken bones of animals are found choking the crevices and fissures of rocks. Around Palermo, Sicily, the hills disclosed extraordinary quantities of bones of hippopotami "in complete hecatombs." Twenty tons of bone breccia were shipped to Marseilles to furnish charcoal for use in factories.

To account for what he found, Prestwich concluded that at the end of the Ice Age or during the Post-Glacial Period, Western Europe and the Mediterranean coasts much have been submerged and immense flooding occurred. The animals retreated, as the waters advanced, "deeper into the amphitheatre of hills until they found themselves embayed . . . the animals must have thronged together in vast multitudes, crushing into the more accessible caves, and swarming over the ground at their entrance, until overtaken by the waters and destroyed."[4]

2. *On Certain Phenomena*, p. 47-48.
3. *Ibid.*
4. *Ibid.*, pp. 51-52.

Prestwich, who is regarded as the greatest authority on the Ice Age in England, concluded, "The agency, whatever it was, must have acted with sufficient violence to smash the bones."[5] He added: "Certain communities of early man must have suffered in the general catastrophe."[6]

The Columbia Plateau of Washington, Oregon and Idaho, occupies about two hundred thousand square miles. It is formed by lava flows which reach depths of hundreds and thousands of feet. At places the lava reaches a depth of 5,000 feet or more. The lava deposits appear very fresh to the observer. Apparently lava flowed as a mighty flood in that region, only a few thousands of years in the past.

In 1889, when boring an artesian well at Nampa, Idaho, drillers extracted a small figurine of baked clay from a depth of 320 feet after piercing basalt lava fifteen feet thick. No one has challenged the finding, except on preconceived opinions based on the a priori assumption that the lava must be of extreme antiquity.

During middle Pleistocene times a strange breed of early man arose. They had large brains, but primitive features which included lower cranial vaults, heavy ridge bones over the eyes and sharply receding chins. They were stocky and heavy limbed. These were the classic Neanderthal men.

Neanderthal man was almost human in many respects. He dwelled in caves, hunted wild game to survive, and crudely buried his dead.

But his differences outweighted his similarities, according to anthropologists. The paleontological evidence shows that the society of Neanderthal man was extremely primitive, he created no lasting forms of art, and was not able to articulate a true language.

Neanderthal's remains have been unearthed at locations widely scattered in Europe. His remains were first found at the Neander Valley, Germany, near a tributary stream of the Rhine River. In 1856 workmen were quarrying for limestone in the

5. p. 67.
6. p. 74.

area and blasted open a small cave about 60 feet above the stream. As they dug into the floor of the cave, they unearthed ancient bones of some creature—the skullcap, ribs, part of the pelvis, and some limb bones were saved.

The bones were shown to a local science teacher, J. K. Fuhlrott, who realized they came from a most extraordinary man. He concluded they belonged to some poor brute who perished in the Noachian flood.

In the year 1908 a magnificent series of Neanderthal fossils was found. The skeleton of an old man was unearthed in a cave near the village of La Chappelle-aux-Saints. At a nearby cave at Le Moustier, a skeleton of a Neanderthal youth was uncovered. Near La Ferrassie an adult male Neanderthal and later the remains of several children were found.

As the years passed, Neanderthal remains were found all over Europe, from Rumania and the Crimea to the western lands of Spain and the Isle of Jersey. In 1921 bones resembling Neanderthal were found in Northern Rhodesia, from a cave in Broken Hill, just north of the Zambesi River.

In 1931 fragments of eleven very primitive men were unearthed from the banks of the Solo River, on the island of Java. The fossils suggested a relationship with the Neanderthals, although the skulls were even somewhat thicker. Later the fossil remains of a Neanderthal boy were found in the desolate Alai Mountains of south central Russia.

During the 1930s a joint Anglo-American expedition was digging for fossils in Palestine, in the slopes of Mount Carmel. At Mugharet et-Tabun they found a female skeleton which was definitely Neanderthal in type, but with a slightly higher than usual skull and a more verticle forehead. Then, from a second cave called Mugharet es-Skhul they found the remains of 10 individuals, some resembling Neanderthals, and some a bit more advanced. One approached the appearance of modern man a little—he had the Neanderthal thick brow ridge, but a steeper forehead, a more delicate jaw, and the chin was more pronounced.

All in all, Neanderthal man seems quite human. William Straus of Johns Hopkins University and A. J. E. Cave of St.

Bartholomew's Hospital Medical College in London, examined the fossil from La Chappelle-aux-Saints, and wrote:

"If he could be reincarnated and placed in a New York subway—provided that he were bathed, shaved and dressed in modern clothing—it is doubtful whether he would attract any more attention than some of its other denizens."[7]

Anthropologists believe that Neanderthal man appeared on earth about 100,000 years ago. Anthropologists have learned a great deal about these primitive men, from surrounding geological deposits, pollen found in the deposits, which can be identified under a microscope, and stone tools found at the site. Wherever early man lived, he often left an abundance of stone tools around. Writes Constable, "One cave in Lebanon, occupied by men for an estimated 50,000 years, has yielded more than a million flints."[8]

Many Neanderthal peoples utilized a technique of making stone tools called the Acheulean. In the Acheulean tradition, the tool was sculpted from a stone by chipping away until the rock was the desired shape. These tools were first discovered at the French town of Saint Acheul, near Amiens. The Acheulean tradition included an object called a hand ax, a flat, oval or pear-shaped tool with cutting edges along each side of its 5 or 6 inch length.

Neanderthal man lived during the Pleistocene Ice Age. He was one of the early Hunters. He must have been a first rate hunter and subsisted largely off the herds of reindeer, woolly rhinos and mammoths.

Nevertheless, the Neanderthals remained limited in many ways. They did not reach the Americas, although a few strong individuals may have reached the southern part of Siberia. George Constable says of them: "And in many other ways, they did not measure up to the men who came after them. The Neanderthals never really grasped the potential of bone as a material for tools; they did not know about the art of sewing, which would require bone needles; they did not know how to

7. George Constable, *The Neanderthals*, p. 27.
8. *Ibid.*, p. 41.

weave baskets or make pottery; and their stone tools were inferior to those of the people who lived after them."[9]

In 1971 Philip Lieberman of the University of Connecticut and Edmund Crelin of Yale began investigating the language capabilities of Neanderthal man. They made a series of measurements of the neck vertebrae, and base of the skull, of the fossil found at La Chapelle-aux-Saints. From this information they determined the length of the vocal tract that produces speech. The measurements suggested that Neanderthal man lacked a modern pharynx. As a result, he was unable to utter the vowel sounds in the words bar, boo, beep, and bought. He could not form the consonnants *g* and *k*. Compared to modern man, his vocabulary must have been very limited, consisting of fewer consonants and a narrow choice of vowel sounds.

On the other hand, Rhodesia man had a slightly more modern pharynx, according to Lieberman and Crelin. Their findings, however, are extremely controversial.

Evidence from Neanderthal sites shows that whatever else they were, they were cannibals. They sometimes killed one another and ate one another. In 1899 at Krapina, Yugoslavia, the mutilated remains of some 20 Neanderthals including men, women and children were found. Skulls had been smashed in. Limbs had been split lengthwise, apparently so the marrow could be sucked out. There were traces of charring, perhaps indicating that the meat had been cooked before being eaten.

In 1965 in a cave at Hortus, France, the charred and shattered human bones of about 20 Neanderthals were found. The human bones were mixed up with animal bones, as if the ancient inhabitants of the cave drew no distinction between eating human and animal flesh.

Why did Neanderthals eat human flesh? Did hunger drive them to this end? Anthropologists believe the answer lies more in the realm of ritual. As in some primitive societies today, natives believe that they can acquire strength and courage by eating the flesh of an enemy. As if to support this contention, at the Solo River in Java 11 skulls were dug up, but no other re-

9. *Ibid.*, p. 58.

mains were found except two leg bones. The facial bones had been smashed off every skull. Not a single jaw or tooth remained. The opening where the spinal cord connects with the brain—called the foramen magnum—in all but two of the skulls had been widened by hacking with tools. This discovery may indicate that like modern cannibals, the Neanderthals widened the opening to the skull so they could reach into it and scoop out the brains and eat them.

Skulls without bodies have been found also in Europe, leading researchers to think there may have existed a worldwide Neanderthal skull cult during Pleistocene times. At Ehringsdorf, Germany, the jaw of an adult and the remains of a 10-year-old child and the cranium of a woman were dug up. The woman had been clubbed on the forehead and decapitated. The foramen magnum had been enlarged, as at Solo River. Similarly at Monte Circeo in Italy workmen found in a cave a single skull, surrounded by an oval ring of bones. The skull was Neanderthal. The man had been killed by a blow to the temple, and once again, the foramen magnum had been enlarged.

Such barbaric customs may seem horrible, but no less so than some tribes in the world today. The head-hunting tribes of New Guinea have a custom where when a child is born they kill a man from another tribe. The father of the infant beheads the enemy, opens the foramen magnum, extracts the brain, bakes it with starch made from the pith of a palm, and eats it. The tribe believes that the newborn child cannot be given a name unless this ritual takes place.

Whatever happened to the Neaderthal race?

In 1907 a caravan travelling through central Asia prepared to make camp. Suddenly a member of the group uttered a startled yelp. On the crest of a ridge silhouetted against the setting sun stood a huge slouching figure of a man or ape, or man-ape. For a while the shaggy being stared back, and then lumbered off. The travelers gave chase, but were outdistanced and never caught it.

This was the first encounter recorded between modern man and the so-called Asian beastmen, called Yetis or Abominable Snowmen.

In 1921 an English mountain climber, Colonel Howard Bury, spotted enormous footprints in the snow during a trip to Mount Everest. Since then the legend of the Abominable Snowmen has snowballed. Today Soviet academicians take the strange tales of travellers seriously. They have compiled a thick dossier on the subject.

According to most reports, the Abominable Snowmen walk with bent knees; they have large jaws and sloping foreheads. They have naked, stooped bodies which are sparcely covered with reddish hair. They cannot talk or speak, but utter only cries like some animal. They subsist by eating a diet of small game and roots.

Says George Constable:

"A few Soviet anthropologists feel that enough is known about the Abominable Snowmen to indicate their real identity: they are the last surviving Neanderthals. Presumably these half-human relics of the ice age have managed to hang on in the Asian heartland because the harsh climate suits their tastes and, more important, because ordinary mortals do not covet the region enough to kill them off."[10]

Constable is skeptical of the story, himself, mentioning no trustworthy photographs have ever been taken.

Nevertheless, something did happen to the Neanderthals—for they perished as a race. They disappeared from the world scene. Writes Constable:

"The disappearance of the Neanderthals seems to have the makings of a soul-stirring play, with the world as a stage, and the happiest ending imaginable—the ascendancy of ourselves. The only trouble is that no one really knows what happened. The actors performed behind a lowered curtain, and all anyone has been allowed to see is the beginning and end. The twists and turns of the drama that brought about the replacement of the Neanderthals constitute the greatest of all prehistoric mysteries."[11]

At many sites, Neanderthal layers fade to sterile layers which

10. *Ibid.*, p. 123.
11. *Ibid.*, p. 124.

are followed by Cro-Magnon layers. It was once thought that the Neanderthal race, therefore, became extinct before Cro-Magnon man came on the scene. However, there are exceptions to this sequence. At some sites, later layers show that toolmaking became better rather than declined. Sometimes there is no break between Neanderthal layers and Cro-Magnon tools, indicating that the site was occupied continuously.

The tools of the Cro-Magnon culture were definitely superior to Neanderthal tools. The evidence is that a change-over occurred very quickly.

No Neanderthal fossil has been given a more recent date than 40,000 years ago. The oldest fossil of Cro-Magnon man dates to about 26,000 years ago. Says Constable, "There is a fossil gap, and it holds secure the Neanderthal mystery."[12]

What happened during this 15,000 year gap? On one side of the gap are the ancient, brutish Neanderthals, with their heavy brow ridges—and on the other side are the distinctly modern appearing Cro-Magnons, with definite artistic ability.

The Neanderthals apparently perished during the Wurm glaciation. Some of them may have survived, and intermarried with later Cro-Magnon types. Neanderthal features may be occasionally seen by strolling through a crowd at an airlines ticket counter, at a subway station, or waiting for a local bus. Could the Neanderthals, or a few of their surviving descendants, have become the famed *Nephilim* in the Biblical record?

Neanderthal man obviously lived upon the earth long before the time of the Biblical Adam, who, we are told by the Scriptures, was created in the Garden of Eden some 6000 years ago.

Cro-Magnon man, also, lived upon the earth long before the Biblical Adam and Eve. They date from about 26,000 years ago to perhaps 10,000 years ago.

The *Nephilim* are mentioned several times in the Old Testament. We read: "The *Nephilim* were on the earth in those days; and also after that, when the sons of God [i.e., descendants of Adam through his son Seth] came in unto the daughters of men,

12. p. 127.

and they bare children to them, the same became mighty men which were of old, men of renown" (Genesis 6:4).

The King James Version translates *Nephilim* as "giants." The Hebrew word *nephil* literally means "bully" or "tyrant." They must have been a fearsome race.

While the children of Adam were multiplying upon the earth, in a veritable population explosion, says the *Revised Standard Version*, "The Nephilim were on the earth in those days." Perhaps they were descended from pre-Adamic races upon the earth. Perhaps they came from the ancient Neanderthal types of millennia before.

The Nephilim were named as a giant race in Numbers 13:33. There, however, the context implies that the people found by the spies were like the very Nephilim of old—that is, similar to them.

The Septuagint translated the Hebrew *Nephilim* in Genesis 6 as "giants." Interestingly, the ancient Greeks had a myth about a group of giants known as Titans, against whom Zeus had to do battle. The primeval titans—the Nephilim—may also have been descended from the line of Cain. These ancient texts are not clearly understood today, and much more archaeological research is needed to bring them into clear and consistent focus.

Nevertheless, the evidence shows that no fossil link or intermediate between Neanderthals and Cro-Magnons has ever been found in Western Europe, one of the richest fossil fields in the world. No fossil even comes close to fitting into the middle ground. There is no link. Most scientists therefore shut the western Neanderthals out of the line leading to Cro-Magnon man.

What led to the demise of the Neanderthals? Many theories have been suggested, including invading Cro-Magnons, rickets due to lack of vitamin D, and ecological catastrophe.

Judging from the rigors that existed upon earth, at the beginning and at the end of the Pleistocene Ice Age, it would seem very likely that the demise of the Neanderthal man can readily be explained in terms of a global, universal catastrophe. That is, Neanderthal man in Western Europe was very likely exterminated in a series of holocausts which struck the earth about 40,000 years ago, during the Wurm glaciation.

There can be no doubt that preAdamic races of mankind—from the so-called man apes of the Australopithecines and Homo erectus to Neanderthal man and Cro-Magnon man—walked the earth before Adam was ever created.

If we take the Biblical account literally—and many other ancient peoples possess legends of mankind being righteous in the past, before a "fall," and living in a tropical paradise such as Eden—then Adam and Eve were a "new creation," different from all their predecessors on this planet.

According to the Hindoos, in the first age man was free from evil and disease, had all his wishes granted, and lived long. The Greek traditions tell us that in the first age man was free from evil and trouble, went about naked, and enjoyed communion with the gods. The Chinese have a tradition of a happy age, when men had an abundance of food, surrounded by peaceful animals. Mongolians and Tibetans have similar stories. Around the world different tribes have traditions of a more civilized state or condition. The original story of the Garden of Eden, was, no doubt, told by Adam to Methuselah, and by Methuselah to Noah, and by Noah to his sons. In the cultures that originated among the descendants of Noah's children the story remained intact in its rudimentary form, although it became grossly modified as to detail.

All these traditions go back to the same primeval event—the Garden of Eden as matter-of-factly set forth in the Scriptures.

As if to corroborate the Biblical account, in 1932 Dr. E. A. Speiser of the University Museum of Pennsylvania, was excavating 12 miles north of Nineveh. Near the bottom of the Tepe Gawra Mound he found a seal, which he dated at about 3500 B.C. and called "strongly suggestive of the Adam and Eve story"—it was of a naked man and a naked woman, walking as if utterly downcast and broken-hearted, followed by a serpent! The seal is about an inch in diameter, engraved on stone, and is called the "Adam and Eve" Seal.

Another seal found among ancient Babylonian tablets, now in the British Museum, seems definitely to refer to the Garden of Eden story. In the center is a Tree; on the right, a Man; on the left, a Woman, plucking Fruit; behind the Woman, a Serpent, standing erect, as if whispering to her. "These old records, carved on stone and clay, at the very dawn of history, in the original home of man, preserved under the dust of the ages, and now at last brought to light by the spade of the archaeologist, are evidence that the main features of the Biblical story of Adam became deeply fixed in the thought of primitive man."[13]

Also, as if to support the Biblical record, the Sumerian King List shows eight antediluvian kings before the flood, and begins with the statement, "When kingship was lowered from heaven the kingship was in Eridu."[14] A later form of the same list preserved by Berossus, priest of Marduk at Babylon under Antiochus I (281-261 B.C.) contains ten names. This tradition of ten antediluvian kings may correspond with the biblical record of ten patriarchs from Adam to Noah.[15]

Is the Garden of Eden story historical? Was there ever such a man as "Adam"? Thus far we have seen that the Biblical record has been proven to be historical when it discussed such prodigies as Joshua's Long Day, the Tower of Babel, Sodom and Gomorrah, the Exodus, and the Noachian Deluge. Why should we doubt it this time? The Biblical chronicle states that there was a town called "Adam," obviously named after the progenitor of the modern human race (Joshua 3:16). The city of Adam today may be identified with Tell ed-Damiyeh, some fifteen miles up the Jordan River from Jericho.

Adam and Eve, then, were a new creation of "Man." They were modern man in every sense of the word. They had full intelligence. Adam could give names to all the creatures brought before him (Genesis 2:19-20). He was capable of full thought, rationality, and the ability to make judgments.

---

13. Halley, *Bible Handbook,* p. 72.
14. Finegan, *Light from the Ancient Past,* p. 29.
15. *Ibid.,* p. 30.

In Genesis 2:7 we read: "And the Lord God formed man of the dust of the ground, and breathed into his nostrils the breath of life; *and man became a living soul.*" Modern man is uniquely different from all his predecessors. He possesses a "spirit" which makes him special, which separates modern man, who was formed and fashioned after God's very own image and likeness (Genesis 1:26-27), from all his wide ranging predecessors. Some of them, like Cro-Magnon man, may have looked like modern man. Some of them may have even had extremely primitive societies, and built very crude communal dwelling places. But none of them, apparently, had the "spirit" in man which makes him truly unique among all God's creations. As Elihu told Job, "But there is a *spirit in man:* and the inspiration of the Almighty giveth them *understanding*" (Job 32:8).

This spirit was absent from Adam's predecessors. They lacked understanding. They were apparently like clay images, a potter's vessel, upon which the Hand of the Almighty sculpted and fashioned their form, attributes, and being. But they were not fully conscious of their own self existence as we are self-aware and conscious. They were similar to "models," made of clay. They were forerunners—they were, if you please, clay prototypes of true man. They might be called, in the strict sense of the word, "experimental models" which served a purpose and were then cast aside, or allowed to die out, much as all animals die sooner or later. They did not possess the "spark" of divinity—the "spirit in man"—which makes him unique and sets him apart from the birds, fish, and beasts of the earth.

True man is different from all his predecessors because he possesses a *mind.* Other man-like beings possessed brains, but modern man possesses the power of mind. It distinguishes him from all the animals of the earth. True man's capacity for intelligent thinking far surpasses all animals. He learns all he needs to in order to survive, and then keeps on learning. His gift of language gives him the ability to grasp and handle abstract ideas, to formulate new theories about his own existence, to generate new mental concepts, to wrestle with the very ideas of creation, origin, God, the purpose of life. Man is capable of *original* thought. He doesn't merely live out his days carrying on a pattern of instinctive behavior. Generation after generation of birds build the same type of nest; beavers build the same dams their predecessors built; there is no originality. But modern man can think rationally, can progress from the methods of his forebears. He can think up *new* ideas, new concepts, he can imagine, he can create.

True man has the capacity to wonder about and investigate himself. He inquires about his origin, his future. He can appreciate beautiful art, music, humor, satire, creativity.

As Pierre Teilhard de Chardin wrote: "Admittedly the animal knows. But it cannot know that it knows . . . In consequence it is denied access to a whole domain of reality in which we can move freely. We are separated by a chasm—or a threshold—which it cannot cross. Because we are reflective we are not only different but quite other. It is not a matter of change of degree, but a change of nature, resulting from a change of state."[16]

The vast gap between animal brain and the mind of true man has never been satisfactorily bridged. We are indeed unique. We have the ability to be self-aware, and our self-awareness is the most compelling of all realities. As individuals, we can experience our own unique self-awareness and individuality. We possess the wonderful divine gift of a conscious existence.

The human mind—the product of the "spirit in man" which God imparted to Adam and all his descendants—is the great gift which sets modern man apart from all the Pre-Adamic races and breeds uncovered by the spade or archaeology and anthropology.

16. *The Phenomenon of Man,* in *Evolution of Man,* ed. by Louise B. Young, 1970, p. 316.

Chapter Thirteen

Dinosaur Extinctions

The earth was once very different from what we see around us today. Seventy million years ago great saurian reptiles roamed the marshes and shorelines and plains of the world.

The world of that time was known as the Mesozoic Era. Geologists divide the Mesozoic into three periods—the Triassic, the Jurassic, and the Cretaceous.

That was the time of the great dinosaurs. In the Mesozoic Era reptiles took over land, air and sea. If you were to be transported to the world of Mesozoic times, in a time capsule, you would be astonished. Nothing would look familiar.

The Mesozoic was a time of transition and change in the plant realm. Revolutionary changes in plant life occurred. Very few types of plants alive today existed then. Ferns were characteristic of the Mesozoic Era, and plants called "cycads." These were gymnosperms which bore true flowers quite similar to flowers of more recent plants of tropical regions. Cycads were so prevalent in the Jurassic that it has been called the "Age of Cycads."

Trees of the Mesozoic were often similar to palm trees, small, medium and large. Ancient conifers appeared throughout the world of that time. The first true pine trees appeared in the Late Jurassic and spread widely during Cretaceous times. The giant sequoia was common by the Cretaceous period.

During the mid-Cretaceous flowering plants, or angiosperms, appeared and rapidly spread over the world. Literally thousands of species including many that still exist suddenly leaped into prominence. Forests of angiosperms contributed to the formation of coal deposits during Cretaceous times.

Mesozoic seas contained shrimps, crabs, crayfish, and lobsters. The first true crabs and earliest barnacles appeared during the Jurassic period.

But the strangest thing to greet your eyes would have been the giant reptiles. These huge reptiles became rulers over the earth. They spread dramatically. In the Triassic period, the first sea-dwelling Plesiosaurs and Ichthyosaurs, along with the first crocodiles, appeared. The long-necked Plesiosaurs caught fish, it is believed, by snapping out their elongated necks, much as seasnakes do today. Ichthyosaurs resembled in body form fast-swimming fishes and porpoises. Large ones ranged up to thirty feet in length. They were very fishlike in appearance and had a completely boneless dorsal fin.

The Plesiosaurs and Mosasaurs were impressive sea creatures. The Plesiosaurs, with short, stubby body and tail, somewhat like a turtle but without the shell, generally had very long necks. Mosasaurs, which attained lengths of thirty feet, were giant sea lizards which could snap off an entire flipper of the huge turtle Archelon which lived in the sea at that time.

On the land, both small and large dinosaurs roamed. Among the sauropods were the famous Brontosaurus, an animal which reached a length of eighty feet, one of the largest land animals ever to have lived. It dieted largely on soft sea plants and vegetation. Related to the huge Brontosaurus were Brachiosaurus and Diplodocus. These creatures were also capable of being quite at home in the water. Despite their huge size, these monsters of the ancient world had only a whiplash tail to use as a defensive weapon.

Among the huge land-dwelling dinosaurs were the carnivorous flesh-eaters. These varied greatly in size, ranging from the size of a chicken to the terrifying Tyrannosaurus Rex, forty feet long, standing twenty feet high. With an enormous head and teeth and very small forelegs, it stood upon its two hindlegs and balanced with its tail. The greatest land carnivore of all time, it must have been a fearsome sight to behold.

Duck-billed dinosaurs, such as Edmontosaurus, appear to have been dwellers of swampy areas. A quick dash to the water may have saved their lives many times from an attacking Tyrannosaurus. Although they, too, were often very large, they were inoffensive plant eaters.

Stegosaurs and Ankylosaurs utilized heavy bony plates for defense from the carnivorous dinosaurs. The Stegosaurus had a row of large bony plates down its back and spikes on its tail for protection from predators. The Ankylosaurus was squat, very heavy and almost completely protected by bony plates within its skin—in appearance something like a land-dwelling turtle or mole. It probably had much power in its tail.

The Ceratopsians, or horned dinosaurs, could defend themselves readily. Similar in shape to a modern rhinocerous they were a formidable foe in any encounter. Triceratops, one of these mobile juggernauts, was about twenty-five feet long, nearly a third of this length taken up by the head. Half the length of the skull was formed by a bony shell or hood that protected the neck. Two imposing horns which could impale any lethargic foe came straight out from the head, side by side.

Even in the skies, the reptiles dominated that ancient world. The Pterosaurs, flying reptiles, flourished from the early Jurassic to the end of the Mesozoic. They possessed a skin membrane, a wing supported in front by forearm bones and the greatly enlarged fourth digit of the forefoot and attached to the body behind. Most of them were rather small, some about the size of a sparrow. But Pteranodon of the late Cretaceous was a huge flying monster—he was toothless, but had a very long bill and a bony extension from the back of his head. His wing-span was some twenty five feet across, greater than any known bird today. Pteranodon apparently preyed upon small schools of fish swimming near the surface of lakes and lagoons.

Interestingly, remains of dinosaurs have even been found high up in the Arctic Circle, in the remote islands of Spitsbergen. In 1960 a party of geologists led by Professor Anatol Heintz of the University of Oslo discovered a number of huge footprints, each one three-toed and between 25 and 30 inches long. There was no doubt they were viewing the footprints of a large dinosaur. Apparently left millions of years ago, the prints proved to be of a gigantic blunt-toed plant-eating dinosaur, Iguanodon. This creature stood 15 feet tall and walked erect on two ponderous hind legs. The spot where the tracks were found is only 800 miles from the North Pole!

This find convinced many geologists that the world of the dinosaurs must have been essentially tropical with mild climates existing throughout the globe, and no polar ice caps. The suggestion has also been made that since a bulky plant-devouring creature such as Iguanodon lived in an area where today there is no sunlight four months of the year, and since vegetation requires daily sunlight to flourish, perhaps the North Pole in that ancient world was located somewhere else. The study of magnetism in rocks seems to demonstrate that in former geologic ages the poles were not located where they are now.

What was the world like in the Mesozoic Era? The greater part of the earth was relatively flat. The great mountain ranges had not yet been pushed up, such as the Andes, Rockies, Alps and Himalayas. Vast, shallow inland seas existed.

Weather conditions were much the same worldwide. There was mild cooling in winter and slight warming in summer, but seasons as we know them did not exist.

Besides the dinosaurs, the world of that age was inhabited by snakes up to 50 feet long, and giant deadly crocodiles with six-foot jaws.

These incredible creatures ruled supreme in the world for 135,000,000 years.

But then they all died out. Something happened to drastically alter that ancient, peaceful, serene world. The great dinosaurs, which had been king, became extinct.

Says Edwin H. Colbert: "No one is sure why the dinosaurs became extinct. Some 70 million years ago they began dying off; after a few million more years, dinosaur evidence vanishes totally from the fossil record"[1].

Declared J. D. Ratcliff, in "The Case of the Vanishing

1. *Marvels and Mysteries of the World Around Us,* "When Dinosaurs Roamed the Arctic," p. 33.

Dinosaurs": "The greatest riddle about the dinosaurs is why they vanished from the earth they had dominated so long . . . Whatever disaster struck them down was global in extent; they had disappeared completely by the end of the Mesozoic period"[2].

"The close of the Cretaceous, and thus of the Mesozoic Era, witnessed a profound change in the life of the world"[3].

The reptiles which dominated earth, sky and sea all vanished. Dinosaurs, Pterosaurs, Ichthyosaurs, Plesiosaurs and Mosasaurs all disappeared.

Was the demise of the dinosaurs accompanied by global cataclysm? What does the evidence show?

Under normal conditions comparatively few fossil remains are preserved for posterity to someday uncover. But the record written in the rocks of the earth reveals that some geologic formations contain uncounted millions of fossils, indicating millions of creatures were buried at the same time.

In the *Journal of Paleontology,* N.D. Newell points out that Robert Broom, a paleontologist of South Africa, estimated there are 800,000,000,000 skeletons of vertebrate animals in the Darroo formation[4].

Such immense fossil graveyards are found around the world. In Alberta, Canada, a rich bed of fossil dinosaurs has been found east of Steveville. Many fine skeletons of dinosaurs and other reptiles have been quarried from a fifteen mile stretch of a local river in that region, a veritable "dinosaurian graveyard."

The Morrison Formation in Wyoming has yielded rich deposits of dinosaur remains. Reported W. D. Matthews: "In the Bone-Cabin Quarry . . . we came across a veritable Noah's ark deposit, a perfect museum of all the animals of the period.

"Here are the largest of the giant dinosaurs closely mingled with the remains of the smaller but powerful carnivorous dinosaurs which preyed upon them, also those of the slow and

2. *Our Amazing World of Nature,* p. 285.
3. *The Illustrated Library of Nature,* vol. 15, p. 1806.
4. Newell, N.D., "Adequacy of the Fossil Record," May 1959, *Journal of Paleontology,* p. 492.

heavy moving armored dinosaurs of the period, as well as the lightest and most bird-like of the dinosaurs.

"Finely rounded, complete limbs from eight to ten feet in length are found, especially those of the carnivorous dinosaurs, perfect even to the sharply pointed and recurved tips of their toes"[5].

For such perfect perservation burial was necessary immediately. To find so many skeletons so closely mingled indicates very unusual, ie., catastrophic conditions, which caught the dinosaurs by surprise and either forced them to group together seeking shelter, or brought them together in heaps after their death.

Carl Dunbar writes of the demise of hapless millions of dinosaurs and the end of that distinguished era: "It is as if the curtain were rung down suddenly on the stage where all the leading roles were taken by reptiles, especially dinosaurs, in great numbers and bewildering variety, and rose again immediately to reveal the same setting but an entirely new cast, a cast in which the dinosaurs do not appear at all, other reptiles are mere supernumeraries and the leading parts are all played by mammals"[6]. Imagine the dramatic scene. In the theatre of that ancient world, the supreme kings and bullying tyrants were those incredible dinosaurs—Tyrranosaurus, Brontosaurus, Plesiosaurus, Mosasarus, Tricetatops, and a host of other leading figures. They reigned supreme on earth and in the seas. The Pterosaurs and other flying reptiles ruled the skies. They had done so for millions of years.

But then with sudden swiftness they all vanished from the scene. They all disappeared. They left not a single survivor. They perished on all continents. They vanished from north, south, east and west. Their graveyards are found around the world, in California, Colorado, Nebraska, Canada, Belgium, India, South Africa, Australia.

At the end of the Mesozoic Era, great changes occurred in the fauna of the world. Almost all fossiliferous areas show that

5. *Dinosaurs,* pp. 136-138.
6. Dunbar, *Historical Geology,* p. 426.

large groups were exterminated on the land and in the oceans. Even the ammonite cephalopods, the belemnites, the large rudistid pelecypods, and ancient oysterlike pelecypods became extinct.

Vast changes also occurred in the flora of the world. After mid-Cretaceous times the chief, dominant plants were no longer the ferns and cycads, but rather the flowering angiosperms.

The Cretaceous period terminated in the Rocky Mountain Revolution. Large mountain ranges were raised at that time, including the Alps, Himalayas and Andes. The mountain ranges bordering the Pacific, and the granitic masses of the Andes and Rockies, are mostly of Cretaceous age.

Climate also was affected. Large lava flows and igneous activity, erupting volcanoes and earthquake action occurred over vast areas. Immense flooding of low-lying continental basins occurred. Says Stokes in *Essentials of Earth History:* "The degree to which Cretaceous seas rose and covered the African continent lends weight to the possibility that the rise in sea level was world-wide and not merely a matter of subsidence of individual continents"[7].

A major breakup of continental land masses occurred during the mid-Mesozoic times. Until the Cretaceous period, there was no South Atlantic Ocean. The Indian Ocean may also date from Cretaceous time.

New oceans were formed, new mountain ranges were raised up, as the continents broke apart. During that same time, old life forms were destroyed and new life forms were created to replace them. These periods of macro-changes in the environment were also periods of "sudden multiple creations" of new life forms—"new and virile forms which often seem to have sprung into existence from nowhere . . . and to have become dominant almost simultaneously over a large part of the world"[8].

Stokes points out that during the extensive Cretaceous

7. p. 258.
8. Arkell, W. J., 1957, "Introduction to Mesozoic Ammonoidea, p. 81-129, in Moore, R.C. Editor, *Treatise on Invertebrate Paleontology.*

floodings, at least 30 percent of the continents were submerged and many species were destroyed. Great climatic changes occurred.

The destruction of the world-ruling dinosaurs, after a reign of 135,000,000 years, seems impossible to believe. Yet it happened. Their extinction must have been dramatic.

Many theories have been proposed—and many disposed of—to account for so tremendous an event. Did egg-laying mammals exterminate the great saurian reptiles? It seems impossible. Did climate changes? No doubt climate fluctuations and changes played an important part—but what, then, triggered the vast changes in climate? Did mountain-building cause widespread changes of climate? Then what accounted for the sudden onset of vast mountain-building?

Was the break up of large land masses responsible? But what, then, triggered the break up of the primeval continents?

Some of the theories to explain the global destruction and extinction of dinosaurs deal with astronomical events, including increased penetration of cosmic rays to the earth, and a global collision with a giant meteor.

William Stokes says: "Even more spectacular is the theory that the impact effects of a tremendous meteor from space may have killed all dinosaurs simultaneously over the entire earth. Heat and shock waves, it is suggested, might wreak more destruction among large animals that could find no shelter than among smaller animals"[9].

Carl O. Dunbar asserts: "It is difficult to account for the simultaneous extinction of great tribes of animals so diverse in relationships and in habits of life. Perhaps no single cause was responsible. The great restriction and final disappearance of the epeiric seas at the end of the era, the rise of highlands from Alaska to Patagonia, a sharp drop in the temperature accompanying the Laramide uplift, the vanishing of the swampy lowlands, and the vastly changed plant world have all been invoked to account for the extinction, and the consequent rising of the weak and lowly into new kingdoms. Whatever the cause,

9. *Essentials of Earth History,* p. 441.

the latest Mesozoic was a time of trial when many of the hosts were 'tried in the balance and found wanting'—wanting in adaptiveness to the new environment. Walther has picturesquely called it 'The time of the great dying' "[10].

But what caused the phenomena mentioned by Dunbar? Derek V. Ager points out: "The greatest problems in the fossil records, however, are the sudden extinctions. . . . For any one ecological group, such as the dinosaurs, it is comparatively easy to find a possible cause. It is much less easy when one has to explain the simultaneous extinction of several unrelated groups, ranging from ammonites to pterodactyls, living in different habitats at the end of the Mesozoic"[11].

The theories advanced to account for such widespread extinctions fall short. Most of them relate to climatic oscillations and the composition of the earth's atmosphere. These, in turn, seem to point to extraterrestrial phenomena. Says Ager: "We are always forced back on seeking some control outside and greater than the earth"[12].

Uniformitarian principles are inadequate to account for such massive and overwhelming extinctions globally. Derek Ager admits, "I feel that we rely too much on the present state of affairs, too much on uniformitarianism, when interpreting the fossil record, especially in those groups that are now completely extinct or but a shadow of their former selves"[13].

Professor Harold C. Urey, Nobel prize winning biochemist, strongly supports *extraterrestrial* causes for mass extinctions. Rare collisions between earth and comets, he suggests, produced vast quantities of energy resulting in high temperatures and high humidities that may have had a disastrous effect on land and marine faunas.

The dinosaurs lasted upon earth, we are told, for over one hundred million years. And yet they perished from off the earth in less than one million years.

10. *Historical Geology,* p. 348.
11. Ager, *The Nature of the Stratigraphic Record,* 1973, pp. 20-21.
12. *Ibid.,* p. 25.
13. *Ibid.,* p. 26.

Writes Jacques Bergier: "Furthermore, it is impossible to pretend that they represented an evolutionary failure: any species that lasts a hundred million years must be considered fully adapted. Yet few species that were contemporaries of those reptiles survive—for example, certain crabs, which have not changed in three hundred million years. In fact, in less than one million years the giant reptiles entirely disappeared.

"How and why?

"We can scarcely maintain that it was because of a change in climate; for even when the climate changes, the oceans hardly vary, and many of these reptiles lived in the oceans.

"It is impossible to believe that a higher form of life was able to exterminate them. This would have required a considerable army, whose traces we would certainly have found.

"One amusing hypothesis is that our ancestors, the mammals, might have fed on dinosaur eggs. But it is only that: an amusing hypothesis: the icthyosaurs deposited their eggs in the oceans, out of their adversaries' reach.

"It has been said that the grasses changed, and that the new grasses were too tough for the big reptiles. A completely unlikely hypothesis: large numbers of vegetation types survived, on which they could have fed perfectly well"[14].

None of these answers hold water. What then did happen?

Two Soviet scientists, V. I. Krasovkii and I.S. Chklovski, both of whom are eminent astrophysicists, explain the end of the dinosaurs by hypothesizing a star explosion occurred at a relatively small distance from our solar system—a supernova at five or ten parsecs from us that would have increased the density of radiations coming from space.

The English radio astronomer Hanbury Brown lends credence to this theory. He believes he has detected traces of the explosion of a supernova fifty thousand years ago at a distance of only forty parsecs from our solar system.

Two U.S. scientists have also studied the problem, K. D. Terry of the University of Kansas, and W. H. Tucker of Rice

14. Bergier, *Extraterrestrial Visitations from Prehistoric Times to the Present*, pp. 1-2.

University. They have observed stars that actually produce such radiation bombardments when they explode. Says Bergier, "It is possible that seventy million years ago a violent bombardment may have coincided with a diminution in the earth's magnetic field, bringing about a wave of mutations in which the dinosaurs died . . ."[15].

In the opinon of Bergier, "The destruction of the dinosaurs certainly came from the cosmos and not from our solar system"[16]. He goes on to speculate that these explosions of supernova may have been controlled by superbeings. In 1957 in a broadcast on French television he asserted that the star explosion that killed the dinosaurs was deliberately induced, "designed to set off a slow process of evolution leading to intelligent life; that we were created by extremely powerful beings. Knowledgeable both of the laws of physics and of the laws of genetics, these beings—who could truly be called gods—set in motion a series of events that will not stop with man but will continue until this evolution results in other gods, beings equal to their creators"[17].

Needless to say, his hypothesis received an immense uproar. But perhaps he was closer to the truth than even he suspected. We will discuss this possibility in a subsequent chapter. There may be something in the hypothesis that a supernova close to the solar system exploded about the end of the Mesozoic and triggered the massive dying of the dinosaurs and other forms of life on earth.

The cause definitely seems to have been extraterrestrial. No terrestrial cause or agency would have been sufficient to kill off millions of dinosaurs, leaving not a trace, in a relatively short span of time.

So it seems that we are forced to look to astronomy—to the cosmos—for an answer. Is there any clue in the solar system itself, which might give us a hint of the answer?

In the Transvaal there exists an eroded granite dome 26 miles

15. *Ibid.*, p. 4.
16. *Ibid.*, p. 14.
17. p. 4.

wide, called the Vredevoort Ring. It might be 250 million years old, according to scientists. "This must have been formed by an asteroid a mile in diameter, hitting with the explosive force of a million-megaton bomb" we are told[18].

Astronomers believe major meteorites strike the earth once every 10,000 years. Such an encounter may explain the demise of the saurian kings 70,000,000 years ago.

Consider the following facts:

1. Hundreds of thousands of various sized asteroids orbit between the orbits of Mars and Jupiter.

2. These asteroids are irregular, fragment-like, with odd, unaccountable shapes.

3. Four irregular-shaped small asteroid like bodies now orbit Jupiter as satellites, apparently captured asteroids.

4. The planet Mars has numerous craters, or astroblemes ("star wounds").

5. Greek cosmology-mythology. The ancient Greeks mention a former planet, one of the sisters in the heavens, who fled the heavens, plucked out her hair, and was changed into a comet after an affair with Zeus (Jupiter).

6. The odd satellites of Mars, Deimos and Phobos.

Patten, Hatch and Steinhauer point out: "It is estimated there are 50,000 asteroids, battered fragments of a former planet. Orbits of 1,800 have been calculated, and 90 per cent of them have orbits with either their aphelion or, more often, their perihelion in the vicinity of 200,000,000 miles from the sun. These fragments are remains of a former planet, possibly one-half the size of our Moon, which fragmented when another, somewhat larger planet (we propose Mars) nearly collided with it"[19].

Many astronomers have speculated that the asteroids between Mars and Jupiter could be the cosmic debris of an ancient planet which was torn apart in some celestial cataclysm. Generally, the theory has been ignored, or put on the shelf, by

18. *The Universe,* David Bergamini, p. 80.
19. *The Long Day of Joshua and Six Other Catastrophes,* pp. 88-89.

most modern astronomers because it seems so difficult to explain an entire planet virtually blowing apart!

Nevertheless, when we realize the former planet, which some have called "Electra," may have been half the size of our moon, then perhaps an explanation is not so incredible. If such a planet had an eccentric orbit, and passed too close to another planet, gravitation forces could have created enormous stresses within the smaller body. Over a period of time, and perhaps several close encounters, these stresses and the unrelenting pull of gravity might cause such a planet to explode into fragments.

It is possible that the former planet Electra—or the fragments and debris left over from its destruction—could well have triggered the cosmic catastrophe which layed low the dinosaurs at the close of the Cretaceous period, 65 million years ago.

The former planet which disintegrated may have had a diameter of 1,000 miles—half the Moon's diameter, and one fourth the diameter of Mars. The largest asteroid's diameter is 480 miles. Iapetus, the second largest satellite of Saturn, interestingly has a diameter of 1,000 miles.

The fact that the four outermost satellites of Jupiter are small irregular shaped rocks, and orbit Jupiter in retrograde motion, suggests that they were once part of the former planet.

Deimos and Phobos, the two satellites of Mars, were probably fragments of this ancient planet. The four outer satellites of Jupiter, Andastea, Pan, Poisedon, and Hades, vary in size from about 10 to 25 miles in diameter, similar to Deimos and Phobos.

Phobos, about eight miles in diameter, is irregular in shape, fragment-like, changes magnitudes, and was very difficult for astronomers to detect. When Asaph Hall announced in 1877 that he had located two hitherto unreported moons on Mars, a genuine shock rocked astronomical circles. In naming the two moons, Hall chose the names of those two tiny mythical companions of Mars in Greek cosmology—Deimos ("Panic") and Phobos ("Fear").

Mars, being such a small planet, was thought too small to capture moons. But once they were seen, astronomers had to accept their existence. Astronomers point out that Jupiter, 3000 times the mass of Mars, only captured four asteroids. For Mars to have been able to capture two trabants seemed amazing.

But if Mars was indeed involved in a cosmic encounter with the former planet Electra, and Jupiter also, then the captured asteroids or planetary fragments makes very good sense.

Amazingly, Jonathan Swift who published *Gullivers' Travels* in 1726, one hundred and fifty years before Asaph Hall discovered the two moons of Mars, actually wrote of them in his book!

According to Swift the two Martian moons were well known to the astronomers of Laputa. Swift recounted:

"... they have likewise discovered two lesser Stars or Satellites, which revolve about Mars, whereof the innermost is distant from the centre of the Primary Planet exactly three of his Diameters, and the outermost five; the former revolves in the Space of ten hours, and the latter in Twenty-one and a Half; so that the Squares of their periodical Times are very near in the same Proportion with the Cubes of their Distance from the Center of Mars, which evidently shews them to be governed by the same Law of Gravitation, that influences the other heavenly Bodies"[20].

For Swift to describe the distances of these two satellites from Mars in terms of Mars' diameter implies measurement and calculation. The Laputans said Phobos was three Mars diameters from the planet (12,420 miles). Modern instruments reveal it is actually 7,897 miles away. The Laputans said Phobos orbited Mars every 10 hours. Modern measurements show the actual time is 7 hours 39 minutes. The Laputans put the diameter of Deimos' orbit as five Mars diameters (20,700 miles). It is actually 16,670 miles. They put the revolution of Deimos at 21½ hours. It is actually 30 hours 18 minutes.

How did Jonathan Swift know? Was he merely guessing?

Isaac Asimov calls it "an amazing coincidence." He adds, "However, his guess that Phobos would rise in the west and set in the east because of its speed of revolution is uncanny. It is undoubtedly the luckiest guess in literature."

20. Jonathan Swift, *Gulliver's Travels,* p. 134.

To ascribe Swift's detailed description to mere guesswork is, however, laughable. He must have been familiar with certain records which described the two satellites of Mars. Perhaps, as some have suggested, his friend and contemporary, William Whiston, a leading astronomer, historian, and catastrophist, helped Swift calculate these facts. But where did the records come from? Alas, no body knows where Jonathan Swift obtained his information. The information may have been developed from ancient Greek myths about Mars and its two companions, Deimos and Phobos.

Perhaps at some ancient time the planet Mars had a different orbit—or the earth did—or they both did—and they passed relatively close to each other. Viewers from the earth could at that time have detected the two small companions of Mars. Their ancient sightings gave rise to the mythology of the god Mars and his two tiny companions.

This may seem like science fiction—But science fiction often becomes science fact. It is usually only a matter of time.

Other evidence for ancient catastrophism in the solar system can be adduced from studies of the Moon and planet Mars. Close up photographs of Mars sent back to earth from Mariner spacecraft show the surface of Mars is crater-ridden. Huge craters, such exist on the moon, cover the surface of Mars. These craters are signs of massive meteoric impacts. The surface of Mars has been compared to an ancient battle field.

One tenth the mass of the earth, with a meteor ravaged surface, Mars seems to possess the scars of ancient conflicts. It seems amazing to astronomers, but Mars—unlike the other planets of the solar system—has a day almost equal to the earth's day. The time of axial rotation of Mars is 24 hours, 37 minutes and 23 seconds; the earth's day is 23 hours, 56 minutes, 4 seconds. No other two planets are so alike in the duration of their day.

Another striking resemblance between the two planets is the inclination of their axis of rotation. The equator of Mars in inclined 24 degrees to the plane of its orbit, whereas the equator of the earth is inclined 23½ degrees to the plane of its ecliptic.

Such a similarity is unequalled among all the other planets of the solar system.

"Is it possible that the axis of rotation and the velocity of rotation of Mars, stabilized and supported in their present position and rate by certain forces, were influenced originally by the earth at the time of contact? Mars, being small as compared with the earth, influenced to a lesser degree the rotation of the earth and the position of its poles"[21].

The solar system's anomalies in many cases bear testimony to the fact that in ancient times there were great disruptions among the planets. Even the rings of Saturn—three rings composed of countless particles of ice or frost-covered gravel which circle the planet at different speeds—bespeak evidence of ancient catastrophism.

Saturn, the most remote planet known in antiquity, is the only planet which would float in water. Its low density is 13 percent of the earth's. One of its moons, Phoebe, like four of the moons of Jupiter, is retrograde in motion and may well be a captured asteroid.

The rings of Saturn, thousands of miles wide, are less than ten miles thick. They rotate exactly in the plane of the planet's equator. The center ring is opaque, the outer ring is nearly so, and the inner ring is semi-transparent. Each of the rings is composed of many individual particles, each one in its own orbit like a tiny satellite. Clerk Maxwell showed that a system of rings could be stable only if it consisted of discrete particles. Cecilia Payne-Gaposchkin suggests that the rings of Saturn may be the remains of an ancient satellite which was broken up within the tidal "danger zone" very near the planet's surface[22].

The moon reveals evidence of bombardment from space. Most of the great craters were created by small asteroids—mountains of rock—hurtling in from space and colliding with the surface. So many asteroids have impacted on the moon that its entire surface was smashed into a new shape.

The crater of Tycho, nearly sixty miles across, is merely one

21. *Worlds in Collision,* pp. 363-364.
22. *Introduction to Astronomy,* p. 222.

of many lunar craters, by no means one of the largest. The far side of the moon, photographs from space and Apollo space shots show, was hammered so violently by meteors that the entire original crust was shattered and torn apart. The blasts of crashing asteroids and meteors released huge volcanic eruptions covering vast sections of the moon with flowing lava. The maria are actually huge lava seas.

Mars, also, and even Venus, we know to be covered with huge craters from twenty to hundreds of miles in diameter.

But the earth also shows evidence of ancient collisions with astral bodies. In addition to the 4,000 foot Barringer Crater in Arizona, and the Vredevoort Ring in South Africa, in Canada hundreds of craters exist, many of them several miles in diameter. Hudson's Bay was very probably formed by the impact of a comet, or asteroid, from outer space. Scientists are also convinced that the Sea of Japan was created in a similar fashion.

We now know, therefore, that interplanetary collisions have occurred in ancient times. The earth, Mars, Venus, and the moon all bear the scars of such ancient encounters. Very possibly a former planet, Electra, was involved in these ancient interplanetary encounters of a cataclysmic kind.

Such encounters are the most likely explanation for the worldwide upheavals, volcanic eruptions, and global cataclysms resulting in the extinction of the entire world of the dinosaurs, at the close of the Mesozoic Era, and the world of Pleistocene times. Such encounters also explain the global cataclysms recorded in the legends of ancient peoples and in the pages of Holy Scripture.

Chapter Fourteen

The Pre-Adamic World

What was the world like before the creation of Adam? Why did God create the world millions or billions of years ago? Or did He?

Many Christians today believe as an article of faith that the Bible teaches the earth was created 6,000 years ago. They dispute all the evidence of geology, paleontology and radiometric dating techniques. They argue that such evidence is invalid, grossly misunderstood, and misinterpreted. Some Neo-Creationists claim that all the earth's strata was due to the Noachian deluge, or the original process of Creation. They claim all Creation took place during a six day period approximately 6,000 years ago.

What is the truth? We have shown in the pages of this book that the Bible is a reliable historical witness. However, the Bible nowhere says Creation occurred 6,000 years ago. Nor does it teach that the earth is flat, although Medieval theologians often assumed so and threatened anyone who would teach otherwise with excommunication and torture. The Middle ages were a sad time in theological history. The supposedly enlightened Church pressured scientists such as Bruno and Galileo with the threat of bodily harm if they chose to believe the earth revolved around the sun.

Biologist George Simpson was right when he observed, "As a matter of fact, most of the dogmatic religions have exhibited a perverse talent for taking the wrong side on the most important concepts of the material universe"[1].

Catholic theologians made a great mistake in the Middle Ages. They assumed the Scriptures taught things about the material universe which were, in fact, false interpretations or assumptions. Perhaps for the masses, it was enough to listen to and believe dogmas with the stamped sanction of "Church authority." But for thinking men, "Renaissance Man," for scientists who wished us to "prove all things," as the Scriptures themselves tell us to do (I Thessalonians 5:21), mere recitation of Church authority or tradition was not enough.

One author characterizes the problem this way: "The emotionally precious view of earth's centrality in a fixed, unchanging universe was crystallized by Ptolemy in the second century A.D., and then taken over by the Christian (ie., Catholic) Church. What had been ancient pagan punishments for contradicting pagan theology became orthodox Christian punishments for questioning orthodox Christian dogma. Despite man's continued secret probing, fourteen centuries brought no serious challenge"[2].

In 1543 Copernicus published his theory of a heliocentric solar system. Although he was a Catholic priest, his theory met with strong opposition from the established Church. In 1600 Giordano Bruno, who endorsed Copernicus' theory, was burned alive at the stake in Rome for his stubborn heretical beliefs, among which was the heliocentric solar system!

Galileo Galilei observed in 1604 that Copernicus had been right. Through the telescope, he observed that the earth and other planets do revolve around the sun.

But the clerics of that day did not agree. Martin Luther lambasted the heliocentric or sun-centered solar system. He reasoned that since Joshua had commanded the *sun* to stand still, it must have been the sun which was moving around the earth. One archbishop of the Catholic Church lampooned the followers of Galileo with a Scriptural pun: "Ye men of Galilee,

1. George Gaylord Simpson, *This View of Life,* p. 214.
2. Robert Gorney, *The Human Agenda,* p. 27.

why stand ye gazing up into the heavens?" he asked, quoting Acts 1:11 in the New Testament.

During the Inquisition, the Catholic Church resisted the pressures of rational thinking men with the pronouncement: "If earth is a planet, and only one among several planets, it cannot be that any such great things have been done specially for it as Christian doctrine teaches. If there are other planets, since God makes nothing in vain, they must be inhabited; but how can their inhabitants be descended from Adam? How can they trace their origin to Noah's ark? How can they have been redeemed by the Saviour?"[3]

Galileo's theory was branded by the Church as "of all heresies the *most abominable,* the most pernicious, the most scandalous."

During the Middle Ages when ecclesiastical authority reigned supreme, the science of geology was attacked as "a dark art," as "infernal artillery," and as "calculated to tear up in the public mind every remaining attachment to Christianity."[4] When scientists accumulated data to show the earth is far older than Archbishop Ussher's date of 4004 B.C., they were vigorously assailed as "infidels," as "atheists," and "heretics."

Archbishop Ussher had concluded from his studies of the Bible that Creation must have been October 23, 4004 B.C. When fossil evidence was unearthed to indicate the earth was far older than that, the fossils were dismissed by some Church leaders as deliberate deceptions of the devil!

Unfortunately, some of this Medieval thinking still exists, today. Galileo, Copernicus, Kepler, Newton—these men were willing to challenge the dogmas of their day. They were called buffoons, they were labeled heretics, they were held up to shame and contempt by ecclesiastical authorites. But they advanced the cause of truth.

Today, too, we must at times take up shield and sword of the

3. *Ibid.,* p. 28.
4. p. 53.

mind and spirit and challenge the Goliaths of modern dogma and conventional orthodoxy.

We must remember the impassioned words of Oliver Cromwell, ruler of England centuries ago, when he said: "I beseech you, in the bowels of Christ, think it possible you may be mistaken."

Why is it that people sometimes insist upon wearing blinders upon their eyes? Why won't they read, study, learn, compare, challenge, and "prove all things," holding in abeyance things which they cannot prove one way or another? Why do people insist upon dogmas? The attitudes of many people is like the nervous captain of a ship lowering the anchor down to twenty feet, and then assuming that it must have reached bottom, because that's all the line left on the anchor!

In 1832 citizens of Lancaster, Pennsylvania refused to allow their schoolhouse to be used for a discussion about railroads. They said: "Railroads are impossible and a great infidelity. If God had intended that his intelligent creatures should travel at the frightful speed of 17 miles an hour by steam he would have foretold it in the Holy Prophets. Such things as railroads are devices of Satan to lead immortal souls down to hell."

Some religious people, today, still ascribe the entire geologic record to the Flood of Noah's time. Theologians used to turn to the Flood to explain the effects of erosion, mountain building, volcanism, and fossil remains. In the infancy of geological science, such a tendency could be well understood, and even pardoned. But, today, after tons of geologic evidence, it seems strange that some religious folk still cling to the out-dated, antiquarian notions of the pre-scientific age. In order to rigorously cling to their notions of the Flood and a shortened chronology of the earth, they reject almost all the evidence of 150 years of geological investigation!

But we should not condemn them too strongly, because on the other side of the fence we have the Neo-Darwinian evolutionists and the school of anti-catastrophism—those muddleheaded geologists and paleontologists who have been brainwashed to the exact opposite conclusion. That is, they stand on "uniformitarian" geology, and will not admit to any earth-shaking, global catastrophes in the past. They discount all human testimony, all traditions, all legends from around the world; they ignore or attempt to explain away all evidence of a geological nature which supports any kind of catastrophism. Uniformitarian theory has, for all practical purposes, become to them another religion.

What we see, then, is dogmatic individuals with blinders on clinging to two opposing viewpoints, neither of which is right, neither of which is supported by the facts. Both unwilling to compromise, adamant in their authority, staunch in their belief. Both interpreting the evidence to fit their own theory.

I discuss this problem in greater detail in my book *The First Genesis: A New Case for Creation.* In that particular volume, I take issue with both the neo-Creationists who refuse to accept the evidence of an earth which has existed for millions of years, and also with the neo-Darwinists who refuse to admit the striking geological evidence for Creation.

Why does it seem so difficult for people to obtain a balance? Why do we humans become emotionally involved with a particular belief, afraid, nervous, fearful and glandular? Emotional attachment to a false world concept, or fable, is a dangerous thing. It is a little like falling in love with the wrong person—it hurts.

Infatuation with a false belief or theory can hurt just as bad as romantic infatuation. After the honeymoon, the young couple have to deal with reality. If they were hasty, and rushed into marriage with the wrong person, the trauma and life long pain and regret can be considerable. Even so, if you have clung to out-moded beliefs, or concepts which are not really in the Scriptures, unlearning that false "knowledge" can be difficult and painful at times. It is much more difficult to unlearn false beliefs than to learn something right the first time!

So it is with geology and the existence of the world before Adam's time.

All the geological and paleontological evidence proves beyond the slightest scintilla of a doubt that there was a world before Adam. All the dating techniques of scientists—carbon 14 dating methods, uranium-argon, potassium-thorium, tree ring analysis or dendrochronology, racemization and thermaluminescence—as well as observation and logic—conclusively show that the rocks under our feet, the bones of ancient animals, and even the charcoal campfires of Paleo-Indians, Neanderthal man, and other ancient hominid remains, are much older that 6,000 years. *There was a world before Adam.* In fact, there were many ages before Adam, and these ages can be carefully distinguished through the study of paleontology, paleo-ecology, and related scientific disciplines.

The evidence is indisputable. Many independent dating techniques demonstrate that various hominid creatures lived about 500,000 years ago. More primitive types lived as long ago as 1-2,000,000 years. Those creatures, in some cases, were familiar with fire, used crude chipped stone tools such as hand axes, notched and saw-toothed implements, scrapers, engravers. They were pre-Adamic creatures living in a pre-Adamic world. A world which ended in a great catastrophe.

And before their time, other worlds existed. The world of the dinosaurs ended about 70,000,000 years ago. That world, too, ended in a cosmic catastrophe.

The pre-Adamic world was a world of growth, change, and progress. It was a world where new life forms were introduced from time to time.

It is not my intention to review the various methods used by scientists to probe into the age of the earth. Such matters I discuss in *The First Genesis: A New Case for Creation.* If you are interested, you will find much more information about the different dating techniques, and how they have altered our knowledge about the world, in that volume.

The fact that this world has been in existence for many millions of years is no longer a matter for debate. It is academic. Any serious author, today, must face squarely the many indications of *time* found in the geological record.

Neo-Creationists believe we must choose either the Bible or science, particularly scientific dating methods. One typical Neo-Creationist argues:

"The Bible-believing scientist must face squarely the question, In the area of natural science which shall supercede, the clear assertions of God's inspired Book, or modern man's interpretation of what he thinks he sees in nature?"

This particular author continues: "According to Bible chronology only a few thousand years have passed since the creation of the ancestors of our modern plants and animals . . . Contrariwise, if one accepts the assumption that the inorganic radioisotope clocks were reset wherever they became associated with fossil-bearing material, then apparently at least 600 million years have passed since plants and animals first appeared successively from that time over a duration of some 600 million years"[5].

The truth is, there is no contradiction between the Biblical record and scientific knowledge of the earth's past. Those who wish to uphold the Bible in the face of new evidence regarding early hominids, homo erectus, homo habilis, or other discoveries of Primitive Man-like creatures, need not worry. There is no evidence that such creatures evolved into Modern man. Rather, they lived long ago in a world before Adam was created—another world—another age—another time.

Such discoveries tell us much about the ancient history of the earth. They tell us nothing, one way or the other, about the Scriptures.

In the pages of Genesis, as it relates to the original creation of the universe, we read the simple, matter-of-fact statement: "In the beginning, God created the heaven and the earth" (Genesis 1:1, *King James* Version). The *Amplified* Bible renders this verse: "In the beginning God (prepared, formed, fashioned,) and created the heavens and the earth." The *Good News* Bible states: "In the beginning, when God created the universe . . ." The *Moffatt* Translation: "When God began to form the universe . . ." The *Goodspeed* Translation: "When God began to create the heavens and the earth . . ."

What exactly does the book of Genesis tell us? That God created the universe—the heavens and the earth—in a period of time called, simply, "the beginning." How long ago that primeval creation occurred we are not told anywhere in the

5. Frank Lewis Marsh, *Life, Man and Time,* pp. 67-68.

Scripture. To determine that, God has given us brains and intellect!

That time of beginning could well have been six to ten billion years ago. Astronomers calculate that a "Big Bang" took place at that time, out of which the entire cosmos was created.

Verse two of Genesis, chapter one, continues:

"And the earth was without form, and void; and darkness was upon the face of the deep" (*King James* Version).

Is this verse describing the original creation as being formless and void? If so, it would seem a contradiction. Verse one tells us God created the heavens and the earth. When God creates something, it is beautiful, grand, and majestic. In the 38th chapter of the book of Job, we read:

"Where wast thou when I laid the foundations of the earth? declare, if thou hast understanding. Who hath laid the measures thereof, if thou knowest? or who hath stretched the line upon it? Whereupon are the foundations thereof fastened? or who laid the corner stone thereof? When the morning stars sang together, and all the sons of God shouted for joy?" (vs. 4-7).

If the original earth had been created a chaotic ruin, formless and void, the angels would not have "sang together" or have "shouted for joy."

Isaiah 45:18 adds more light on this enigmatic passage. The prophet declares: "For thus saith the Lord that created the heavens; God himself that formed the earth and made it; he hath established it, he created it *not in vain,* he formed it to be inhabited: I am the Lord; and there is none else" (*King James* Version).

The Hebrew word translated "vain" here is *tohu* and means "to lie waste," "a desolation," "a desert." It can also be translated "confusion," "empty place," "without form," "nothing," "wilderness." It is the very same word used in Genesis 1:2, where we read the earth "was without form."

One place says God created the earth and it "was without form"; in another place we read God did *not* create the earth "without form." Is this a contradiction? Not at all!

The key to understanding this apparently complex problem lies in the little word "was." It can also be translated "became." In fact, in Genesis 19:16 it is translated "became." We read: "And Lot's wife *became* a pillar of salt."

What happened, then, is this: When God originally created the earth, it was indeed a lovely place. He created it with no waste, no wilderness, no desolation. It was inhabited. The angels leaped for joy, and shouted with admiration and enthusiasm when they beheld the primeval earth.

But then something happened. It *became* "tohu"—that is, waste, a ruin, a desolation. The original earth suffered a great cataclysm—a cosmic catastrophe. The Hebrew words translated "without form and void" in Genesis 1:2 literally mean a desolation, a wilderness, an empty, uninhabited ruin. These words, *tohu* and *bohu* are very strong words and denote catastrophe. They strongly suggest that some sort of primeval cataclysm, or several such cataclysms, occurred.

Destruction!

Paroxysm!

Chaos!

Scripture gives no data for determining how long ago the universe was created. And in the first chapter of Genesis, it only records three creative acts: 1) the heavens and the earth (verse 1); 2) new animal life (verses 20-21); and 3) human life, Adam and Eve (verses 26-27). The first creative act referred to the dateless past. The creation of new forms of animal life, and Adam and Eve, occurred approximately 6,000 years ago. Obviously, then, the first chapter of Genesis is not describing the original creation of the heavens and earth as occurring in seven consecutive days.

After the chaos and destruction which occurred, in verse two of Genesis one, God began a process of re-creation, reconstruction, if you please, which lasted for seven days. Verse 16 of Genesis one does not describe the sun and moon and stars being created on the fourth day. How could light have been created on the first day, but the sun and stars which impart light not till the fourth day? The original Hebrew for "made" in verse 16 actually means "made to appear, made visible." The sun and moon were created "in the beginning." The light came from the sun, of course, but the vapor in the earth's atmosphere diffused the light. After the great cataclysm, the earth was cut off from the light of the sun, moon and stars. Darkness prevailed everywhere. As verse two says: "And the earth was (became) without form and void (*tohu* and *bohu*); and *darkness* was upon the face of the deep. And the Spirit of God moved upon the face of the waters".

What do we see then? An earth destroyed, in pitch darkness, covered by water, the continents submerged, due to some great cataclysm.

During the process of reconstruction or re-creation, God first caused the light from the sun to penetrate the atmosphere once again, in a diffused manner (Genesis 1:3-5), allowing day and night to become discernible. He created order in the atmosphere (verses 6-8). He caused the dry land to appear once again (verse 10). He caused the earth to once again bring forth life, plants, vegetation, of all kinds. As the turgid clouds and atmospheric disturbances cleared away, He caused the sun, moon and stars to once again become visible from the earth's surface (verses 14-18).

Then, having refashioned the surface of the earth, and having prepared it, God created new living creatures—new animal life of all kinds, from great whales to small fish, from elephants to rodents, from flying birds to flying fish and insects—to re-populate the earth, and to replenish it (verses 20-25).

Something had happened to the Pre-Adamic earth. It had been overwhelmed in a mighty catastrophe, or a long series of catastrophes, which is briefly described in verse 2 of Genesis chapter 1.

But what happened?

The world before Adam came to an abrupt, screeching end. It was cut short by flooding and upheaval, stroke upon stroke of catastrophe. This one short enigmatic, much misunderstood verse of the Bible, contains within its cryptic message a story that will amaze you. This one little verse may hold a clue as to what happened to the earth, after the original time when it was created, beautiful, and to be "inhabited," and before the time of Adam and Eve, when it had to be refashioned, reshaped, refurbished, and rebuilt.

This one verse, in essence, may cover a time span of millions of years. If God originally created the earth six to ten billion years ago, and over millions of years created various and sundry life forms, causing them to become buried in massive burials to form deposits of coal, peat, and oil and natural gas; if He spent millions of years preparing the world for the eventual time when He would create Man in His own image; who are we to complain?

Vast periods of time, and many successive ecological niches, had to exist in the earth, for algal reefs of hundreds of feet to grow in place. Much time was required for vast quantities of vegetation to live, grow, and die, and to become entombed, to create vast deposits of coal in Kansas, Oklahoma, Illinois, Indiana, Kentucky, West Virginia and Pennsylvania.

This vast period of time God put to good use.

As Robert Macdonald shows, in a paper entitled "Geology":

"The fossil record contains hundreds of zones, each with its own particular faunal assemblage. What is the chance that such an invariant worldwide sequence of life forms could be built up if they all lived contemporaneously, and the sequence in which they are found were only a burial order? How could a burial order based not on water sorting, but on environments do the job? . . .

"Suppose that in a worldwide catastrophe, one group of organisms were brought in from one area and deposited, then another assemblage from another area were deposited on top of that, and so on. A local sequence of life forms would be built up. But the chances would be against the deposition of fossils in the same order in a local sequence in another area. Consider the chance that the same order would occur in all sequences worldwide. It would be nil!

"There is no way to account for the sequence in faunal succession by one catastrophe. Nor is there any way to account for this sequence by a series of catastrophes, or by a long drawn-out catastrophe. If all these Paleozoic and Mesozoic organisms were contemporaneous, there would inevitably have been some mixing of early and late forms.

"The only explanation is that each geologic horizon does indeed represent a different time in the past during which a unique assemblage of life forms was living and being deposited in many parts of the world. Slow or incremental deposition is therefore essential to give time for worldwide changes in populations of fauna whose remains preserved as fossils vary from one stratum to another."

During the geologic ages of the earth's past, life went on in a normal fashion for millions of years. Fossil reefs obviously grew in the place in which they are found. Standing trees, with their roots in place, tracks and trails both on land and on the sea bottoms, layer upon layer containing burrows and borings made by animals just as they do in the sea-bottoms today, all show that most of the geologic column was created over millions of years, not in the Flood of Noah's time, or some other isolated catastrophe.

Although the record in the earth's strata clearly shows that great catastrophes did take place, in the earth's past, the record also shows that there were periods of millions of years in which no violent cataclysms occurred. During these calm, relatively nonviolent periods, great creative processes were going on. Cyclothems of coal were formed. As Macdonald points out, coal is commonly found in a sequence of beds called a cyclothem—a cycle of beds repeated over and over again, perhaps dozens of times. Much time would be needed for such deposits to be made, one on top of another.

How, then, are we to understand the "Pre-Adamic world"? What was it like?

Robert Macdonald gives a good answer:

"The fossil record shows that new organisms appeared in the record from time to time, and at other times groups of organisms have become extinct. This shows that at times God created new organisms, and at other times, species were destroyed or allowed to die out. There is a continuity to this pre-Adamic world. It would appear that there is no record of the complete destruction of all life during that period before Adam."

Macdonald continues: "I therefore do not consider the pre-Adamic world as a series of creations, but one creation, even though the acts of new life forms were not all simultaneous.

"Why the sequence of life we find in faunal succession? What possible reason could there be for God creating the organisms of the pre-Adamic world 'by stages' instead of all at one time? Perhaps a better question would be 'Why a pre-Adamic world at all?' Human answers to these questions are bound to be somewhat speculative since God has not revealed this knowledge, but a few ideas have been proposed.

"It has been suggested that there was pre-Adamic life so that the *angels* could have something to rule over and work with. This seems a likely possibility, but there must be more to it."

Robert Macdonald goes on:

"The first life forms created apparently were bacteria, algae and possibly worms, 'simple' organisms that could survive in a barren and sterile environment. The points in the sequence which mark the first appearance of new life forms indicate where God created new species, and added them to an already viable ecological system. These new organisms were added from time to time as the environment became prepared for them by the former ecological system.

"The succession of life forms added by creation was one of generally increasing complexity and size. Thus the sequence observed in faunal succession was not a result of evolution, but one necessitated by practicality. It took a few 'simple' small varieties of organisms in the beginning to prepare the way for more numerous varieties of larger and more complex organisms, and so on."

Macdonald asserts:

"Understanding the reasons for this sequence imparts an understanding of at least one possible purpose of the pre-Adamic creation—to prepare the earth for man. This preparation was not only of the environment, but also of the fossil fuels and our mineral resources which made possible the industrial revolution."

The world before Adam can only be understood by studying the evidence of that world contained within the earth's strata. The Scriptures allude to such a world in the very briefest of terms. But there is not a word in the Bible that would lead one to understand the physical life on earth existed before Adam. The Bible is largely silent about that ancient world. It remains, therefore, for the study of geology and paleontology to guide us and to provide information about that by-gone world.

The fact that geology shows us that various forms of animal and plant life became extinct, at different periods of the earth's geologic past, would indicate that God allowed these extinctions for a purpose. At times, to accomplish His purpose, the extinctions were widespread and general, and involved catastrophe.

At the end of the Cretaceous period, the dinosaurs were exterminated. However, frogs, turtles, lizards, snakes and crocodiles continued on through the boundary, into a new world. The destruction, although vast and global in nature, was not universal.

Fundamentalists, who attempt to account for all life remains and fossils within the past 6,000 years, simply dismiss the 100 miles of evidence in the geologic column!

As Bertrand Russell, the famous philosopher, once wrote: "The world was created in 4004 B.C., complete with fossils, which were inserted to try our faith. The world was created suddenly, but was made such as it would have been if it had evolved. There is no logical impossibility about this view. And similarly, there is no logical impossibility in the view that the world was created five minutes ago, complete with memories and records."[6]

Theodosius Dobzhansky, professor of genetics at the University of California, at Davis, and professor emeritus at the Rockefeller University, points out it is foolish to try to make the Bible into a primer on natural science. If the radiometric evidence is wrong, if the duration of the geological and paleontological record is grossly distorted, he adds, then the Creator must have seen fit to play deceitful tricks on geologists and biologists. If fossils were placed by the Creator where we find them now, so as to deliberately give the appearance of great age and antiquity, then God must be absurdly deceitful. Dobzhansky added: "This is as revolting as it is uncalled for."

6. *An Outline of Philosophy,* p. 27.

Sir Albert Einstein once said, "I shall never believe that God plays dice with the world." The God revealed in the pages of the Bible is a loving Creator. He is not malicious, spiteful, capricious, or a "Practical Joker." Nor is He a cosmic Magician pulling rabbits out of a hat.

The God of the Bible is a Creator—a Builder—a Designer—an Architect, Engineer, Supreme Draftsman, and Originator. Everything He does is with plan and purpose. Nothing is haphazard. His original creation was perfect. And every addition He has made was perfect, for the purpose for which He designed it.

Creation is an ongoing process. It is still continuing, today. Each new life which is born is, in effect, a "new creation."

But if God is not the architect of violence, catastrophe, and cataclysm, then what was the cause of the various global catastrophes which occurred in the earth's past?

Who is the author of destruction?

What really happened aeons ago?

Chapter Fifteen

Elohim

Long, long ago, in a time far remote, there was a great star war for control of the universe. It was the greatest galactic struggle of all time. We possess records of that ancient conflict which have survived through many millennia. Those records tell of incredible events which have occurred. Those records are not musty old manuscripts hidden in some secret monastery in Tibet, Nepal or India. They have been very accessible to modern man. They have been with us for centuries—but not properly understood or interpreted.

This chronicle of ancient star wars which occurred, before the time of man, and thereafter, is contained right in the pages of your family Bible!

There has been a protracted conflict raging in the universe since time immemorial. In several places in the Scriptures this war is spotlighted. It involves the story of Lucifer, and the world of angels.

Books have been written about angels, but few people understand the angelic world—the purpose of angels, why they exist, or what they look like. Mythology has all but buried the truth under reams of superstition and nonsense. What are angels? Do they really exist? What do they have to do with our story?

And what about Lucifer? Who was he? What did he do?

In this chapter, we are not dealing with mythology and fable. We are dealing with stark reality. The Bible is a book of fact. Reality. Truth. And it reveals the existence of a world of angels.

The Bible is an authentic record of ancient history. It contains special revelation to man of knowledge of the past, present and future. It is a source of information about the very nature of man himself. For the Bible tells us of an ancient celestial conflict, a "space war," which puts all fiction to shame.

According to Scripture, long ago, even before the earth was created, there was a spirit world, a world of created super-beings.

The Bible reveals that the Creator of all things is the true God. In Genesis 1:1 we read: "In the beginning GOD created the heaven and the earth." The Hebrew word for God here is *Elohim* and is a uni-plural word. It literally means "The Mighty Ones." It denotes more than one individual Person—even as our English words "family," "church," "congregation" denote more than one individual.

Who was this "Elohim"?

In verse 26 of this same chapter we read: "And GOD (Elohim) said, Let *us* make man in *our* image, after *our* likeness . . ."

Was God like the absent-minded professor, always talking to Himself? Or doesn't this denote more than One Person in the Godhead?

Notice also the account of the building of the Tower of Babel: "And the LORD (Elohim) said, Behold, the people is one, and they have all one language; and this they begin to do: and now nothing will be restrained from them, which they have imagined to do. Go to, let *us* go down, and there confound their language, that they may not understand one another's speech" (Genesis 11:6-7).

Who were the Persons in the Godhead, revealed in Scripture? One was known as the "Ancient of days". This personage is described in the book of Daniel. Daniel the prophet recorded: "I beheld till the thrones were cast down, and the Ancient of days did sit, whose garment was white as snow, and the hair of his head like the pure wool: his throne was like the fiery flame, and his wheels as burning fire. A fiery stream issued and came forth from before him: thousand thousands ministered unto him, and ten thousand times ten thousand stood before him: the judgment was set, and the books were opened" (Daniel 7:9-10).

The other personage of the Godhead is the "Word" or "Logos" of God. In the New Testament book of John we read: "In the beginning was the Word, and the Word was with God, and the Word was God. The same was in the beginning with God. All things were made by him; and without him was not anything made that was made" (John 1:1-3). Thus the Ancient of days and the Word—*Logos* in Greek, or the "Spokesman"—together created the heavens and the earth. Without the Word, John said, "was not anything made that was made."

This Word or *Logos* the Bible reveals actually became flesh and dwelt among us 1900 years ago as Jesus Christ. "And the Word was made flesh, and dwelt among us, (and we beheld his glory, the glory as of the only begotten of the Father,) full of grace and truth" (John 1:14).

Speaking of Jesus Christ, the apostle Paul later wrote: "Who is the image of the invisible God, the firstborn of every creature: For *by him* were all things created, that are in heaven, and that are in earth, visible and invisible, whether they be thrones, or dominions, or principalities, or powers: all things were created by him, and for him: And he is before all things, and by him all things consist" (Colossians 1:15-17).

Jesus told the apostle John, in the book of Revelation: "I am Alpha and Omega, the beginning and the ending, saith the Lord, which is, and which was, and which is to come, the Almighty" (Revelation 1:8). John turned around and beheld the One speaking to him. He described the sensational event thus: "And I turned to see the voice that spake with me. And being turned, I saw seven golden candlesticks; And in the midst of the seven candlesticks one like unto the Son of man, clothed with a garment down to the foot, and girt about the paps with a golden girdle. His head and his hairs were white like wool, as white as snow; and his eyes were as a flame of fire; And his feet like unto fine brass, as if they burned in a furnace; and his voice as the sound of many waters. And he had in his right hand seven stars: and out of his mouth went a sharp two-edged sword: *and his countenance was as the sun shineth in his strength.* And when I saw him, I fell at his feet as dead. And he laid his right hand upon me, saying unto me, Fear not; I am the first and the last: I am he that liveth, and was dead; and, behold, I am alive for evermore. Amen; and have the keys of hell and of death" (Revelation 1:12-18).

Jesus, the Word made flesh, was the second member of the Godhead in the beginning. He took part in the entire creation—nothing was created without his participation. He and the One He called the "Father," also known as the "Ancient of days," created the entire Universe—all the stars, planets, and far-flung galaxies. Scientific investigation suggests that that original time of Creation was between 10 and 15 billion years ago. At that time, evidence suggests, the entire Cosmos was initially created in a great explosion, commonly referred to as the original "Big Bang."

The Big Bang Theory postulates that there once existed a huge primordial cloud composed of matter—this cloud may have contained a "soup" of all the fundamental particles which exist within the atom. Hubble's constant indicates the "Big Bang" occurred 10,000,000,000 years ago—that was the time when the universe started expanding, with the galaxies flying outward toward the infinite reaches of space. By noting the present observable speed of these far away retreating galaxies, Hubble suggested that about 10,000,000,000 years ago they must have all been closely packed together in a huge primeval cloud. As temperatures in the cloud shot upward, and intense radiation filled the universe, a tremendous explosion rocked the entire mass, creating galaxies, stars, and the various components of the universe, and hurling them outward at fantastic speeds.

As Lincoln Barnett points out: "If the universe is running down and nature's processes are proceeding in just one direction, the inescapable inference is that everything had a beginning: somehow and sometime the cosmic processes were started . . ."

He adds: "Most of the clues, moreover, that have been discovered at the inner and outer frontier of scientific cognition suggest a definite time of creation . . .

"Every theory rests ultimately on the prior assumption that someting was already in existence."[1]

The Bible nowhere states how long it required for God to create the heavens and the earth. Whether He did it instantaneously, or over millions of years, is not the question. Scientific evidence may be adduced to show that the solar system itself is approximately 5×10^9 years old. The oldest surface rocks on the earth appear to be 3.5×10^9 years old. From an abundance of lead isotopes found, it is estimated that the earth, the moon and meteorites have an age of 4.7×10^9 years.

That original Creation, and all creation which has occurred since that time, requires the existence of a Creator. Dr. Werhner von Braun put the case succinctly: "Anything as well ordered and perfectly created as is our earth and universe must have a Maker, a Master Designer. Anything so orderly, so perfect, so precisely balanced, so majestic as this creation can only be the product of a Divine Idea.

"There must be a Maker; there can be no other way."

The Bible tells us that this Great God created the entire cosmos through the power of His Holy Spirit. His Spirit pervades all space. It is the "power of God" (Luke 1:35). It is the spirit energy out of which all the cosmos was fashioned and formed. It is the creative energy of the omnipotent, omnipresent God.

God's spirit is everywhere. Jeremiah the prophet recorded God as saying: "Am I a God at hand, saith the Lord, and not a God afar off? Can any hide himself in secret places that I shall not see him? saith the Lord. *Do not I fill heaven and earth?* saith the Lord" (Jeremiah 23:23-24).

"I have made the earth, the man and the beast that are upon the ground, by my great power and by my outstretched arm . . ." God says (Jeremiah 27:5).

Isaiah tells us more about God's greatness: "Who hath measured the waters in the hollow of his hand, and meted out heaven with the span, and comprehended the dust of the earth

1. Lincoln Barnett, *The Universe and Dr. Eistein*, pp. 104-106.

in a measure, and weighed the mountains in scales, and the hills in a balance? Who hath directed the Spirit of the Lord, or being his counsellor hath taught him?. . . . Have ye not known? Have ye not heard? Hath it not been told you from the beginning? Have ye not understood from the foundations of the earth? It is he that sitteth upon the circle (Hebrew *chuug* meaning a "sphere") of the earth, and the inhabitants thereof are as grasshoppers; that stretcheth out the heavens as a curtain, and spreadeth them out as a tent to dwell in" (Isaiah 40:13-22).

Moffatt translates this verse, "He sits over the round earth." The *Critical and Experimental Commentary* states that this expression is "applicable to the globular form of the earth."

The fact that God "stretcheth" out the heavens as a curtain, and "spreadeth them out" as a tent, may be an indication of the *expanding universe.*

This great God says: "To whom then will ye liken me, or shall I be equal? saith the Holy One. Lift up your eyes on high and behold who hath created these things, that bringeth out their host by number: he calleth them *all by names* by the greatness of his might, for that he is strong in power; not one faileth . . . Hast thou not known? Hast thou not heard, that the everlasting God, the Lord, the Creator of the ends of the earth, fainteth not, neither is weary? There is no searching of his understanding" (Isaiah 40:25-28).

The stars of the billions of retreating galaxies have been compared to grains of sand on the seashore. The great God says He knows each one of them by "name"! Nothing escapes His detection. He also is aware of every sparrow that falls, and every hair on the top of your head (Matthew 10:29-30; Luke 12:6-7).

This great God, the Bible tells us, inhabits Eternity (Isaiah 57:15). His name is Holy (same verse). He is from everlasting to everlasting—the Eternal God.

This great God revealed in the Bible has several names. The two personal names of God in the Hebrew Scriptures are Elohim and Jehovah (or, more correctly, Yahweh). The former calls attention to the fullness of divine power. The latter means "He who is," and thus declares the divine Self-existence.

These terms are varied or combined with others to bring out or emphasize certain attributes of the Godhead, such variations or combinations being rendered in our English version, "God Almighty," "The Living God," "The Most High," "The Lord," or "The God of Hosts." The English word "God" is identical with the Anglo-Saxon word for "good," and therefore it is believed that the name God refers to the divine goodness.

The divine title Elohim occurs 2,700 times in the Bible. Its first occurrence connects it with creation, and gives it its essential meaning of *the Creator.*

Jehovah is indicated in the Authorized Version by small capital letters, "LORD," and by "GOD" when it occurs in combination with *Adonai,* in which case "Lord GOD" means *Adonai Jehovah.* The Jehovah titles, found in the Hebrew canon, are:

1. *Jehovah-Jireh*—Jehovah will see, or provide (Gen. 22:14).
2. *Jehovah-Ropheka*—Jehovah that healeth thee (Exo. 15:26).
3. *Jehovah-Nissi*—Jehovah my banner (Exo. 17:15).
4. *Jehovah-Mekaddishkem*—Jehovah that doth sanctify you (Exo. 31:13; Lev. 20:8; 21:8; 22:32; Ezek. 20:12).
5. *Jehovah-Shalom*—Jehovah sends peace (Judges 6:24).
6. *Jehovah-Zebaoth*—Jehovah of hosts (I Sam. 1:3 and frequently).
7. *Jehovah-Zidkenu*—Jehovah our righteousness (Jer. 23:6; 33:16).
8. *Jehovah-Shammah*—Jehovah is there (Ezek. 48:35).
9. *Jehovah-Elyon*—Jehovah most high (Psa. 7:17; 47:2; 97:9).
10. *Jehovah-Roi*—Jehovah my Shepherd (Psa. 23:1).

JAH is Jehovah in a special sense and relationship—Jehovah as having become our Salvation (Exodus 15:2), He who is, and was, and is to come. It occurs 49 times in the Bible (see Psalm 68:4, 18).

EL is essentially *the Almighty*—Elohim in all His strength and power. It is rendered "God" as *Elohim* is, but *El* is God the Omnipotent. *Elohim* is God the *Creator* putting His omnipotence into operation. *El* is the God who knows all (Gen. 14:18-22) and sees all (Gen. 16:13) and that performs all things for His people (Psa. 57:2).

ELOAH is Elohim, who is to be worshipped. *Eloah* is God in connection with His will rather than His power. The first occurrence associates this name with worship (Deuteronomy 32:15, 17). Hence it is the title used whenever the contrast is with false gods or idols. *Eloah* is essentially "the living God" in contrast to inanimate idols.

ELYON first occurs in Genesis 14:18 with *El* and is rendered "the most high (God)." It is *El* and *Elohim,* not as the powerful Creator, but as "the possessor of heaven and earth." It is *Elyon* as possessor of the Earth who divides the nations "their inheritance." In Psalm 83:18 He is "over all the earth." This title occurs 36 times. *Elyon* is the Dispenser of God's blessings in the earth.

SHADDAI is in every instance translated "Almighty." It is God (*El*), not as the source of strength, but of grace; not as Creator, but as the *Giver. Shaddai* is the All-bountiful. The title does not refer to His creative power but to His power to supply all the needs of His people. It first occurs in Genesis 17:1 where he shows Abraham that He who called him out to walk alone before him could supply all his need.

ADON is one of three titles (*ADON, ADONAI, ADONIM*) all generally rendered "Lord." Each has its own special usage and association. They all denote *headship* in various aspects. They have to do with God as "overlord."

ADON is the Lord as Ruler in the earth. *ADONAI* is the Lord in His relation to the earth; and as carrying out His purposes of blessing in the earth. *ADONIM* is the plural of *Adon. Adonim* carries with it all that *Adon* does, but in a greater and higher degree; and more especially as owner and proprietor. An *Adon* may rule others who do not belong to him. Hence without the article it is often used of men. But *Adonim* is the Lord who rules His own.

God told Moses, the Hebrew patriarch, that He had appeared to Abraham, Isaac and Jacob by the name of "God Almighty"—*Elohim*—but not by His name *Jehovah* or *Yahweh*

(Exodus 6:3). In revealing His name to Moses, He stated: *"I AM THAT I AM"* (Exodus 3:14). God is the eternal, Self-existing One. He was, and is, and ever more shall be, the *"I AM."*

This great God created all things in heaven and earth. Nothing was made that did not suit His purpose and plan from the beginning. We find in the Bible that He also created the angels. In the Bible angels are sometimes called "the sons of God"—that is, sons by an act of special creation.

What does the Bible reveal about the world of angels?

The angels, or "sons of God," were created before the foundations of the earth were laid (Job 38:4-7). They shouted for joy at its completion (verse 7).

The fact that in Scripture "stars" and "angels" are often interchangeable expressions should be clear from the words of Jesus who told the apostle John: "Write the things which thou hast seen, and the things which are, and the things which shall be hereafter; The mystery of the seven stars which thou sawest in my right hand, and the seven golden candlesticks. The seven stars are the angels of the seven churches; and the seven candlesticks which thou sawest are the seven churches" (Revelation 1:20).

The Hebrew word for angel—*malak*—and the Greek word *angelos* both mean the same thing, "messenger." Although the word in some cases is used of human messengers (ie., Isa. 43:19; Mal. 2:7), its most common usage in Scripture is in reference to certain spiritual and superhuman beings who are "messengers of God." Few books in the Bible—such as Ruth, Nehemiah, Esther, the epistles of John and James—make no mention of angels.

We must depend wholly upon the Scriptures for our knowledge of the spirit world and the existence of angels. What does the Bible tell us about them?

There are many passages of Scripture in which the expression "angel of God" is used for a manifestation of God himself. In Genesis 22:11-14 we find that an "angel of the LORD" called to Abraham out of heaven—and Abraham subsequently called the name of that place "Jehovah-jireh" (verse 14). The "angel of the LORD" called to Abraham a second time (verse 15), "And said, By myself have I sworn, saith the Lord . . . that in blessing I will bless thee, and in multiplying I will multiply thy seed as the stars of the heaven, and as the sand which is upon the sea shore . . ." (verses 16-18).

Likewise, in Exodus 3:2 we find that "the angel of the LORD appeared unto him (Moses) in a flame of fire out of the midst of a bush: and he looked, and, behold, the bush burned with fire, and the bush was not consumed." This angel, it turns out, was the Eternal God Himself (verses 4-6).

Exactly what are angels? The apostle Paul declared, "Are they not all ministering spirits, sent forth to minister for them who shall be heirs of salvation?" (Hebrews 1:14). In this same chapter, Paul quoted the Old Testament: "Who maketh his angels spirits and his ministers a flame of fire" (verse 7). The quotation comes from Psalm 104:4. But in the 103rd Psalm, in verse 20, we read: "Bless the LORD, ye his angels, that excel in strength, that do his commandments, hearkening unto the voice of his word."

During the history of man upon the earth, angels repeatedly appeared to men. Angels, the Bible tells us, are spirit beings that cannot die (Luke 20:36). Jesus told His disciples: "But they which shall be accounted worthy to obtain that world, and the resurrection from the dead, neither marry, nor are given in marriage: Neither can they die any more: for they are equal unto the angels; and are the children of God, being the children of the resurrection" (Luke 20:35-36).

The angels in heaven always behold the face of the Father—the Ancient of days (Matthew 18:10). A picture of the throne of God in heaven is given to us in the book of Daniel, which we already referred to. In Daniel 7:9 the throne of God is "like the fiery flame, and his wheels as burning fire. A fiery stream issued and came forth from before him: thousand thousands (millions) ministered unto him, and ten thousand times ten thousand (hundreds of millions) stood before him" (verses 9-10). These spirit beings, ministering before God, are the angels.

A more graphic picture of the throne of God is given to us in the book of Revelation. John describes what he saw:

"And immediately I was in the spirit: and, behold, a throne was set in heaven, and one sat on the throne. And he that sat was to look upon like a jasper and a sardine stone: and there was a rainbow round about the throne, in sight like unto an emerald. And round about the throne were four and twenty seats: and upon the seats I saw four and twenty elders sitting, clothed in white raiment; and they had on their heads crowns of gold. And out of the throne proceeded lightnings and thunderings and voices: and there were seven lamps of fire burning before the throne, which are the seven Spirits of God. And before the throne there was a sea of glass like unto crystal: and in the midst of the throne, and round about the throne, were four beasts (living creatures) full of eyes before and behind. And the first beast was like a lion, and the second beast like a calf, and the third beast had a face as a man, and the fourth beast was like a flying eagle. And the four beasts had each of them six wings about him; and they were full of eyes within: and they rest not day and night, saying, Holy, holy, holy, Lord God Almighty, which was, and is, and is to come. And when those beasts (living creatures) give glory and honour and thanks to him that sat on the throne, who liveth for ever and ever, the four and twenty elders fall down before him that sat on the throne, and worship him that liveth for ever and ever, and cast their crowns before the throne, saying, Thou art worthy, O Lord, to receive glory and honour and power: for thou hast created all things, and for thy pleasure they are and were created" (Revelation 4:2-11).

Here the Throne of the Creator God is pictured. Before it are seven lamps of fire, which are seven Spirits of God. Round about the Throne were 24 seats, sat upon by 24 elders. Also round about the Throne were four living creatures, each one possessing six wings—one like a lion, one like a calf, one as a man, and one like a flying eagle. John continued in the next chapter: "And I beheld, and I heard the voice of many angels round about the throne and the beasts (living creatures) and the elders: and the number of them was ten thousand times ten thousand, and thousands of thousands" (Rev. 5:11).

What are these mysterious creatures? Let us allow the Bible to explain. Isaiah the prophet had a similar vision. He described it thus: "In the year that king Uzziah died I saw also the Lord sitting upon a throne, high and lifted up, and his train (or, the skirts thereof) filled the temple. Above it stood the *seraphims*: each one had six wings; with twain he covered his face, and with twain he covered his feet, and with twain he did fly. And one cried unto another, and said, Holy, holy, holy, is the LORD of hosts: the whole earth is full of his glory" (Isaiah 6:1-3).

Here we find that seraphim were angelic beings which possess six wings. These seraphim must be the four living creatures the apostle John saw and depicted in Revelation, chapter four.

Another amazing description of the throne of God is found in the mysterious book of Ezekiel the prophet.

Ezekiel writes:

"Now it came to pass in the thirtieth year, in the fourth month, in the fifth day of the month, as I was among the captives by the river of Chebar, that the heavens were opened, and I saw visions of God.

"In the fifth day of the month, which was the fifth year of king Jehoiachin's captivity, the word of the Lord came expressly unto Ezekiel the priest, the son of Buzi, in the land of the Chaldeans by the river Chebar; and the hand of the Lord was there upon him.

"And I looked, and, behold, a whirlwind came out of the north, a great cloud, and a fire infolding itself, and a brightness was about it, and out of the midst thereof as the colour of amber, out of the midst of the fire. Also out of the midst thereof came the likeness of four living creatures. And this was their appearance; they had the likeness of a man. And every one had four faces, and every one had four wings. And their feet were straight feet; and the sole of their feet was like the sole of a calf's foot: and they sparkled like the colour of burnished brass. And they had the hands of a man under their wings on their four sides; and they four had their faces and their wings. Their wings were joined one to another; they turned not when they went; they went every one straight forward.

"As for the likeness of their faces, they four had the face of a man, and the face of a lion, on the right side: and they four had the face of an ox on the left side; and they four also had the face of an eagle. Thus were their faces: and their wings were stretched upward; two wings of every one were joined one to another, and two covered their bodies. And they went every one straight forward: whither the spirit was to go, they went; and they turned not when they went.

"As for the likeness of the living creatures, their appearance was like burning coals of fire, and like the appearance of lamps: it went up and down among the living creatures; and the fire was bright, and out of the fire went forth lightning. And the living creatures ran and returned as the appearance of a flash of lightning" (Ezekiel 1:1-14).

These creatures, with four wings, and four faces, like burnished brass, appearing like lamps of fire, may be identified with the "seven lamps" or "seven Spirits" mentioned in Revelation 4:5. They are actually super-powerful angelic beings.

Let us continue:

"Now as I beheld the living creatures, behold one wheel upon the earth by the living creatures, with his four faces. The appearance of the wheels and their work was like unto the colour of a beryl: and they four had one likeness: and their appearance and their work was as it were a wheel in the middle of a wheel. When they went, they went upon their four sides: and they turned not when they went. As for their rings, they were so high that they were dreadful; and their rings (strakes) were full of eyes round about them four. And when the living creatures went, the wheels went by them: and when the living creatures were lifted up from the earth, the wheels were lifted up. Whithersoever the spirit was to go, they went, thither was their spirit to go; and the wheels were lifted up over against them: for the spirit of the living creature was in the wheels (or, the spirit of life was in the wheels). When those went, these went; and when those stood, these stood; and when those were lifted up from the earth, the wheels were lifted up over against them: for the spirit of the living creature (spirit of life) was in the wheels.

"And the likeness of the firmament upon the heads of the living creature was as the colour of the terrible crystal, stretched forth over their heads above. And under the firmament were their wings straight, the one toward the other: every one had two, which covered on this side, and every one had two, which covered on that side, their bodies. And when they went, I heard the noise of their wings, like the noise of great waters, as the voice of the Almighty, the voice of speech, as the noise of an host: when they stood, they let down their wings.

"And above the firmament that was over their heads was the likeness of a throne, as the appearance of a sapphire stone: and upon the likeness of the throne was the likeness as the appearance of a man above upon it. And I saw as the colour of amber, as the appearance of fire round about within it, from the appearance of his loins even upward, and from the appearance of his loins even downward, I saw as it were the appearance of fire, and it had brightness round about. This was the appearance of the likeness of the glory of the Lord. And when I saw it, I fell upon my face, and I heard a voice of one of them that spake" (Ezekiel 1:15-28).

This amazing eye-witness account of one who saw the throne of God, and the mysterious creatures surrounding it, was recorded to provide us with information about the throne of God. This world of the spirit exists! These beings are real!

Ezekiel describes the scene further in chapter 10 of his prophecy:

"Then I looked, and, behold, in the firmament that was above the head of the cherubims there appeared over them as it were a sapphire stone, as the appearance of the likness of a throne. And he spake unto the man clothed with linen, and said, Go in between the wheels, even under the cherub, and fill thine hand with coals of fire from between the cherubims, and scatter them over the city. And he went in in my sight. Now the cherubims stood on the right side of the house, when the man went in; and the cloud filled the inner court.

"Then the glory of the LORD went up from the cherub, and

stood over the threshold of the house; and the house was filled with the cloud, and the court was full of the brightness of the LORD's glory. And the sound of the cherubims' wings was heard even to the outer court, as the voice of the Almighty God when he speaketh.

"And it came to pass, that when he had commanded the man clothed with linen, saying, Take fire from between the wheels, from between the cherubims; then he went in, and stood beside the wheels. And one cherub stretched forth his hand from between the cherubims unto the fire that was between the cherubims, and took thereof, and put it into the hands of him that was clothed with linen: who took it, and went out.

"And there appeared in the cherubims the form of a man's hand under their wings. And when I looked, behold the four wheels by the cherubims, one wheel by one cherub, and another wheel by another cherub: and the appearance of the wheels was as the colour of a beryl stone. And as for their appearances, they four had one likeness, as if a wheel had been in the midst of a wheel. When they went, they went upon their four sides; they turned not as they went, but to the place whither the head looked they followed it; they turned not as they went. And their whole body, and their backs, and their hands, and their wings, and the wheels, were full of eyes round about, even the wheels that they four had.

"As for the wheels, it was cried unto them in my hearing, O wheel. And everyone had four faces: the first face was the face of a cherub, and the second face was the face of a man, and the third the face of a lion, and the fourth the face of an eagle. And the cherubims were lifted up. This is the living creature that I saw by the river of Chebar.

"And when the cherubims went, the wheels went by them: and when the cherubims lifted up their wings to mount up from the earth, the same wheels also turned not from beside them. When they stood, these stood; and when they were lifted up, these lifted up themselves also: for the spirit of the living creature was in them.

"Then the glory of the LORD departed from off the threshold of the house, and stood over the cherubims. And the cherubims lifted up their wings, and mounted up from the earth in my sight: when they went out, the wheels also were beside them, and every one stood at the door of the east gate of the LORD's house; and the glory of the God of Israel was over them above. *This is the living creature that I saw under the God of Israel by the river of Chebar; and I knew that they were the cherubims.* Every one had four faces a piece, and every one *four wings*; and the likeness of the hands of a man was under their wings. And the likeness of their faces was the same faces which I saw by the river of Chebar, their appearances and themselves: they sent every one straight forward" (Ezekiel 10:1-22).

The Ezekiel account is the fullest account of the Throne of God found in the Scriptures. It tells us the most about the mysterious super-angelic beings called cherubim. Notice that they have *four* wings apiece, whereas the seraphim have *six* wings each.

Notice, too, that these mysterious creatures travel in straight lines, associated with equally mysterious "wheels." What are these? Could they be associated with some of the strange, mysterious "UFO" sightings in modern times? Could they be the same as some of the mysterious "flying saucers" people claim to have seen darting through the skies in straight lines? Or hovering over the earth, before rising out of sight like a flame of light?

Ezekiel says he saw these creatures, and these "wheels," rising up from the House of the Lord—that is, the Temple—in Jerusalem approximately 718 B.C. Could he have been describing from a first-hand, eye witness account, what we, today, would term a "UFO"—"unidentified flying object"?

Much remains to be learned about the Throne of God, and the incredible panoply of creatures that surround it—the 24 "elders," the seraphim with six wings, the cherubim with four wings, the wheels, the myriad hosts of angels. The Bible also speaks of *arch-angels,* or super-powerful angels, such as Gabriel and Michael.

Of one thing you may be certain, however. The angels of the Bible, when they appeared to men, never had "wings" but appeared as powerful men, in a human form. Never did they appear as sweet little "cherubs," with bows and arrows, to smite the love-sick.

An angel of the Lord appeared to many of the children of Israel to rebuke them for turning aside from the right path, in the days of the Judges of Israel (Judges 2:1, 4).

An angel of the Lord appeared to Gideon, when the land of Midian prevailed against Israel (Judges 6:1-2; verse 11-12). "Then the angel of the LORD put forth the end of the staff that was in his hand, and touched the flesh and the unleavened cakes (which Gideon had prepared as an offering); and there rose up fire out of the rock, and consumed the flesh and the unleavened cakes. Then the angel of the LORD departed out of his sight. And when Gideon perceived that he was an angel of the Lord, Gideon said, Alas, O Lord God! for because I have seen an angel of the Lord face to face. And the Lord said unto him, Peace be unto thee; fear not: thou shalt not die" (verses 21-23).

Often men had trouble at first discerning that they were talking with angels of the Lord. One appeared to the wife of Manoah, telling her she would conceive and bear a son (Judges 13:2-3). "Then the woman came and told her husband, saying, A man of God came unto me, and his countenance was like the countenance of an angel of God, very terrible: but I asked him not whence he was, neither told me his name" (Judges 13:6). Later, the angel also appeared to Manoah: "And Manoah said unto the angel of the LORD, I pray thee, let us detain thee, until we shall have made ready a kid for thee. And the angel of the LORD said unto Manoah, Though thou detain me, I will not eat of thy bread: and if thou wilt offer a burnt offering, thou must offer it unto the Lord. *For Manoah knew not that he was an angel of the Lord.* And Manoah said unto the angel of the Lord, What is thy name, that when thy sayings come to pass we may do thee honour? And the angel of the Lord said unto him, Why askest thou thus after my name, seeing it is secret (or, wonderful)? So Manoah took a kid with a meat offering, and offered it upon a rock unto the Lord: and the angel did wondrously; and Manoah and his wife looked on. For it came to pass, when the flame went up toward heaven from off the altar, that the angel of the LORD ascended in the flame of the altar.

And Manoah and his wife looked on it, and fell on their faces to the ground. But the angel of the LORD did no more appear to Manoah and to his wife. Then Manoah knew that he was an angel of the Lord'' (Judges 13:15-21).

The numbers of angels is very great. Jesus Christ, when He was on the earth, asked His disciples, ''Thinkest thou that I cannot now pray to my Father, and he shall presently give me more than twelve legions of angels?'' (Matthew 26:53). A legion in the Roman army contained 6,000 infantry, besides a contingent of cavalry.

The Bible refers to angels as ''strong'' (Rev. 5:2) and ''mighty'' (Rev. 18:21). Their appearance is often brilliant and dazzling. At the resurrection of Christ, two angels appeared at the tomb. ''And, behold, there was a great earthquake: for the angel of the Lord descended from heaven, and came and rolled back the stone from the door, and sat upon it. His countenance was like lightning, and his raiment white as snow: and for fear of him the keepers did shake, and became as dead men'' (Matthew 28:2-4).

John says in Revelation, chapter 10: ''And I saw another *mighty* angel come down from heaven, clothed with a cloud: and a rainbow was upon his head, and his face was as it were the sun, and his feet as pillars of fire'' (verse 1).

Angels are called ''holy ones'' in many places in the Scriptures (Daniel 4:13, 23; 8:13; Matthew 25:31).

The Scriptures also reveal that there are specific titles and agencies belonging to various angels (Ephesians 1:21).

The righteous angels serve God without ceasing. Whether they are pictured surrounding God's Throne, praising Him, or busy upon some mission to earth, they always serve their Creator with dispatch and fidelity. They compose a great angelic *army* which will follow Christ to the earth in the future to establish the Kingdom of God upon the earth, in its divine fulness and splendor (Revelation 19:11-15, especially verse 14). When Christ returns in His glory, all the holy angels will come with him (Matthew 25:31).

We read the same event described in Matthew 24:30-31: ''And then shall appear the sign of the Son of man in heaven:

and then shall all the tribes of the earth mourn, and they shall see the Son of man coming in the clouds of heaven with power and great glory. And he shall send his angels with a great sound of a trumpet, and they shall gather together his elect from the four winds, from one end of heaven to the other."

The apostle Paul tells us something else about angels: "There are also celestial bodies, and bodies terrestrial: but the glory of the celestial is one, and the glory of the terrestial is another. There is one glory of the sun, and another glory of the moon, and another glory of the stars: for one star differeth from another star in glory" (I Corinthians 15:40-41). "Stars," remember, are often symbols for angels. In this passage Paul not only is comparing the physical sun, moon and stars, but also showing us that angels, which are celestial, have a special glory, comparable to "stars," and differ from one another in glory.

Among the most glorious angels are the archangels such as Michael and Gabriel. When Christ returns, the voice of the archangel will accompany him (I Thessalonians 4:16). The apostle Jude writes: "Yet Michael the archangel, when contending with the devil he disputed about the body of Moses, durst not bring against him a railing accusation, but said, The Lord rebuke thee" (Jude 9). The archangel who appeared several times to Daniel was Gabriel (Daniel 8:16; 9:21). Gabriel also appeared to Zacharias, the father of John the Baptist: "And the angel answering said unto him, I am Gabriel, that stand in the presence of God; and am sent to speak unto thee, and to shew thee these glad tidings" (Luke 1:11-20).

The Throne of God is a center of vast, incredible, intense activity. It is the source of all Energy. To obtain even a glimpse of such a regal, holy Throne must fill our minds with awe. No wonder those of ancient times, when they beheld a glimpse of the Throne of God, feared lest they would be struck dead on the spot!

Millions of mighty angels, capable of flight without wings, with the speed of light—lightning fast—serve the Omnipotent Creator.

But aeons ago, something disastrous happened. A great rebellion broke out among the angels. A great, incredible STAR

WAR erupted and threatened the entire Universe! It was the greatest rebellion of all time.

The entire future of the Universe was at stake!

Chapter Sixteen

The Greatest Battle

Aeons ago, according to the Bible, there was an ancient cosmic war—a celestial battle for control of the Universe. That war has been continuing ever since that ancient time. Today it dramatically involves mankind.

According to the Scriptures, there are three heavens—1) the atmosphere around the earth, where the birds fly "in the midst of heaven" (Genesis 1:20); 2) the starry heavens, where the solar system and galaxies are; and the "third heaven," where God's Throne is located (II Cor. 12:2-4).

This "third heaven" is where the holy angels dwell, worshipping and praising God. The Bible indicates that from time to time the angels present themselves before the Throne of God. "Now there was a day when the sons of God came to present themselves before the LORD, and Satan came also among them" (Job 1:6). The angels are "sons of God" by the act of divine creation (Job 38:7).

We know very little about what happens in the "third heaven" except what the Bible tells us.

The apostle Paul relates: "It is not expedient for me doubtless to glory. I will come to visions and revelations of the Lord.

"I knew a man in Christ above fourteen years ago, (whether in the body, I cannot tell; or whether out of the body, I cannot tell: God knoweth;) such a one caught up to the *third heaven.*

"And I knew such a man, (whether in the body, or out of the body, I cannot tell: God knoweth;)

"How that he was caught up into paradise, and heard

unspeakable words, which it is not lawful for a man to utter" (II Corinthians 12:1-4).

A vision of heaven given to the apostle John is recorded in the book of Revelation, chapters 4-5. The Bible relates that there exists a heavenly city which God is presently preparing for the saints. In due time it will come down out of heaven to the earth. John recorded:

"And I saw a new heaven and a new earth: for the first heaven and the first earth were passed away; and there was no more sea. And I John saw the holy city, new Jerusalem, coming down from God *out of heaven,* prepared as a bride adorned for her husband. . . .

"And he carried me away in the spirit to a great and high mountain, and shewed me that great city, the holy Jerusalem, descending out of heaven from God, having the glory of God: and her light was like unto a stone most precious, even like a jasper stone, clear as crystal; and had a wall great and high, and had twelve gates, and at the gates twelve angels, and names written thereon, which are the names of the twelve tribes of the children of Israel" (Revelation 21:1-2, 10-12).

This great city will have three gates on the north, south, east and west sides (verse 13). The wall around the city will have twelve foundations, and in them the names of the twelve apostles (verse 14). The base of the city will lie in the shape of a square, each of the four sides being 12,000 furlongs in length. A furlong, equal to the Greek stadium, was about 202 yards in length. Thus each side of the city will be approximately 1,500 miles—and the height of the city will be the same (Rev. 21:16).

The wall of the city will be approximately 288 feet in height around the perimeter of the city (verse 17).

John continues his description: "And the building of the wall of it was of jasper: and the city was *pure gold*, like unto clear glass. And the foundations of the wall of the city were garnished with all manner of precious stones. The first foundation was jasper; the second, sapphire; the third, a chalcedony; the fourth, an emerald; the fifth, sardonyx; the sixth, sardius; the seventh, chrysolite; the eighth, beryl; the ninth, a topaz; the tenth, a chrysoprasus; the eleventh, a jacinth; the twelfth, an amethyst.

"And the twelve gates were twelve pearls; every several gate was of one pearl: and the street of the city was pure gold, as it were transparent glass" (Rev. 21:18-21).

The nations of those men and women who are saved—will inherit that heavenly city (Rev. 21:24). Jesus Christ told John, *"He that overcometh shall inherit all things;* and I will be his God, and he shall be my son" (Rev. 21:7). God has a tremendous destiny planned for mankind.

John continues: "And he [the angel] shewed me a pure river of water of life, clear as crystal, proceeding out of the throne of God and of the Lamb. In the midst of the street of it, and on either side of the river, was there the tree of life, which bare twelve manner of fruits, and yielded her fruit every month: and the leaves of the tree were for the healing of the nations. And there shall be no more curse: but the throne of God and of the Lamb shall be in it; and his servants shall serve him: and they shall see his face; and his name shall be in their foreheads.

"And there shall be no night there; and they need no candle, neither light of the sun; for the Lord God giveth them light: and they shall reign for ever and ever" (Rev. 22:1-5).

Notice—the saints, those who overcome, those who serve God, shall *reign with Him* in that future world of tomorrow! They will reign as kings over the earth (Rev. 5:10). They will inherit all things with Christ, their elder brother, the captain of their salvation (Hebrews 2:10; 5:9).

God the Father has appointed Christ to be the "heir of all things" (Hebrews 1:1). Moffatt puts it plainly: "HEIR OF THE UNIVERSE!"

We are to be joint heirs with Him—of the Universe! As Paul wrote to the Romans: "The Spirit itself beareth witness with our spirit, that we are the children of God; and if children, then heirs; heirs of God, and JOINT-HEIRS WITH CHRIST; if so be that we suffer with him, that we may be also glorified together. For I reckon that the sufferings of this present time are not worthy to be compared with the glory which shall be revealed in us" (Rom. 8:16-18).

The apostle John puts it even plainer in his first epistle: "Beloved, now are we the sons of God, and it doth not yet appear what we shall be: but we know that, when he shall appear, we shall be like him; for we shall see him as he is" (I John 3:2).

We will be like Him! Glorified! Immortal! With eternal life! We will be rulers of the world to come! We will, with Him, inherit the Universe! Can your mind comprehend it?

In awe of the destiny of man, Paul humbly wrote: "For unto the *angels* hath he not put in subjection the world to come, whereof we speak. But one in a certain place testified, saying, *What is man,* that thou art mindful of him? or the son of man, that thou visitest him? Thou madest him a little lower than the angels; [temporarily, while we are in this mortal fleshly body] thou crownedst him with glory and honour, and didst set him over the works of thy hands [man was given dominion over the earth at the time of his creation—Genesis 1:26-27]: Thou hast put *all things* in subjection under his feet. For in that he put *all* in subjection under him, *he left nothing that is not put under him.*"

These are very deep sayings of the apostle Paul. Paul continues: "But now we see *not yet* all things put under him" (Hebrews 2:5-8).

"NOT YET"!

No, today man has dominion over the earth only. And, in his mortal, fleshly, carnal nature, he has made a miserable botch of the earth! At this point, man does not deserve to rule over anything else, or he would mess it up, too! Can you imagine mankind unleashed upon the hapless universe? Can you imagine man polluting not the earth only, but the entire cosmos with his dirt, debauchery, and degradation?

But God does intend—eventually—for mankind—changed, glorified, made immortal—to rule over the entire COSMOS!

Paul wrote that we see "not yet" all things put under the control of man. He added, "But we see Jesus, who was made a little lower than the angels for the suffering of death, crowned with glory and honor; that he by the grace of God, should taste death for every man. For it became him, for whom are all things, and by whom are all things, in bringing *many sons unto glory,* to make the captain of their salvation perfect through sufferings" (Heb. 2:9-10).

In that future world, we shall even rule over—if your mind

can comprehend it—the angels! The apostle Paul put it plainly: "Do ye not know that the saints shall judge the world? . . . Know ye not that we shall *judge angels*?" (I Corinthians 6:2-3).

At that time of course we shall be given new celestial bodies. Paul wrote that Jesus Christ, our high priest and King, is He "Who shall change our vile body, that it may be fashioned like unto his glorious body, according to the working whereby he is able even to subdue all things unto himself" (Philippians 3:21).

And what is His body like? Read again Revelation, chapter 1, verses 13-17. His body is glorious—His countenance shines as the sun in its full strength! We shall then be like that—immortal, spirit beings—sons of God by the resurrection from the dead!

Christians—truly begotten sons of God—those who have repented of their sins, accepted Christ as Saviour, and received His Holy Spirit as a begettal—are forerunners of a new world—a new Age! They are now in training to inherit all things, the entire Universe! They will someday be glorified, even as Christ, their Saviour, the Captain of their salvation, and Elder Brother.

As Paul wrote, "For both he that sanctifieth and they who are sanctified are all of one: for which cause he is not ashamed to call them brethren" (Heb. 2:11).

Why has this knowledge been hidden from mankind? Why haven't you heard your true potential destiny before? Why have even many of the churches been ignorant of the destiny of mankind? Why is there a veil cast over the eyes of all nations?

Why, indeed?

God's Plan has been manifest from the very beginning. Ages ago God determined what He would do. When He created mankind, it was for this supreme glorious Purpose.

God ordained this plan, from the foundation of the world. As Paul wrote: "Blessed be the God and Father of our Lord Jesus Christ, who hath blessed us with all spiritual blessings in heavenly places in Christ: According as he hath chosen us in him before the foundation of the world, that we should be holy and without blame before him in love: Having predestinated us unto the adoption of children [Greek, *sonship*] by Jesus Christ to himself, according to the good pleasure of his will, to the praise of the glory of his grace, wherein he hath made us accepted in the beloved. In whom we have redemption through his blood, the forgiveness of sins, according to the riches of his grace; wherein he hath abounded toward us in all wisdom and prudence; Having made known unto us the mystery of his will, according to his good pleasure which he hath purposed in himself: That in the dispensation of the fulness of times he might gather together in one all things in Christ, both which are in heaven, and which are on earth; even in him: In whom also we have obtained an inheritance, being predestinated according to the purpose of him who worketh all things after the counsel of his own will: That we should be to the praise of his glory, who first trusted in Christ" (Ephesians 1:3-12).

God has a great purpose planned for mankind, if we only have eyes to see it. It far surpasses the mind and ken of man. In our frail, mortal bodies, we can but catch the barest outline of it shining resplendently, majestically, like some flaming distant fiery diamond.

As Paul said: "For now we see through a glass darkly; but then face to face: now I know in part; but then shall I know even as also I am known" (I Corinthians 13:12).

Paul declared the purpose of God, saying: "Now this I say, brethren, that flesh and blood cannot inherit the kingdom of God; neither doth corruption inherit incorruption. Behold, I shew you a mystery; We shall not all sleep, but we shall all be changed, in a moment, in a twinkling of an eye, at the last trump: for the trumpet shall sound, and the dead shall be raised incorruptible, and we shall be changed. For this corruption must put on incorruption, and this mortal must put on immortality. So when this corruptible shall have put on incorruption, and this mortal shall have put on immortality, then shall be brought to pass the saying that is written, Death is swallowed up in victory" (I Cor. 15:50-54).

All mankind should know the purpose of life. But very few

really understand it. Why? The answer is clear: Their minds have been blinded by "the god of this world."

Paul wrote: "But as it is written, Eye hath not seen, nor ear heard, neither have entered into the heart of man, the things which God hath prepared for them that love him. But God hath revealed them unto us by his Spirit: for the Spirit searcheth all things, yea, the deep things of God" (I Cor. 2:10).

The world lies in deepest ignorance of the plan and purpose of God. As the apostle Paul declared so plainly: "But if our gospel (the Greek word for "good news") be hid, it is *hid to them that are lost:* In whom the god of this world hath *blinded* the minds of them which believe not, lest the light of the glorious gospel [good news] of Christ, who is the image of God, should shine unto them" (II Corinthians 4:3-4).

Their minds are blinded. A veil is drawn over their eyes. But those of us who are the advance called out ones, the "chosen" ones, to whom God has revealed His purpose—"But we all, with open face beholding as in a glass the glory of the Lord, are changed into the same image from glory to glory, even as by the Spirit of the Lord" (II Cor. 3:18).

Who is the "god of this world" who has blinded the minds of men and nations? Paul also called him " . . . the prince of the power of the air, the spirit that now worketh in the children of disobedience" (Ephesians 2:2).

Because of this evil prince, the world walks in the "vanity of their mind, having the understanding darkened, being alienated from the life of God through the ignorance that is in them, because of the *blindness* of their heart: who being past feeling have given themselves over unto lasciviousness, to work all uncleanness with greediness" (Ephesians 4:17-19).

This prince—this "god"—is identified in many passages of the Scriptures as the 'devil.' This being is the avowed, sworn enemy of mankind. He seeks to destroy man, especially the children of God.

Paul charges every Christian: "Put on the whole armour of God, that ye may be able to stand against the wiles of the devil.

"For we wrestle not against flesh and blood, but against principalities, against powers, against the *rulers of the darkness of this world,* against spiritual wickedness [or, *wicked spirits*] in high places. Wherefore take unto you the whole armour of God, that ye may be able to withstand in the evil day, and having done all, to stand. Stand therefore, having your loins girt about with truth, and having on the breastplate of righteousness; and your feet shod with the preparation of the gospel of peace; Above all, taking the shield of faith, wherewith ye shall be able to quench all the fiery darts [missiles, or bolts] of the wicked [one]. And take the helmet of salvation, and the sword of the Spirit, which is the word of God: Praying always with all prayer and supplication in the Spirit, and watching thereunto with all perseverance and supplication for all saints" (Ephesians 6:11-18).

The Spirit of God, and His Word, give us power to stand up against this wicked enemy in high places—to beat him in every spiritual encounter.

We must be vigilant against this foe. Peter warns us in strong terms: "Humble yourselves therefore under the mighty hand of God, that he may exalt you in due time; Casting all your care upon him; for he careth for you. Be sober, be vigilant; because your adversary the devil, as a roaring lion, walketh about, seeking whom he may devour: Whom resist steadfast in the faith, knowing that the same afflictions are accomplished in your brethren that are in the world" (I Peter 5:6-9).

This wicked enemy is compared to a roaring lion, hungry, seeking prey—stragglers—from the innocent flocks of sheep. We must stand our guard, be alert to every danger, every wile and subtle device of the devil, which he would use to lure us away from the Word of God, or entice us into the ways of the world, or inveigle us with the charms of lust, the passions of the flesh, or pride and avarice.

The purpose God is working out here below requires that we learn patience. We must love and obey the commands of our Creator, as summed up in the Ten Commandments, which themselves are summed up in the beautiful two great commandments—love for God, and love for our neighbor.

Jesus Christ, when He walked upon the earth, had an encounter with the devil. It was no doubt the greatest battle of all time—more significant than the battle of Troy, the battle of Carthage, Trafalgar, the battle of Britain, or even the battle of Midway. It was the greatest battle of all human history.

The story is given in Matthew, chapter four, and also in Luke, chapter four.

"Then was Jesus led up of the Spirit into the wilderness to be tempted of the devil. And when he had fasted forty days and forty nights, he was afterward an hungred. And when the tempter came to him, he said, If thou be the Son of God, command that these stones be made bread" (Matthew 4:1-3).

The devil attempted to strike where Jesus must have been weakest. After fasting forty days, he was no doubt extremely hungry, perhaps very close to physical death, lacking in physical energy. His whole body must have cried out, ached, for food.

But Jesus resisted the impulse to do as the devil insinuated. The devil had said, "If thou be the son of God." Jesus knew there was no question of "if." He knew who he was. He knew he had nothing to prove to the devil; he knew, too, that the devil really knew who he was. This was merely a trick to catch him off guard, to sidetrack him from the real battle of the mind.

"But he answered and said, It is written, Man shall not live by bread alone, but by every word that proceedeth out of the mouth of God" (Matt. 4:4).

Jesus used the Word of God to defeat the devil. He cited Scripture. He kept close to the Father in Spirit, and knew that the Word of God would cut right to the heart of every issue. As long as he was fortified with the Word of God, the devil couldn't destroy him.

But then the devil used a new tact. He came from a different direction. This time *he* quoted Scripture!

"Then the devil taketh him up into the holy city, and setteth him on a pinnacle of the temple, and saith unto him, If thou be the Son of God, cast thyself down: for it is written, He shall give his angels charge concerning thee: and in their hands they shall bear thee up, lest at any time thou dash thy foot against a stone" (Matt. 4:5-6).

Again, the devil used the subtily implanted doubt—he said

"If." But this did not anger, annoy, or irritate Christ. He was above such human frailties and foibles. The lack of respect shown by the devil did not tempt him in the least. And Christ was ready for the devil's ploy of using Scripture. Knowing the Bible even better than the devil he turned the Scripture right back on him—

"Jesus said unto him, It is written again, Thou shalt not tempt the Lord thy God" (verse 7).

Jesus knew the real issue wasn't whether God the Father would rescue him if he fell off a roof or high place. The real issue was whether he would succumb to the charms and enticements of the devil—come under his control, under his influence, under his power of suggestion. Jesus did not budge. He stood as a tower of strength.

The devil's third attempt was a clever, oblique approach. This time he did not attack Christ head on, or challenge him. This time he acted as a close friend, he sidled up to him, and showed him all the kingdoms of the world, their riches and glory. All this wealth and power, he offered to the human Christ Jesus. He didn't have to earn them; he didn't have to sweat, or work hard, suffer, in order to obtain this power. It was all offered—immediately, upon one very easily met condition.

"Again, the devil taketh him up into an exceeding high mountain, and sheweth him all the kingdoms of the world, and the glory of them; and saith unto him, All these things will I give thee, if thou wilt fall down and worship me." (Matt. 4:8).

That's all he had to do. But the devil was really seeking to destroy Christ—to tempt him to renounce God, and to sin—to disqualify as your Saviour and mine!

If Christ had succumbed to this blandishment, it would have been all over. Picture yourself there under mental pressure and turmoil, with all the kingdoms of the world easily within your grasp. Would you have been tempted—just a little? No troubles, no trials, no tests in life—just having your own way in every thing! All the wealth—all the riches—all the fame, honor and glory—all the emeralds, diamonds, sapphires, and precious stones of every description—all the beautiful buildings, gardens, and fountains—all the beautiful women, as many as you chose, as often as you wished—all the servants, pomp and ceremony your heart could wish.

Imagine it!

But Jesus did not succumb. Rather than have everything this world had to offer, and its "god," he chose the hard and narrow path, the rocky road, the way of trials, tests, troubles, and eventual death, so you and I could have a Saviour!

Jesus, straightened up, stood tall, and thundered to the devil in a voice of complete command:

"Get thee hence, Satan: for it is written, Thou shalt worship the Lord thy God, and him only shalt thou serve" (Matthew 4:10).

Jesus won the encounter. "Then the devil leaveth him, and, behold, angels came and ministered unto him" (verse 11).

As hungry, tired and worn out as Jesus must have felt, after fasting 40 days and 40 nights, the devil was still no match for him. By drawing upon the strength of the Word of God, he conquered the arch enemy, the foe of all mankind!

And now God Almighty says to us—because Jesus was a conqueror, a champion, a winner, a victor—"And we know that all things work together for good to them that love God, to them who are the called according to his purpose. For whom he did foreknow, he also did predestinate to be conformed to the image of his Son, that he might be the firstborn among many brethren. Moreover whom he did predestinate, them he also called: and whom he called, them he also justified: and whom he justified, them he also glorified. What shall we then say to these things? If God be for us, who can be against us? He that spared not his own Son, but delivered him up for us all, how shall he not with him also freely give us all things? Who shall lay any thing to the charge of God's elect? It is God that justifieth. Who is he that condemneth? It is Christ that died, yea rather, that is risen again, who is even at the right hand of God, who also maketh intercession for us. Who shall separate us from the love of Christ? shall tribulation, or distress, or persecution, or famine, or nakedness, or peril, or sword? As it is written, For thy sake we are killed all the day long; we are accounted as sheep for the slaughter. *Nay, in all these things we are MORE THAN CONQUERORS through him that loved us.*

"For I am persuaded, that neither death, nor life, nor angels, nor principalities, nor powers, nor things present, nor things to come, nor height, nor depth, nor any other creature, shall be able to separate us from the love of God which is in Christ Jesus our Lord" (Romans 8:29-39).

Powerful words, those!

We are indeed more than conquerors. And yet we are not physical conquerors as Alexander the Great, Caesar, or Napoleon—all mortal men who died. We are spiritual warriors and conquerors of the spirit!

Paul put it plainly:

"For though we walk in the flesh, we do not war after the flesh: (For the weapons of our warfare are not carnal, but mighty through God to the pulling down of strong holds:) Casting down imaginations, and every high thing that exalteth itself against the knowledge of God, and bringing into captivity every thought to the obedience of Christ" (II Corinthians 10:4-5).

Our warfare is spiritual! And that warfare goes on throughout our lives.

Paul wrote to the evangelist Timothy: "Fight the good fight of faith, lay hold on eternal life" (I Tim. 6:12). He charged him: "Wherefore I put thee in remembrance that thou stir up the gift of God, which is in thee by the putting on of my hands. For God hath not given us the spirit of fear; but of power, and of love, and of a sound mind" (II Tim. 1:6-7).

Paul exhorted Timothy: "Thou therefore endure hardness, as a good soldier of Jesus Christ. No man that warreth entangleth himself with the affairs of this life; that he may please him who hath chosen him to be a soldier" (II Tim. 2:3-4).

Paul knew it is difficult to be a Christian. He fought against the pulls of the world, the flesh, and the devil. Paul wrote these blazing words:

"Know ye not that they which run in a race run all, but one

receiveth the prize? So run, that ye may obtain. And every man that striveth for the mastery is temperate in all things. Now they do it to obtain a corruptible crown; but we an incorruptible. I therefore so run, not as uncertainly; so fight I, not as one that beateth the air: But I keep under my body, and bring it into subjection: lest that by any means, when I have preached to others, I myself should be a castaway" (I Corinthians 9:24-27).

The saints are those who seize hold of the Kingdom of God, and take it by force! Jesus said we must strive to enter in at the strait gate, for many would try to do so, and their effort would not be enough—they would not be able (Matt. 7:13-14). He said, "strive"—the Greek word is *agonizomai,* and means strive as if in sheer agony. Have you ever striven to do something so hard that beads of perspiration broke out all over your face and body? You may have seen a weightlifter striving to lift 400 pounds over his head, grunting, groaning, wheezing, puffing, his muscles bulging, his face red with blood-flushed effort and tension, his jaw firmly set. Or you may have seen a runner, struggling with every ounce of strength and determination left within him, pounding the track with his feet, forcing his legs to respond to the commands of his mind, driving himself toward that fluttering finish line, beads of sweat blurring his vision, his arms pumping, his body arched, his breath coming fast and furiously, as he struggles forward, forward, forward . . . on to victory, snapping the tape!

So it is with the Christian life. It is not easy. It teaches grace, grit, gumption and guts. It teaches you to be a true Winner!

We are to work out our own salvation with fear and trembling (Philippians 2:12-13). Through the power of faith, we are to conquer all enemies. "For whatsoever is born of God overcometh the world: and this is the victory that overcometh the world, even our faith" (I John 5:4).

"Love not the world," John said, "neither the things that are in the world. If any man love the world, the love of the Father is not in him. For all that is in the world, the lust of the flesh, and the lust of the eyes, and the pride of life, is not of the Father, but is of the world" (I John 2:15-16).

Faith is our final victory! But how do we obtain this miracle-working faith?

Paul declared: "I am crucified with Christ: nevertheless I live; yet not I, but Christ liveth in me: and the life which I now live in the flesh I live by the faith of the Son of God, who loved me, and gave himself for me" (Galatians 2:20).

It is the faith of Jesus Christ dwelling in us, and working mightily in us, that makes victory possible—that actually makes us into champions of faith—that molds us into the image of Christ!

It is not something we struggle, strive, and work out ourselves, through our own efforts. Paul said: "For by grace are ye saved through faith; and that not of yourselves: it is the gift of God: not of works, lest any man should boast" (Ephesians 2:8-9).

We must claim his promise. We must repent of our sins, and all those works of the flesh which separate us from God. We must draw near to Him in prayer, seeking Him, asking His forgiveness, claiming the sacrifice of Christ on our behalf, and forsaking our own ways of darkness, and turn to His way of light, peace, patience, gentleness, goodness, and faith.

We must drink deeply of the fountain of living waters, which is his Holy Spirit: "But the fruit of the Spirit is love, joy, peace, longsuffering, gentleness, goodness, faith, meekness, temperance (self control): against such there is no law" (Galatians 5:22-23).

The god of this world— the arch enemy of mankind—the prince of the power of the air—stands opposed to us. He doesn't want God's plan for mankind to be fulfilled. He is jealous. He is envious. In the garden of Eden, he tempted Adam and Eve to forsake the commands of God, and to experiment for themselves, to take and taste of the forbidden fruit. In the guise of a serpent, a snake, full of subtilty and cunning, he craftily beguiled them into disobeying their Creator. And ever since then he has been waging a running war with mankind, deceiving, leading men astray, tempting, seducing, and ensnaring them in evil.

But when did this warfare begin? How did the devil come to exist? How—why—did he turn against God and attempt to thwart God's Plan?

When did the devil become a "devil"?

What really happened aeons ago?

Chapter Seventeen

Lucifer—Apollyon

Who—or what—is this being we call the "devil"? Flip Wilson used to say in his comedy routine, "The devil made me do it!" The devil, usually pictured with red body suit, long tail, horns and a pitchfork, is a part of popular mythology.

In the religious mythology of the world, the term devil is generally applied to the prince of evil spirits. In several different Western religions, notably Zoroastrianism, Judaism, Christianity and Islam, the devil is viewed as a fallen angel who in pride tried to usurp the position of the one and only God, and who has constantly tried to thwart man's beneficial relationships to the deity.

Zoroastrianism, a religion founded by the 6th century B.C. prophet Zoroaster, calls the devil Ahriman, the Destructive Spirit and Fiend. The devil with his hordes of other demons defiled all of creation with darkness.

Islamic theology is rich with references to Iblis, the personal name they give to the devil, who also is known as Shaytan (Satan) and "Enemy of God." According to the *Koran,* Iblis is the tempter of Eve. In Islamic legend, Iblis is the leader of the *jinn*—spiritual creatures who can do good or evil—and believed himself to be superior to the other angels.

In addition to the major Western religions, the devil was an important figure in Gnosticism, and Manichaeism. Even today there are small sects and cults which literally worship the devil as the "Prince of Darkness."

Our word "devil" actually comes from the Greek word *diabolos* which means "accuser," "slanderer." This name particularly applies to him because he is known as the "accuser of the brethren" (Rev. 20:10). In this role, he accuses God's people before the Throne of God. In the book of Job we find he belittled and accused Job before God, and was given limited power or authority by God to cause certain afflictions to befall Job, as a means to test his character, integrity, and spiritual state.

We read: "Now there was a day when the sons of God came to present themselves before the Lord, and Satan came also among them. And the Lord said unto Satan, Whence comest thou? Then Satan answered the Lord, and said, From going to and fro in the earth, and from walking up and down in it. And the Lord said unto Satan, Hast thou considered my servant Job, that there is none like him in the earth, a perfect and an upright man, one that feareth God, and escheweth evil?

"Then Satan answered the Lord, and said, Doth Job fear God for nought? Hast not thou made an hedge about him, and about his house, and about all that he hath on every side? Thou hast blessed the work of his hands, and his substance is increased in the land. But put forth thine hand now, and touch all that he hath, and he will curse thee to thy face.

"And the Lord said unto Satan, Behold, all that he hath is in thy power; only upon himself put not forth thine hand. So Satan went forth from the presence of the Lord" (Job 1:6-12).

The Hebrew word *satan* literally means "an adversary, opponent." The Greek word *Satanas* has the same meaning. Satan is another name for the devil, or chief of fallen angels.

Satan has been given many names in Scripture—he is also called the Devil, the Dragon, the Evil One, the Angel of the Bottomless Pit, the Prince of this World, the Prince of the Power of the Air, the God of this World, Apollyon, Abaddon, Belial, Beelzebub.

The first mention of Satan in the Bible is in the book of Job (except in the sense that he tempted Eve, in the guise of a serpent, in the garden of Eden). The account in Job reveals that Satan mixes with the sons of God—angels—among whom he no longer has any essential belonging. He arbitrarily roams about and seeks his own, but is still used as a servant by God. In this passage of Scripture Satan is shown as the spy of evil, the accuser of man to God, the faultfinder, the supreme Critic. He maintained that Job's reverence for God was really nothing more than self-interest. God had blessed Job, and defended him from all evil—so why wouldn't Job revere and worship God? This was Satan's line of reasoning.

God allowed Satan to test Job—to bring trials upon him, as a test of his character. Satan went about his job with great activity. He immediately inspired a marauding band of robbers to attack Job's estate, leading off his cattle and killing his servants (Job 1:14-15). Satan was also capable of causing a great fire to fall from heaven, burning up Job's sheep and other servants (verse 16). He caused another band of cutthroats to rustle Job's camels and kill the servants taking care of them. Finally, Satan stirred up a great whirlwind or tornado which ripped apart the house where Job's children, his sons and daughters, were partying, killing them all (verses 18-19).

Truly Satan is the "prince of the power of the air" and the "god of this world." In these capacities he functioned using his powers to bring havoc and disaster upon the estate and family of Job.

Satan again presented himself before God's Throne, his mission accomplished. This time the Lord said to Satan, "Hast thou considered my servant Job, that there is none like him in the earth, a perfect and an upright man, one that feareth God, and escheweth evil? and still he holdeth fast his integrity, although thou movedst me against him, to destroy him without cause" (Job 2:1-3).

Satan had lost that encounter—that battle. Job continued to worship the Living God (Job 1:20-22). So Satan had to fall back to another position. He exclaimed: "Skin for skin, yea, all that a man hath will he give for his life. But put forth thine hand now, and touch his bone and his flesh, and he will curse thee to thy face. And the Lord said unto Satan, Behold, he is in thine hand; but save his life.

"So went Satan forth from the presence of the Lord, and smote Job with sore boils from the sole of his foot unto his crown. And he took him a potsherd to scrape himself withal; and he sat down among the ashes. Then said his wife unto him, Dost thou still retain thine integrity? curse God, and die. But he said unto her, Thou speakest as one of the foolish women speaketh. What? shall we receive good at the hand of God, and shall we not receive evil? In all this did not Job sin with his lips" (Job 2:4-10).

This great historic encounter between man and his supreme Adversary illustrates many vital lessons. We see clearly that Satan can do nothing against one of God's people, without express divine permission. And he can only act within the express limitations set by God. We see that Job knew that these sore trials and tests were actually the ultimate responsibility of God. In faith he knew that God must have had a reason for allowing these troubles to befall him, although he did not at the time know what that reason was.

Fourthly, we see at this point that Satan did not attack Job's wife. Rather, he used her to attempt to get Job to curse God. But Job stood firm, and rebuked her for her lack of loyalty and submission to God.

Even so, today, Satan is the accuser of God's people. When trials come, we can be sure that it is Satan's hand. But he could do nothing except God allow it.

These tests and trials God allows to strengthen us spiritually, to teach us to rely completely upon Him, to commit our lives, fortunes, families and everything to His care and keeping, for He cares for us (I Peter 5:7).

But the devil, or Satan, is the chief opponent, the great false accuser—"the accuser of our brethren . . . which accused them before our God day and night. And they overcame him by the blood of the Lamb, and by the word of their testimony; and they loved not their lives unto the death" (Revelation 12:10-11).

Satan is the deceiver of this whole world which is cut off from God (Rev. 12:9). He corrupts the minds of men, turns them against their Creator. He is also the creator of false, diabolical, counterfeit religions in the earth. Satan is so clever, his deceptive power is so great, that if it were possible even true Christians could be subverted and led astray.

Jesus warned: "For there shall arise false Christs, and false prophets, and shall shew great signs and wonders; inasmuch that, if it were possible, they shall deceive the very elect" (Matthew 24:24).

The apostle Paul warned, similarly: "And then shall that Wicked be revealed, whom the Lord shall consume with the spirit of his mouth, and shall destroy with the brightness of his coming: Even him, whose coming is *after the working of Satan* with all power and signs and lying wonders, and with all deceivableness of unrighteousness in them that perish; because they received not the love of the truth, that they might be saved" (II Thessalonians 2:8-10).

How does Satan accomplish this? How does he manage to deceive the entire world? Does he come dressed up as the popular mythology pictures him—as a dragon, with long tail, horns, and pitchfork?

Of course not! But, as the apostle Paul warned: "But I fear, lest by any means, as the serpent beguiled Eve through his *subtilty*, so your minds should be corrupted from the simplicity that is in Christ. For if he that cometh preacheth another Jesus, whom we have not preached, or if ye receive another spirit, which ye have not received, or another gospel, which ye have not accepted, ye might well bear with him" (II Corinthians 11:3-4).

Paul was deeply concerned over the Corinthian brethren. He cautioned them: "For such are false apostles, deceitful workers, transforming themselves into the apostles of Christ. And no marvel; for Satan himself is transformed into *an angel of light.* Therefore it is no great thing if his ministers also be transformed as the ministers of righteousness; whose end shall be according to their works" (verses 13-15).

The devil appears as an angel of light! What could be more slick, more cunning, more convincing?

The arch-rebel and supreme critic comes in the guise of righteousness. He insinuates that God's Word isn't completely true. The Scripture really can be broken (contrary to John 10:35). God cannot really be relied upon. We must depend upon ourselves for whatever we want out of life. We must look out for "number one." Its all right to lie, cheat, steal, rob, get drunk, commit adultery, fornication, or murder—under the proper set of circumstances.

Satan's philosophy is "Get, get, get"—"Get it *now,* don't wait." "Indulge your appetites." "Take what isn't yours, if you want it." "You deserve it, any way." "You are better than every body else."

Satan's way of life is scheming, competition, strife, putting down others, exalting the self, pride, vanity, and self-importance. He is the supreme Egotist, the supreme Bigot, the supreme self-centered Rival to God. His way is the way of death, destruction, and disaster.

Satan's attitude was summed up by the apostle James, who wrote: "Who is a wise man and endued with knowledge among you? let him shew out of a good conversation (conduct) his works with meekness of wisdom. But if ye have bitter envying and strife in your hearts, glory not, and lie not against the truth. This wisdom descendeth not from above, but is earthly, sensual, *devilish.* For where envying and strife is, there is confusion (Greek, tumult, unquietness) and every evil work.

"But the wisdom that is from above is first pure, then peaceable, gentle, and easy to be intreated, full of mercy and good fruits, without partiality, and without hypocrisy. And the fruit of righteousness is sown in peace of them that make peace" (James 3:13-18).

The Bible says, "God is not the author of confusion, but of peace" (I Corinthians 14:33). The author of confusion, disorder, and tumult, is the devil. Satan creates disturbances, riots, tumults, insurrections, rebellions, revolution, warfare. He is the essence of unbridled lust.

God tempts no man (James 1:13). Satan is the chief tempter, drawing men away from God through their own lust, and enticing them.

But how did the devil get started on his evil campaign to subvert every plan and purpose of God? Where did the devil come from? What is the origin of Satan?

Did God create him that way? Did God actually create a "devil"?

God is not in business to subvert or contradict Himself. God is not a fool. He would not create a super-powerful being to stand up as His enemy, challenger, and antagonist. Such a thought is absurd!

Jesus told his disciples: "I beheld Satan as lightning fall from heaven" (Luke 10:18).

At some ancient time, some point in history, Satan fell from heaven. When did it happen?

A hint of the truth is given in the gospel according to John. Jesus said to the Pharisees of his day: "Ye are of your father the devil, and the lusts of your father ye will do. *He was a murderer from the beginning, and abode not in the truth,* because there is no truth in him. When he speaketh a lie, he speaketh of his own: for he is a liar, and the father of it" (John 8:44).

Long before becoming a human being, and partaking of human nature, Jesus had been with the Father from the beginning. He was the "Word," the second member of the Godhead. He said to the hypocritical Pharisees of his day: "Verily, verily, I say unto you, Before Abraham was, I am" (John 8:58). He was with God, and was God (John 1:1-3, 14).

At that ancient, primordial time, Jesus saw Satan fall as lightning out of heaven. He saw him when he became a Murderer "from the beginning." He saw him when he first began to harbor thoughts of resentment, vanity, jealousy, greed, avarice, and gluttony. He saw him when he first began to stray from the truth, and began to become deceitful, tricky, clever, guilty of half-truths, slander, gossip, and falsehoods.

Jesus was there.

A much fuller account of the story is provided by the prophet Isaiah. Notice what the prophet was inspired to record:

"How art thou fallen from heaven, O Lucifer, son of the morning! How art thou cut down to the ground, which didst weaken the nations!

"For thou hast said in thine heart, I will ascend into heaven, I will exalt my throne above the stars of God: I will sit also upon the mount of the congregation, in the sides of the north: I will ascend above the heights of the clouds; I will be like the most High. Yet thou shalt be brought down to hell, to the sides of the pit" (Isaiah 14:12-15).

Here the prophet Isaiah describes what happened aeons ago!

Here the first massive STAR WAR is briefly narrated. An archangel by the name of Lucifer, which means "Day star," or "Shining star of the dawn," rebelled against the Almighty God. He attempted to ascend to heaven, to exalt his own throne or seat of authority above the other angels, called "stars of God." He attempted to ascend above the clouds (clouds are in the earth's atmosphere), to rise up and conquer space—to remove God from His Throne—to become "like the Most High." But his abortive attempt failed. He was cast back down to earth in a massive struggle.

Just how big was this cosmic battle for control of the Universe? Why did Lucifer want to be "like the most High?"

In his massive rebellion, Lucifer drew the allegiance of perhaps one third of all the angels. He was a very powerful personality, a mighty angel of God. But his angelic nature, consumed with greed and lust, became a loathsome thing, detestable, unclean, filthy, vile, putrid, ugly, distorted, misshapen, foul. He became characterized as a dragon.

In the book of Revelation, John tells us: "And there appeared another wonder in heaven; and behold a great red dragon, having seven heads and ten horns, and seven crowns upon his heads. *And his tail drew the third part of the stars of heaven,* and did cast them to the earth . . ." (Revelation 12:3-4). During this cosmic conflict it is probable that tens of thousands of meteorites in the solar system were also cast down upon the earth.

John describes this vision further: "And there was *WAR* in heaven: Michael and his angels fought against the dragon; and the dragon fought and his angels, and prevailed not; neither was their place found any more in heaven. And the great dragon was cast out, that old serpent, called the Devil, and Satan, which deceiveth the whole world: he was cast out into the earth, and his angels were cast out with him" (Rev. 12:7-9).

This "war in heaven" must have been catastrophic in nature. It must have been the greatest battle of all time! Armies of angels clashing with each other! The entire cosmos must have been shaken!

Peter speaks of the cataclysmic fall of Lucifer and his

renegade angels this way: "For if God spared not the angels that sinned, but cast them down to hell (Greek, *tartaroo,* a "place of restraint"), and delivered them into chains of darkness, to be reserved unto judgment" (II Peter 2:4). These angels had "sinned." But what is "sin"? The Bible defines it as rebellion, lawlessness. "Sin is the transgression of the law," John wrote (I John 3:4). Further, Paul tells us, "whatsoever is not of faith is sin" (Romans 14:23).

One third of the angelic hosts, apparently, sinned—violated the laws of God—and acted wantonly. They attempted to overthrow the Government of the Creator God. They precipitated violence on a cosmic scale never before heard of or seen! They went astray from the paths of peace, goodness, faith, righteousness.

They looked upon God as a tyrant, a malevolent dictator, not fit for His office, not capable of running the Universe. They wanted *their* way. They wanted their ambitions—*right now*! They wanted to seize God's Throne and take over—He wasn't running things right, in their eyes. Perhaps they were jealous—they thought He was playing favorites and they didn't feel on the "inside group."

Lucifer may well have been jealous of the potential destiny and future of mankind. God very likely had made His plans known to the angelic world "from the foundation of the world," and they knew that ultimately, eventually, He intended for man to be over the angels (Hebrews 2:5-8; I Corinthians 6:3).

The thought of mankind ruling over him apparently did not sit too well with Lucifer. It was the "last straw." He couldn't—or wouldn't—take it any more.

Jude tells us: "And the angels which kept not their first estate, but left their own habitation, he hath reserved in everlasting chains under darkness unto the judgment of the great day" (Jude 6).

These rebellious angels were, Jude says, "Raging waves of the sea, foaming out their own shame; wandering stars, to whom is reserved the blackness of darkness for ever" (Jude 13).

The rebellious angels are largely confined to the earth

today—in chains of darkness, reserved for judgment. The minions of the devil are known as "demons"—wicked spirits. They are disembodied spirits which roam the earth, trying to lead people into sin and rebellion against God. They are responsible for a great deal of the madness, lunacy, insanity and schizophrenia found in the earth among men and women.

The king of demons, or fallen angels, is Satan, formerly known as "Lucifer," or "Light bringer." But he exchanged light for darkness. Lucifer, or Satan, the "Adversary," is also known as *Abaddon,* or *Apollyon,* meaning "A destroyer." He is the "angel of the bottomless pit."

The apostle John, in a vision of the future ahead of us, said:

"And the fifth angel sounded, and I saw a star (angel) fall from heaven unto the earth: and to him was given the key of the bottomless pit [or, abyss]. And he opened the bottomless pit; and there arose a smoke out of the pit, as the smoke of a great furnace; and the sun and the air were darkened by reason of the smoke of the pit. And there came out of the smoke locusts upon the earth: and unto them was given power, as the scorpions of the earth have power. . . . And they had a king over them, which is the angel of the bottomless pit, whose name in the Hebrew tongue is Abaddon, but in the Greek tongue hath his name Apollyon" (Revelation 9:1-3, 11).

When did the original great Rebellion take place? Jesus said it was "from the beginning," that "from the beginning" Satan was a murderer and liar, and the father of such things. "In the beginning," we read, "God created the heavens and the earth" (Genesis 1:1). The angels were created before the earth was founded (Job 38:4-7). This ancient conflict, therefore, was probably millions of years ago—maybe even billions of years ago. Satan's Rebellion, with one third of the angels composing his aggressing army invading heaven, must have been responsible for the chaos and destruction which is recorded in Genesis 1:2—the *tohu* and *bohu* and darkness which covered the earth, long before the creation of Adam and Eve. The cataclysm in Genesis 1:2 is undoubtedly related to the cataclysmic fall of Lucifer from heaven.

How many times Satan's acts have led to destruction and

cataclysm since that original rebellion we are not given to know at this time. His attempts to wage war upon God may have occurred many times over millions of years. The extinction of the dinosaurs may well be connected; the demise of the Pleistocene World may have been directly involved. Satan, as an agent of destruction, attempting to thwart God's Plan, has actually been a tool in God's hand. That is, everything he has done, God has caused to work out for mankind's ultimate good. Even the tests and trials that Satan brings upon us, God causes to work out for our eventual good (Romans 8:29).

Ezekiel tells us more about the ancient world. He tells us that Lucifer originally was one of the two cherubim that covered the throne of God.

In the days of the Exodus, God instructed Moses to make a replica of God's Throne—a sanctuary for God to dwell in. An ark was to be made, overlaid with pure gold (Exodus 25:3-11). A mercy seat of pure gold was to be placed in the ark, symbolizing God's Throne. And God said: "And thou shalt make two cherubims of gold, of beaten work shalt thou make them, in the two ends of the mercy seat. And make one cherub on the one end, and the other cherub on the other end: even of the mercy seat shall ye make the cherubims on the two ends thereof. And the cherubims shall stretch forth their wings on high, covering the mercy seat with their wings, and their faces shall look one to another; toward the mercy seat shall the faces of the cherubims be" (Exodus 25:18-20).

The prophet Ezekiel tells us what happened to one of these two cherubim. "Moreover the word of the Lord came unto me, saying, Son of man, take up a lamentation upon the king of Tyrus, and say unto him, Thus saith the Lord God; Thou sealest up the sum, full of wisdom, and perfect in beauty.

"Thou hast been in Eden the garden of God . . . " (Ezekiel 28:11-13).

Note that this could not be describing a literal king of the City of Tyre. The garden of Eden perished at the Noachian deluge, and Tyre did not become a city until much, much later. This king, as we shall see, was actually a spirit being—a cherubim!

Ezekiel continues:

"Thou hast been in Eden the garden of God; every precious stone was thy covering, the sardius, topaz, and the diamond, the beryl, the onyx, and the jasper, the sapphire, the emerald, and the carbuncle, and gold: the workmanship of thy tabrets and of thy pipes was prepared in thee in the day that thou wast created.

"*Thou art the anointed cherub that covereth*; and I have set thee so: thou wast upon the holy mountain of God; thou hast walked up and down in the midst of the stones of fire.

"Thou wast perfect in thy ways *from the day that thou wast created,* till iniquity was found in thee" (Ezek. 28:13-15).

Consider, for a moment. Ezekiel is describing a beautiful, resplendent, angelic creature—one of the two anointed cherubim that covered God's Throne in heaven! This creature walked upon the holy mountain of God, in the garden of God in Eden. It was a created being—and it was a perfect creation!

But then something happened to change the beautiful nature and character of this brilliant, shining angelic being. "Iniquity" was found in him. A root of bitterness, a root of jealousy, of envy, of hatred, began to spring up (compare Hebrews 12:15).

Ezekiel continues the description of this ancient scene:

"By the multitude of thy merchandise they have filled the midst of thee with *violence, and thou hast sinned:* therefore I will cast thee as profane out of the mountain of God: and I will destroy thee, O covering cherub, from the midst of the stones of fire.

"Thine heart was lifted up because of thy beauty, thou hast corrupted thy wisdom by reason of thy brightness: I will cast thee to the ground, I will lay thee before kings, that they may behold thee.

"Thou hast defiled thy sanctuaries by the multitude of thine iniquities, by the iniquity of thy traffick; therefore will I bring forth a fire from the midst of thee, it shall devour thee, and I will bring thee to ashes upon the earth in the sight of all them that behold thee. All they that know thee among the people shall be astonished at thee: thou shalt be a terror, and never shall thou be any more" (Ezekiel 28:16-19).

What happened eons ago?

Lucifer's heart was lifted up with pride. He became vain because of his beauty and brilliance. His wisdom became corrupted, and channeled into selfish, devious directions. God had said he "sealed up the sum, full of wisdom, and perfect in beauty" (Ezek. 28:12). But this beautiful creature become disloyal, disobedient, and destructive.

If we can reconstruct the scene, it would appear that in that ancient world there was much merchandise and traffic. Trade and commerce existed. The world was populated by millions of angels, and their king was Lucifer. His throne was on the earth. But he wasn't satisfied. he was a great king, and the greatest human king to compare with him was the king of Tyre, the mercantile city, in the days of Ezekiel.

But this angelic king grew restless. he said, "I will ascend into heaven." That shows he was located on the earth. "I will exalt *my throne* above the stars of God" (Isaiah 14:13). That shows he was a king, a ruler—he had a throne on the earth. But he wanted to reign upon the mountain of God, "in the sides of the north" (same verse).

Many verses of the Bible lend support to the theory that God's Throne is located in the northern heavens, in the general direction of the North Star. King David wrote: "Great is the Lord, and greatly to be praised in the city of our God, in the mountain of his holiness. Beautiful for situation, the joy of the whole earth, is mount Zion, on the sides of the north, the city of the great King" (Psalm 48:1-2). The city of God, the heavenly Jerusalem, as we know, is now in heaven (Revelation 21:1-2).

Lucifer wasn't satisfied with kingship over this earth. He wasn't satisfied with being one of the two anointed cherubim that actually covered God's Throne—a position of great importance and supreme respect—very close to the throne itself. He wasn't even happy when God gave him his own throne upon the earth, over millions of angels. His heart seethed with discontent. He wanted what God had! He was created to be a ministering angel—but he wanted to be ministered to, not to minister to others. He didn't want to be a servant. He wanted to be served!

Very likely the straw which finally broke the camel's back was the fact that God intended to create man, and to give him eventual dominion over the earth and the angelic kingdom. This Lucifer could not stand!

He rebelled!

And God dealt severely with his rebellion. God's attitude toward rebellion is revealed in the first book of the prophet Samuel:

"And Samuel said, hath the Lord as great delight in burnt offerings and sacrifices, as in obeying the voice of the Lord? Behold, to obey is better than sacrifice, and to hearken than the fat of rams. For rebellion is as the sin of witchcraft, and stubbornness is as iniquity and idolatry. Because thou hast rejected the word of the Lord, he hath also rejected thee from being king" (I Samuel 15:22-23).

Lucifer was also rejected from being a king. He lost his throne, his kingdom, his power. But he still has limited authority upon the earth, and is the "god of this world," the "prince of the power of the air." He will remain in that position until God is through with him and replaces him.

Ever since that original rebellion, there has been a constant, ongoing, continual struggle between Satan, the "Adversary," and God. Lucifer's name, "Light bringer," was changed to "Satan," meaning "Opponent."

Satan and his fallen angels, now disembodied spirits, roam the earth, in a condition of restraint. They have very little power compared to that which they used to exert. They cannot appear to men in strength and power, as the righteous angels can. They are vague shadows of their former selves. They have lost their intense brightness and brilliance. They are ghostly beings, like the wind, and are called "familiar spirits" that peep and mutter (Leviticus 19:31; 20:27; Isaiah 8:19-20).

In the New Testament mention is made of a plurality of evil spirits, with Satan as their leader (Matt. 8:28; 9:34; 12:26; Luke 11:8, 19). Satan, their leader, Jesus called "Beelzebub," meaning "the god of dung," or "the god of flies." He also called him "Belial," meaning *worthlessness, wickedness,* hence, *recklessness, lawlessness.*

Such evil spirits sometimes possess a human being, or take control of human faculties. Then can manifest super-human strength (Matthew 8:28), and break chains. They have much knowledge—they know their condition of restraint until the final time of judgment (Matt. 8:29). Jesus many times cast demons out of people and charged them not to allow the unclean spirits back (see Mark 1:24; Matthew 12:43-45). Jesus also gave Christians power over unclean spirits, so we don't need to be in fear of them at all (Mark 16:17; Acts 8:6-7; 16:16-18).

Satan is the prince of the demons (Matt. 9:24; 12:24). Demons sometimes enter the bodies of people to afflict them with diseases (Luke 8:30, 32; Matt. 9:33; 17:18; Luke 4:35, 41). Some individuals become as though "mad" because of demoniac influence (Matt. 11:18; Luke 7:33; John 7:20).

The verb "to be demonized" occurs, in one form or another, seven times in Matthew, four times in Mark, once in Luke and once in John. Among the diseases often mimicked by demons were paralysis, blindness, deafness, loss of speech, epilepsy, melancholy, and insanity. The demonized people, or those who fell under the control of a wicked spirit, or even several wicked spirits inhabiting the same body, were incapable of separating their own consciousness and ideas from the influence of the demon, their own identity often being merged, and even lost, in that of their tormentors.

Jesus distinguished between demoniacal possession and all forms of mere disease, although they sometimes occur together. He "cast out the spirits . . . and healed all that were sick" (Matt. 8:16). The people "brought unto him all sick people . . . and those which were possessed with devils, and those which were lunatic" (Matt. 4:24); "they brought unto him all that were diseased, and them that were possessed with devils" (Mark 1:32, 34). Here "lunatics" are specially distinguished from demoniacs.

The actions and utterances in demoniacal possessions are not those of the individual, but of the evil spirits. The demons are the actual agents in such cases. As Matthew said: "The unclean spirits cried," and "the devils besought him" (Matt. 8:31). And, "when the unclean spirit had torn him, and cried with a loud voice, he came out of him" (Mark 1:26; Luke 4:35).

In one case the demons asked and received from Christ permission to pass from a demoniac into a herd of swine, and promptly stampeded into the lake of Galilee. The swine were drowned (Matt. 8; Mark 5; Luke 8).

These fallen spirits always knew of Christ's divinity. One said to Him, "I know thee who thou art, the Holy One of God" (Mark 1:24; Luke 4:34). One asked, "What have we to do with thee, Jesus, thou Son of God?" (Matt. 8:29; compare Luke 4:41; Mark 3:11).

Jesus treated cases of demoniac possession as realities. He is not only described as "charging," "rebuking," "commanding," and "casting out" the unclean spirits, but his direct commands to them are recorded by the gospel writers. The fact that Jesus regarded demons as very real, and not mere figments of the imagination, or mental illness, is evident from the encounter He had with the Pharisees, when He affirmed that his casting out demons by the Spirit of God proved that the Kingdom of God had come unto them (Matt. 12:23-27; Luke 11:17-23).

Jesus gave his followers power over the demons, so they cannot afflict God's people who are close to Him, and diligently serving Him. In fact, He gave his ministry the ability and power to cast out demons, not by magical tricks, or exotic formulas, or exorcism, but always by the word of power, which Jesus intrusted to his disciples, and which the demons always obey.

Because Satan and his demons are restrained, upon the earth, their power is limited. They are frustrated, miserable, filled with hatred and resentment toward God. They are sarcastic, disrespectful, snide, rude, and belittling in nature. Satan, himself, remembered, goes about as a "roaring lion" seeking whom he may devour.

From time to time Satan or one of his demon spirits or fallen angels is used by God to perform a mission upon the earth. In the days of Jehoshaphat, king of Judah, the king of Israel wanted to join armies and fight against the Syrians. Jehoshaphat wanted to inquire of God, first, so the king of Israel paraded out 400 prophets who prophesied success and victory. But Jehoshaphat wasn't convinced. A messenger was sent to call Micaiah the prophet. Micaiah, a true prophet of God, told the kings that disaster would befall them and the battle would end in defeat (I Kings 22:17).

Micaiah added, giving us a glimpse into the strategic planning which goes on around the Throne of God: "Hear thou therefore the word of the Lord: I saw the Lord sitting on his throne, and all the host of heaven standing by him on his right hand and on his left. And the Lord said, Who shall persuade Ahab, that he may go up and fall at Ramoth-gilead? And one said on this manner, and another said on that manner. And there came forth a spirit, and stood before the Lord, and said, I will persuade him. And the Lord said unto him, Wherewith? And he said, I will go forth, and I will be a lying spirit in the mouth of all his prophets. And he said, Thou shalt persuade him, and prevail also: go forth, and do so. Now therefore, behold, the Lord hath put a lying spirit in the mouth of all these thy prophets, and the Lord hath spoken evil concerning thee" (I Kings 22:19-23).

Another example of Satan's continuing warfare against mankind is revealed in I Chronicles 21. We find that "Satan stood up against Israel, and provoked David to number Israel" (verse 1). David, tempted by pride, wanted to know the size of Israel's army, and gave in to the temptation. he took his eyes off the fact that God had given him outstanding success, and began to look to his own resources. Joab, the captain of the host, tried to reason with the king and talk him out of it, but David's wishes prevailed (verses 3-4).

As a result, "God was displeased with this thing; therefore he smote Israel" (verse 7). David quickly repented, and acknowledged his sin, whereupon God gave him three choices—either three years of famine, three months of armed invasion of Israel, or three days pestilence by the "sword of the Lord" and the "angel of the Lord" (verse 12). Forced to choose, David selected the hand of the Lord, trusting in his great mercies.

We read: "So the Lord sent pestilence upon Israel: and there fell of Israel seventy thousand men. And God sent an angel unto Jerusalem to destroy it: and as he was destroying, the Lord beheld, and he repented him of the evil, and said to the angel that destroyed, It is enough, stay now thine hand. And the angel of the Lord stood by the threshingfloor of Ornan the Jebusite. And David lifted up his eyes, and *saw* the angel of the Lord stand between the earth and the heaven, having a drawn sword in his hand stretched out over Jerusalem" (I Chronicles 21:14-16).

This awesome prodigy in the skies over Jerusalem—a figure suspended in the sky, with drawn sword stretched out over the city—left David shaken. Some commentators believe that this fiery destruction involved a comet, with its tail extended like a sword.

The Roman naturalist Pliny classified comets according to their shape. One of his 12 classifications was called *Xiphiae* or *ensiformis* (sword-shaped). After David offered sacrifice on the threshingfloor of Ornan (verse 26), the angel "put his sword back in its sheath" (verse 27). This could also refer to the fact that the blazing comet, at that time, lost its sword-like tail.

Comets, from the Greek *kometes,* meaning "long-haired," have been objects of dread and awe throughout ancient history. Some scholars believe a bright comet appeared over Judea around 7 B.C. The Jewish historian Josephus said a comet was observed in the sky in 66 A.D., hovering like a sword over Jerusalem. In 451 A.D. a comet blazed in the sky as Attila the Hun overran Europe. A comet foreshadowed the death of Caesar. According to the venerable Bede, "comets portend revolutions of kingdoms, pestilence, winds or heat."

But regardless of the exact nature of this prodigy, it was Satan who provoked David to number Israel, leading to all the trouble. Even so today he is the great Tempter, the accuser of the people of God. But soon his reign of evil suggestion and deception will be over. Very soon he will be replaced. His fate is sealed.

Chapter Eighteen

Star Wars to Come

One of the most mysterious enigmas today is the subject of UFOs or so-called "flying saucers."

Many books have been written about UFOs, both pro and con. Religions have sprung up. Some individuals have claimed to be emissaries from far away planets, sent to earth to help bring peace. Closer investigation however has never substantiated their claims. They have offered no proof—no scientifically reliable evidence.

Is our planet being visited clandestinely by spacecraft manned or controlled by intelligent beings from another world?

Scientists speculate that life may exist on other planets, but no man has any real knowledge of such. Astronomer Carl Sagan and others believe that in the entirety of the Universe, there are very likely millions of planets similar to earth on which life as we know it, or not vastly different, could exist. Thousands of such planets may exist within the relatively nearby regions of space, and hundreds of thousands within our own Milky Way galaxy.

Could life exist elsewhere, in the Universe?

Whether or not there is physical life—or highly intelligent life—on other planets, no man knows.

If we regard the Scriptures in this matter, all we can know for certain is that God has a special interest in the earth at this time. The earth is called his "footstool" (Matthew 5:35). It is to the earth that God the Father sent His Son, Jesus Christ, to redeem mankind from his sins (II Corinthians 5:18-21). Through the life and work and death and resurrection of Jesus Christ the entire world can be reconciled to God (verse 19). Christians are actually "ambassadors" of God's Kingdom, here to tell the world this joyful good news!

Obviously the world is special. We have no revelation or trustworthy knowledge that any other of the worlds in outer space ever strayed from the path and became in need of salvation and reconciliation!

However, the Bible does reveal that God is the supreme Creator of all things. Originally, we know, multitudes of angels inhabited the earth. And during those millions of years, perhaps, they were preparing the earth for the eventual creation and rulership of Man.

As Supreme Creator, Designer and Architect of the Universe, as well as Supreme Life-Giver, it is very possible—even very likely—that God also created life forms on multitudes of other planets. There is no reason to believe that the multitudes of other planets are all barren, waste, and empty. As Isaiah stated, God is not the author of confusion, disorder, or emptiness.

Isaiah wrote: "For thus saith the Lord that created the heavens; God himself that formed the earth and made it; he hath established it, he created it *not in vain* (*tohu,* waste, empty, barren), he formed it to be inhabited: I am the Lord; and there is none else" (Isaiah 45:18).

God intended from the very beginning that not just the earth, but the heavens also be *inhabited*! Whether God has already created life on other planets, or whether He intends to do so in the future, only He knows at this time. Moses put it this way: "The secret things belong unto the Lord our God: but those things which are revealed belong unto us and to our children for ever, that we may do all the words of this law" (Deuteronomy 29:29).

Do "flying saucers" exist? And are they extra-terrestrial visitations from another planet or planets?

There is no doubt that many unexplained phenomena occur which nobody understands fully. Many claims have been made by men and women who say they have seen unusual creatures or strange beings who appeared to be unearthly in appearance. Sometimes they seemed to appear out of a strange flying object, perhaps some sort of space craft. Some of these men were put to lie detector tests, and even put under hypnosis, to determine whether they were lying. The tests proved that they sincerely believed that they saw what they said they saw. They themselves were sincerely convinced. But whether they were confused, or misled, or whether they saw what they *thought* they saw, that is another question.

In a nineteen year span of time more than 10,000 sightings of "UFOs" or "unidentified flying objects" were recorded and classified, and Project Blue Book of the United States Air Force was instituted to investigate UFOs. The report concluded: "In our experience, the persons making reports seem in nearly all cases to be normal, responsible individuals. In most cases they are quite calm, at least by the time they make a report. They are simply puzzled about what they saw and hope that they can be helped to a better understanding of it. Only a very few are obviously quite emotionally disturbed, their minds being filled with pseudo-scientific, pseudo-religious or other fantasies.[1]

Opinion surveys indicate that several million Americans believe they have seen objects that could be described as unidentified flying objects, or "UFOs". What could they have seen?

Over a two year period hundreds of cases were investigated by the University of Colorado, under the direction of Dr. Edward U. Condon. A number of alleged UFO photographs were analyzed in depth. Some were successfully explained, but at least one, showing a disk-shaped object in flight over Oregon, is classed as difficult to explain in a conventional way. When the study was completed, it concluded that there is no evidence to justify a belief that extraterrestrial visitors have penetrated our skies. But nevertheless, from time to time we still hear of new sightings, new encounters, strange new bizarre phenomena.

Most UFO sightings have been explained as actual sightings of kites, weather balloons, missiles, the planet Venus, or any number of meteorological phenomena.

But still the sightings persist, and not all of them are so easily explained. What could they be?

---

1. *Scientific Study of Unidentified Flying Objects,* p. 10.

It is not my purpose here to go into great detail describing many alleged sightings of UFOs—you can read about most of them in any number of books. But one thing is certain—the Project Blue Book did not close the lid on the subject of "flying saucers." The controversy, the furor, is as great today as it ever was! And movies such as *Close Encounters of the Third Kind* only serve to stir up interest.

Perhaps three percent, or less, of the actual sightings are difficult or impossible to explain satisfactorily by conventional explanations. Could some of them be actual extra-terrestrial visits? Or is another explanation more likely?

Scientists discount the plausibility of extra-terrestrial visits from alien planets. They point out that inter-stellar or intergalactic travel by spaceship is virtually impossible to any life forms as we know them. Such travel, spanning many light years (and remember, light travels at a speed of 186,000 miles per *second*!), would require tremendous velocities far beyond the capability of man; it would probably require hundreds or thousands of years, for just one "trip," and perhaps many generations of creatures would have to be born, live, and die, on such spaceships in their cross-galactic journies; not to mention the constant danger and incessant bombardment from cosmic rays and other hazardous radiation which itself would destroy any life forms before they reached our planet.

This is indeed a formidable objection to the possibility that extra-terrestrial visitors are keeping planet earth under surveillance.

Another objection is simply this: If creatures have managed to successfully accomplish such lengthy voyages through space, and finally reached earth, why are they so secretive and hesitant about contacting us? Why don't they contact our national and governmental leaders? Why do they hide under a cloak of anonymity and obscurity? Why are they so ephemeral? Why won't they allow their existence to be documented? Why won't they allow themselves to be scrutinized, studied, and carefully observed? Why are they so reluctant, after such a tedious voyage, to communicate? It doesn't make much sense.

But there is another explanation for many of the "unexplained" UFO phenomena, and that explanation involves the existence of the "spirit world."

The Bible carefully documents the existence of a world of both righteous angels and demons. Also, the Bible shows that these angelic creatures from time to time have contacted various men, bringing them messages from the throne of God. Among these men were Abraham, Moses, Joshua, Gideon, the parents of Samson, Ezekiel, Daniel, Zacharias the father of John the Baptist, Mary the mother of Jesus, the two women who went to Jesus' tomb, the disciples when they were gathered to see Jesus ascend into heaven, and the apostle John in the book of Revelation.

In the days of the prophet Elijah a very strange thing occurred. When it was time for Elijah to cease his ministry, and for Elisha to take over in his stead, God determined to take Elijah away. As the two prophets were talking, Elijah told Elisha, "Ask what I shall do for thee, before I be taken away from thee. And Elisha said, I pray thee, let a double portion of thy spirit be upon me. And he said, Thou hast asked a hard thing: nevertheless, if thou see me when I am taken from thee, it shall be so unto thee; but if not, it shall not be so.

"And it came to pass, as they still went on, and talked, that, behold, there appeared *a chariot of fire, and horses of fire,* and parted them both asunder; and Elijah went up by a whirlwind into heaven" (II Kings 2:9-11).

Most people would have recoiled in great fear. Here indeed was a "flying object," a very strange one at that—a completely unexplainable phenomenon by conventional means. Everybody knows that chariots cannot fly! What's more, everybody knows that there are no such things as "horses of fire"! No doubt that most serious scientists would have dismissed this account as the ramblings of a religious "crack pot" observor.

But what Elisha saw most people would have regarded as a true "UFO"!

And most people, if they saw an angel, would probably assume it was a being from outer space. And in the strict sense of the word, they would be correct! For angels, the Bible shows, can indeed "fly."

The strange vision of Ezekiel, of the Throne of God surrounded by cherubim, each of them having a "wheel," and the wheel having a "wheel within a wheel," which moved in straight lines and 90 degree angles, could easily be interpreted as a UFO by human observors. These "wheels," which may be likened to "chariots," could in fact account for some of the mysterious UFO sightings which have never been explained.

Again, however, we must also consider the demonic world and the strange manifestations of demons. Some of the lurid accounts of men being thrown into great agitation and fear by strange beings from outer space, may actually be connected with demonic visions, manifestations, and phenomena. We should remember that the Bible calls Satan the "prince of the power of the air." He does have certain abilities to stage theatrical performances and visual phenomena connected with the atmosphere of the earth.

The multiplying sightings and signs of UFOs in the heavens, seen by millions of people, could be explained as the workings of Satan the devil, who is preparing the world to be deceived.

Prior to the second coming of Christ, Luke records: "And there shall be signs in the sun, and in the moon, and in the stars; and upon the earth distress of nations, with perplexity; the sea and the waves roaring; men's hearts failing them for fear, and for looking after those things which are coming on the earth: for the powers of heaven shall be shaken. And then shall they see the Son of man coming in a cloud with power and great glory" (Luke 21:25-27).

Could it be that the devil, restless and rebellious, overflowing with resentment and hostility, and knowing that Jesus Christ is *soon* going to return, is creating a "diversion" by spiritual manifestations in the skies, leading millions of people to believe that extra-terrestrial beings are spying on the earth, preparatory to a coming extra-terrestrial invasion? Could the devil cunningly be plotting and creating these "UFO" manifestations as a prelude to the second coming of Jesus Christ, so that when Christ does return the nations of the world will automatically *assume* that He is not Christ at all but an Invader from Outer Space?

What plan could be more deceitful, more diabolical, more clever?

We *know* that a spirit world exists. We also know that the devil and his demons are continually waging war right now against mankind—that Satan is the real arch-enemy of man! How clever it would be for him to lead mankind into believing he is our friend, and that Christ is the real enemy—an invader from the nether regions of the Universe!

No doubt that Satan and his hierarchy of demons are behind some of the unexplained and bizarre phenomena connected with the Occult and with certain "UFO" manifestations and weird observations.

The Bible shows that demons can at times manifest themselves as ghostly creatures. The classic account of the witch at Endor, who conjured up an apparition of Samuel the prophet, is a case in point. In this account we find that Samuel the prophet was dead (I Samuel 28:3). He had been buried. At that time King Saul had put away—banished—all wizards and those who possessed familiar spirits (demons) from the land (same verse).

But Saul was going out to battle against the Philistines, and his heart trembled with fear. He sought to find out how the battle would go, and inquired of God, but the Lord answered him not (verse 5). Desperate, Saul sought a woman with a familiar spirit—a witch—to help probe the future (verses 7-8). Saul wanted the woman to bring up Samuel out of the grave, to speak to him (verses 9-11).

An apparition appeared which looked like Samuel, although it really wasn't. No witch has the power to resurrect a person from the grave—only God has that kind of power. But a demon appeared, disguised as Samuel the prophet. The woman said to Saul, "I saw gods [*elohim,* judges] ascending out of the earth. And he said unto her, What form is he of? And she said, An old man cometh up; and he is covered with a mantle. And Saul *perceived* [that is, he *thought*] that it was Samuel [although he never *saw* him for himself!], and he stooped with his face to the ground, and bowed himself" (I Samuel 28:12-14).

The account goes to show that this apparition informed Saul

that the Philistines, upon the morrow, would conquer the army of Israel, and Saul and his sons would perish in the battle.

"Then Saul fell straightway all along on the earth, and was sore afraid, because of the words of Samuel [the apparition which appeared like Samuel]: and there was no strength in him; for he had eaten no bread all the day, nor all the night" (verse 20).

If God would not answer the pleas of Saul, or give him any answer (verse 6), God would surely not resurrect Samuel from the grave to give Saul the answer. This being conjured up by the witch at Endor must have been a familiar spirit, a demon. The entire episode frightened the king greatly.

Even so, some of the strange, frightening encounters some have had with supposed UFOs may very well be similar spirit manifestations created by Satan and/or his host of demons.

This world at the present time is given into the hands of the Devil. He is its "god" (II Corinthians 4:4). He has used all his powers to deceive the world as to the true nature of God (Revelation 12:9). He has successfully deluded billions of people into worshipping him, claiming that he is "God." He has been so successful that when Christ returns in power and might, the entire world will be marshalled together to fight against Him at Armageddon (Rev. 17:14; 16:12-14; 19:11-20).

That day is coming. It will be the final dramatic battle of the star war that has raged down through time.

The apostle John, in Revelation, wrote of future catastrophic events to befall planet earth. He described it thus:

"And I beheld when he [an angel] had opened the sixth seal, and, lo, there was a great earthquake; and the sun became black as sackcloth of hair, and the moon became as blood; And the stars of heaven [meteors, asteroids] fell unto the earth, even as a fig tree casteth her untimely figs, when she is shaken of a mighty wind. And the heaven [the constellations] departed as a scroll when it is rolled together; and every mountain and island were moved out of their places.

"And the kings of the earth, and the great men, and the rich men, and the chief captains, and the mighty men, and every bondman, and every free man, hid themselves in the dens and in the rocks of the mountains; And said to the mountains and rocks, Fall on us, and hide us from the face of him that sitteth on the throne, and from the wrath of the Lamb: For the great day of his wrath is come, and who shall be able to stand?" (Revelation 6:12-17).

After this John speaks of the events to occur when the seventh and last seal is opened. The seventh seal introduces seven angels with seven trumpets.

When these angels sound their trumpets, plagues, catastrophes, meteors, comets, and earth-rending disasters follow. Notice it:

"And the seven angels which had the seven trumpets prepared themselves to sound. The first angel sounded, and there followed hail and fire mingled with blood, and they were cast upon the earth: and the third part of trees was burnt up, and all green grass was burnt up."

Hail and fire—in other words, meteors, bolides, and fiery destruction.

"And the second angel sounded, and as it were a great mountain burning with fire was cast into the sea: and the third part of the sea became blood; and the third part of the creatures which were in the sea, and had life, died; and the third part of the ships were destroyed" (verses 8-9 of Revelation 8).

A great mountain burning with fire—very probably this refers to a massive asteroid which will crash into the sea, destroying vast segments of life.

"And the third angel sounded, and there fell a great star from heaven, burning as it were a lamp, and it fell upon the third part of the rivers, and upon the fountains of waters; And the name of the star is called Wormwood: and the third part of the waters became wormwood; and many men died of the waters, because they were made bitter" (verse 10-11). This "great star" which "burns as a lamp" probably refers to a glowing *comet* and its gaseous tail. The poisonous, noxious gases in the comet's tail will poison the waters of the earth, making them unfit to drink, killing many.

"And the fourth angel sounded, and the third part of the sun was smitten, and the third part of the moon, and the third part of the stars; so as the third part of them was darkened, and the day shone not for a third part of it, and the night likewise" (Revelation 8:12). Tremendous darkness—tenebrous darkness will obscure the sun, moon and stars, causing a third of their light to be cut off from the earth. A turbulent, tortured atmosphere, laden with gases, dust, debris, and the ejection and detritus of hundreds of volcanoes exploding and belching their products into the sky, will create impenetrable darkness in vast regions of the earth, obscuring the light from the heavenly bodies.

Such a time is mentioned in the prophets as occurring at the end of our own "world age." Such events have happened before—at the Flood, at the Exodus and the Conquest of Canaan. It should be no great surprise when they happen once again!

But the world isn't prepared for such extra-terrestrial shocks. The world today has largely forgotten the experiences of its ancestors. The calamities of previous generations have become vague, faint, scarcely believable legends—regarded as "mere myths"—and do not stir fear in the hearts of men, and women, today, as they once did centuries ago. . . .

The apostle Luke wrote: "And there shall be signs in the sun, and in the moon, and in the stars; and upon the earth distress of nations, with perplexity; the sea and the waves roaring; Men's hearts failing them for fear, and for looking after those things which are coming on the earth: for the powers of heaven shall be shaken" (Luke 21:25-26).

Even the powers of the heavens shall be shaken! Even so it seem to the ancients, who thought the sky was falling. But why? What is the real cause?

Great celestial star wars, we see, have raged upon the earth. And that great battle has raged down through the corridors of time and the continuum of eternity. It has taken various forms, shapes, and many different encounters.

In the days of the prophet Daniel, a great struggle took place—one phase of the ongoing "star wars." Daniel had been fasting for three weeks, with no pleasant bread, flesh or wine coming into his mouth. It was the 24th day of the first month, as he was by the side of the great river Hiddekel. Daniel says:

"Then I lifted up mine eyes, and looked, and behold a certain man clothed in linen, whose loins were girded with fine gold of Uphaz: His body also was like the beryl, and his face as the appearance of lightning, and his eyes as lamps of fire, and his arms and his feet like in colour to polished brass, and the voice of his words like the voice of a multitude. And I Daniel alone saw the vision: for the men that were with me saw not the vision; but a great quaking fell upon them, so that they fled to hide themselves."

Daniel later says:

"And behold, a hand touched me, which set me upon my knees and upon the palms of my hands. And he said unto me, O Daniel, a man greatly beloved, understand the words that I speak unto thee, and stand upright: for unto thee am I now sent. And when he had spoken this word unto me, I stood trembling. Then said he unto me, Fear not, Daniel: for from the first day that thou didst set thine heart to understand, and to chasten thyself before thy God, thy words were heard, and I am come for thy words. But the prince of the kingdom of Persia withstood me [that is, fought, resisted, opposed] one and twenty days: but, lo, Michael, one of the chief princes [or, first princes], came to help me; and I remained there with the kings of Persia" (Daniel 10:1-13).

Daniel again collapsed upon the ground. He had no strength left (verses 15-17). But again the angel touched him, strengthened him, and said: "O man greatly beloved, fear not: peace be unto thee, be strong, yea, be strong. And when he had spoken unto me, I was strengthened, and said, Let my lord speak; for thou hast strengthened me. Then said he, Knowest thou wherefore I come unto thee? And now will I return to *fight* with the prince of Persia: and when I am gone forth, lo, the prince of Grecia shall come. But I will shew thee that which is noted in the scripture of truth: and there is none that holdeth with me in these things, but Michael your prince" (verses 19-21).

Apparently this was the archangel Gabriel. The only two

angelic beings mentioned by name in the Bible, other than Lucifer, the fallen angel, are Michael and Gabriel. Gabriel was the angel whom God had used before to communicate visions to Daniel (Daniel 8:16; 9:21-23). Notice that Gabriel, if indeed that is who appeared to Daniel, had a great controversy or battle with the prince of Persia for twenty one days, until the archangel Michael came to help him (Dan. 10:13), and that he was returning to fight the same prince (verse 20). It is very possible that the prince of Persia was none other than Satan, or one of his top lieutenants. Satan was the power behind the throne of the kingdom of Persia, a Gentile world kingdom. The struggle must have been fierce, intense. Any battle lasting twenty one days must have been indeed a furious fight for supremacy.

The devil apparently still thinks he can displace God and conquer Him. We find that in the future the Devil, Satan, the Prince of demons, the Prince of the power of the air, will once again attempt to wage war in heaven, to unseat the Almighty God.

Speaking of the time of the end, the time at the close of this age, John records in Revelation:

"And there was *war in heaven:* Michael and his angels fought against the dragon; and the dragon fought and his angels, and prevailed not; neither was their place found any more in heaven. And the great dragon was cast out, that old serpent, called the Devil, and Satan, which deceiveth the whole world: he was cast out into the earth, and his angels were cast out with him. And I heard a loud voice saying in heaven, Now is come salvation, and strength, and the kingdom of our God, and the power of his Christ: for the accuser of our brethren is cast down, which accused them before our God day and night . . . Therefore rejoice, ye heavens, and ye that dwell in them. Woe to the inhabiters of the earth and of the sea! For the devil is come down unto you, having great wrath, because he knoweth that he hath but a short time.

"And when the dragon saw that he was cast unto the earth, he persecuted the woman which brought forth the man child [Israel and the Church of God]. And to the woman were given two wings of a great eagle, that she might fly into the wilderness, into her place, where she is nourished for a time, and times, and half a time, from the face of the serpent [three and one half years].

"And the serpent cast out of his mouth water as a flood after the woman [he sends forth an army to destroy the Church and kill the saints—compare "flood" here with Daniel 11:22], that he might cause her to be carried away of the flood.

"And the earth helped the woman, and the earth opened her mouth, and swallowed up the flood which the dragon cast out of his mouth. And the dragon was wroth with the woman, and went to *make war* with the remnant of her seed, which keep the commandments of God, and have the testimony of Jesus Christ" (Revelation 12:7-17).

These things are soon to happen! If you have not read my book entitled *THE LAST DAYS,* which discusses the prophecies of the Bible in great detail, especially the books of Daniel and Revelation, then I urge you to write for it. It focuses on the great Star Wars to come—the titanic battles which will soon rage on the earth, immediately before the second coming of Jesus Christ as King of Kings and Lord of Lords (Revelation 17:14).

According to the prophecies of the Bible, after the devil persecutes the saints, and goes to make war upon the rest of her seed, he will marshall the armies of the world to fight against Christ when He returns from heaven. The apostle John says: "And I saw three unclean spirits like frogs come out of the mouth of the dragon, and out of the mouth of the beast, and out of the mouth of the false prophet. For they are the spirits of devils (demons), working miracles, which go forth unto the kings of the earth and of the whole world, to gather them to the battle of that great day of God Almighty" (Revelation 16:13-14).

John continues: "And they gathered them together into a place called in the Hebrew tongue Armageddon" (verse 16).

In this last great climactic battle, the devil and his minions will go down into utter defeat. John records the battle itself:

"And I saw heaven opened, and behold a white horse; and he that sat upon him was called Faithful and True, and in righteousness he doth judge and make war. His eyes were as a flame of fire, and on his head were many crowns; and he had a name written, that no man knew, but he himself. And he was clothed with a vesture dipped in blood: and his name is called The Word of God. And the armies which were in heaven followed him upon white horses, clothed in fine linen, white and clean. And out of his mouth goeth a sharp sword, that with it he should smite the nations: and he shall rule them with a rod of iron: and he treadeth the winepress of the fierceness and wrath of Almighty God. And he hath on his vesture and on his thigh a name written, KING OF KINGS, AND LORD OF LORDS" (Revelation 19:11-16).

John continues this graphic description:

"And I saw an angel standing in the sun; and he cried with a loud voice, saying to all the fowls that fly in the midst of heaven, Come and gather yourselves together unto the supper of the great God; that ye may eat the flesh of kings, and the flesh of captains, and the flesh of mighty men, and the flesh of all men, both free and bond, both small and great. And I saw the beast, and the kings of the earth, and their armies, gathered together to make war against him that sat on the horse, and against his army. And the beast was taken, and with him the false prophet that wrought miracles before him, with which he deceived them that had received the mark of the beast, and them that worshipped his image. These both were cast alive into a lake of fire burning with brimstone" (Verses 17-20).

Can you imagine it? The devil will deceive the nations so completely that they will gather their armies together to fight against Jesus Christ and his angelic hosts! The people of the world will believe he is an invader from outer space—an alien being—a diabolical creature from some other galaxy or planet. They will fight against him bitterly, to the very death. This battle will be fought around the city of Jerusalem. The devil and his last mighty defensive effort to maintain his kingdom and power will be overthrown. His ages old rebellion will be squashed.

What will happen to Satan at that time?

How does God intend to deal with him?

We have already seen that the saints will eventually "judge

the angels" (I Corinthians 6:3). But a clear picture of their judgment and future is given in the book of Revelation.

"And I saw an angel come down from heaven, having the key of the bottomless pit and a great chain in his hand. And he laid hold on the dragon, that old serpent, which is the Devil, and Satan, and *bound him a thousand years,* and cast him into the bottomless pit, and shut him up, and set a seal upon him, that he should deceive the nations no more, till the thousand years should be fulfilled: and after that he must be loosed a little season" (Rev. 20:1-3).

After the saints, resurrected and made immortal, reign over the earth for one thousand years with Christ (verses 4-6), Satan will be loosed again, briefly. John continues:

"And when the thousand years are expired, Satan shall be loosed out of his prison, and shall go out to deceive the nations which are in the four quarters of the earth, Gog and Magog, to gather them together to battle: the number of whom is as the sand of the sea. And they went up on the breadth of the earth, and compassed the camp of the saints about, and the beloved city: and fire came down from God out of heaven, and devoured them.

"*And the devil that deceived them was cast into the lake of fire and brimstone,* where the beast and false prophet [were cast], and shall be tormented day and night for ever and ever" (Revelation 20:7-10).

This mighty burning lake of fire, Jesus said, will be "everlasting fire, prepared for the devil and his angels" (Matthew 25:41). The word for "everlasting" here is *aionion* fire, and means literally "age-lasting fire." Its result wil be forever, although it need not burn forever. It will accomplish the final destruction of these evil fallen spirits. As Ezekiel wrote, the anointed cherub that covered God's Throne, Lucifer, will be devoured by fire. God says: "and I will bring thee to ashes upon the earth in the sight of all them that behold thee" (Ezek. 28:18). Isaiah alludes to the same event (Isaiah 14:15-17, 19-20). Although he is speaking of the king of Babylon as a type, the fact that he means Lucifer is recorded in verse 12, very clearly.

Will the devil then, and his angels, be ultimately destroyed?

Or will their spirits roam forever in the new universe that God will create?

Peter tells us: "But the day of the Lord will come as a thief in the night; in which the heavens shall pass away with a great noise, and the elements shall melt with fervent heat, the earth also and the works that are therein shall be burned up. Seeing then that all these things shall be dissolved, what manner of persons ought ye to be in all holy conversation and godliness, looking for and hasting unto the coming of the day of God, wherein the heavens being on fire shall be dissolved, and the elements shall melt with fervent heat?

"Nevertheless we, according to his promise, look for new heavens and a new earth, wherein dwelleth *righteousness*" (II Peter 3:10-13).

There will be no trace of wickedness in that new world—not the vaguest hint of wickedness (Revelation 21:8). God will finally rid himself ot his arch enemy, this competitor, this arch villain, this age-old rebel.

Some believe that the devil, being a spirit creature, cannot be destroyed or put to death, and that he will simply be cast out into outer darkness, into the infinite regions of space, to foam out his bitterness and hostility for ever. But I am convinced that such is not the case. Christ the Creator took on himself the nature and form of a man, and suffered death—but was resurrected from the dead. Even so, I believe it is certainly within the capability of the Creator God to change Satan from a spirit being into flesh, or physical matter, and then cremate his remains in the lake of fire so that nothing is left but smoke and ashes—so there will be no vestige or hint of his former existence in the New Age to Come!

Malachi puts it plainly: "For, behold, the day cometh, that shall burn as an oven; and all the proud, yea, and all that do wickedly"—and that certainly includes the devil and his legions of demons—"shall be stubble: and the day that cometh shall burn them up, saith the Lord of hosts, that it shall leave them neither root nor branch" (Malachi 4:1).

The great Destroyer will eventually himself be destroyed.

But what about you?

Where are you going to be when the great Star War breaks out again?

Will you be sheltered in a place of protection, nestled in the loving arms of the Almighty in a place of refuge?

Or will you take your chances with the rest of rebellious, deceived mankind?

Jesus warned: "And take heed to yourselves, lest at any time your hearts be overcharged with surfeiting, and drunkenness, and cares of this life, and so that day come upon you unawares.

"For as a snare shall it come on all them that dwell on the face of the whole earth.

"Watch ye, therefore, and pray always, that ye may be accounted worthy to escape all these things that shall come to pass, and to stand before the Son of man" (Luke 21:34-36).

Can you say with David:

"He that dwelleth in the secret place of the most High shall abide under the shadow of the Almighty. I will say of the Lord, He is my refuge, and my fortress: my God; in him will I trust. Surely he shall deliver thee from the snare of the fowler, and from the noisome pestilence. he shall cover thee with his feathers, and under his wings shalt thou trust: his truth shall be thy shield and buckler. Thou shalt not be afraid for the terror by night; nor for the arrow that flieth by day; nor for the pestilence that walketh in darkness; nor for the destruction that wasteth at noonday.

"A thousand shall fall at thy side, and ten thousand at thy right hand; but it shall not come nigh thee. Only with thine eyes shalt thou behold and see the reward of the wicked.

"Because thou hast made the Lord, which is my refuge, even the most High, thy habitation; there shall no evil befall thee, neither shall any plague come nigh thy dwelling. For he shall give his angels charge over thee, to keep thee in all thy ways. They shall bear thee up in their hands, lest thou dash thy foot against a stone. Thou shalt tread upon the lion and adder: the young lion and the dragon shalt thou trample under feet.

"Because he hath set his love upon me, therefore will I deliver him: I will set him on high, because he hath known my name. He shall call upon me, and I will answer him: I will be with him in trouble; I will deliver him, and honour him. With long life will I satisfy him, and shew him my salvation" (Psalm 91).

Can you claim this promise?

Star wars—great celestial battles—are coming on the earth again. Very probably within our lifetime. Millions will die during the "Day of the Lord." Great suffering and trials are ahead of us. Jesus said: "For then shall be great tribulation, such as was not since the beginning of the world to this time, no, nor ever shall be. And except those days should be shortened, there should no flesh be saved [alive]: but for the elect's sake those days shall be shortened" (Matthew 24:21-22).

Are you one of God's elect?

Are you . . . "Elect according to the foreknowledge of God the Father, through sanctification of the Spirit, unto obedience and sprinkling of the blood of Jesus Christ" (I Peter 1:2)?

Are you part of God's "chosen generation, a royal priesthood, a holy nation, a peculiar [purchased] people" (I Peter 2:9)?

Are you one of those destined to rule in the world to come —the Kingdom of God?

Are you in training now to qualify for a high position ruling with Christ during His Millennial reign? Are you growing in grace and knowledge (I Peter 3:18)? Are you overcoming sins, temptations, distractions of the flesh? Are you purging your life of those things which hinder us? Do you fortify your faith with daily Bible study?

The apostle Paul wrote:

"Wherefore, seeing we also are compassed about with so great a cloud of witnesses, let us lay aside every weight, and the sin which doth so easily beset us, and let us run with patience the race that is set before us, Looking unto Jesus the author and finisher of our faith; who for the joy that was set before him endured the cross, despising the shame, and is set down at the right hand of the throne of God" (Hebrews 12:1-2).

Our calling is so great that these "things the angels desire to look into" (I Peter 1:12).

It is worth any and every sacrifice. It is the supreme challenge, and opportunity, of all the ages. It makes our present sufferings, trials and afflictions pale into mere straw by comparison. It dwarfs our present problems as mighty Mount Rushmore dwarfs a tiny pebble. It is as stupendous as the earth itself in comparison to a mere ping pong ball!

Do you understand? Do you grasp the awesome destiny God holds out for you? Do you comprehend? Has it sunk down into the depths of your mind? *Do you see?*

Now is the time to get off the fence—to start working out, in training, for the Greatest Calling ever presented to mankind. Now is your chance to really amount to something. Now is your opportunity to make your life really meaningful and worthwhile!

God has called and chosen you to become one of His sons. He wants you to eventually shoulder the mantle of rulership over the entire Universe, along with our saviour and Elder Brother, Jesus Christ. God wants to glorify you, make you immortal, give you dazzling strength and power and radiance. He wants you to help rule His Kingdom for ever!

But God will never give that kind of awesome power to any being whom He cannot trust. You must prove yourself. You must be an overcomer.

Where are you in the Christian life? Have you even taken step one? Have you really repented of your sins, confessed your human weakness, and given your life over to Christ for Him to use as He decides? Have you buried your past in baptism? Have you arisen from the watery grave of baptism, a new person—a new creation of God? Have you deep within your heart and soul accepted Jesus Christ as your own Saviour, Redeemer, and coming King?

Have you partaken of His Holy Spirit, which empowers us to be overcomers? Have you yet been begotten by that Spirit and is Christ being formed in you? Are you becoming more and more like Him every day?

Is the love of God radiating out in your life, toward God and toward other people? Does the love of God flow through your heart like a mighty river, bringing life and health to all that it touches?

If you haven't made peace with your Creator—isn't it about time you did?

God wants us to become perfect even as He is (Matthew 5:48). But He knows we can never be totally perfect in this life.

He knows that we stumble, and slip into sins, and make mistakes from time to time. But He is ever willing to forgive us, and to pick us up, and set us back on the right path, if we let Him.

He wants us to reflect the character and nature of Jesus Christ more and more throughout our lives. He wants us to repudiate the way of Satan the devil, the way of personal greed, avarice, gluttony, lust, envy, jealousy, pride, vanity, and selfishness. He wants us to learn to be like He is—the Great Giver of everything that is good! He wants us to learn to give, and share, and help others at all times. To have outgoing, overflowing love for our fellow man.

God wants you to be *concerned* about others! To care!

In order for us to grow in godliness, and Christlike character, we must learn to feed daily upon the bread of life—the Word of God. We must absorb its spiritual strength-giving qualities. We must drink in of His Spirit daily. We must pray daily, and have constant communion with God. As we do these things, our thoughts will gradually become more in tune with His thoughts, we will grow in faith, wisdom and understanding. As each of us shoulder our individual burdens, or "cross," and follow Christ, He will give us spiritual strength and enable us to overcome.

Our tremendous destiny is certainly worth the small price which God requires!

Daniel the prophet was inspired to record: "And many of them that sleep in the dust of the earth shall awake, some to everlasting life, and some to shame and everlasting contempt.

"And they that be wise shall shine as the brightness of the firmament; and they that turn many to righteousness *as the stars for ever and ever*" (Daniel 12:2-3).

This is our calling!

This is our destiny!

This is the reason you, and I, were born!

Today, mankind has limited power and dominion over the earth.

But tomorrow, after we learn our lessons, and grow in spiritual maturity, and achieve peace with God through Jesus Christ, He intends for us to rule over the stars—the vast, far flung reaches of the Universe. We will be able to travel faster than light. We may even create new Universes, with new planets, and new galaxies!

What an awesome, mind-boggling, incredible, astonishing destiny and calling! Can your mind really comprehend it?

Today, the earth.

Tomorrow, the stars!